Designers' Identities

Tower Hamlets College
Learning Centre
Withdrawn

123913

£24.95

D1344729

© text 2010 Liz Farrelly

Published in 2010 by
Laurence King Publishing Ltd
361–373 City Road
London EC1V 1LR
United Kingdom
Tel: + 44 20 7841 6900
Fax: + 44 20 7841 6910
email: enquiries@laurenceking.com
www.laurenceking.com

Copyright © 2010

All rights reserved. No part of this
publication may be reproduced or
transmitted in any form or by any
means, electronic or mechanical,
including photocopy, recording or
any information storage and retrieval
system, without prior permission in
writing from the publisher.

A catalogue record for this book is
available from the British Library.

ISBN-13: 978 1 85669 690 6

Design by Intercity
www.intercitystudio.com

Printed in China

Designers' Identities
Liz Farrelly

THE LIBRARY
TOWER HAMLETS COLLEGE
POPLAR HIGH STREET
LONDON E14 0AF
Tel: 0207 510 7763

Laurence King Publishing

Contents

Introduction

'Corporate Identity' just sounds wrong when talking about the personal choices designers make with their own stationery, websites and promotional projects. But for the sake of consistency I've used it, at least initially, to describe the design solutions collected here. 'Designers' Identities' is a bit of a mouthful too. Again, it only barely describes what this book has grown into.

As far as it does what it says on the tin (or in this case, the book cover), a more accurate title would be along the lines of 'lots of examples of how designers present themselves to the world, via the very widest range of means and large amounts of invention, fun, cleverness and class.' 'Lots' being the salient point, as I've included almost twice as many examples as I set out to, overwhelmed as I was by contributions that ticked so many boxes. Not only did they look good (cue the sharp intake of breath on opening the envelope), but they work too. They have stand-out appeal, are easily updated, or offer inventive solutions that do both. Along with the objects came the stories, the reasons why designers did what they did; these proved fascinating and often won the project a place in the book by dint of excellent out-of-the-box thinking.

As I contacted designers, asked them to contribute, and selected the entries, I aimed to bring together examples from a wide geographic range. This must also go wider in the future so, please, designers get in touch! I also wanted to represent designers on all rungs of the career ladder and from differing commercial situations; solo players, team members, collectives, major studios and start-ups; from a recent graduate to a creative director; from someone still in their second decade who is happy Twittering, stickering and blogging, to those who got their first design job when computers still ran on punch cards.

My hope was that the range of circumstances would reveal clever solutions, perfectly adapted to the needs of designers with diverse work and lifestyles. But I've shied away from being too explicit about designers' circumstances, as they change, and you may find out more in the About section of nearly every designer's website. I was more interested in hearing from the designers themselves, so each was sent a few questions – not so many as to interfere with a busy day's work, but not the usual 'fill in this questionnaire' type of deal either. The answers revealed attitudes and motivations, alliances and inspirations, causes and obsessions. Wherever possible, I've quoted the designers directly, so that they may explain their projects. Some people had more to say than others, so a few longer 'break-out' interviews are included too.

With such a range of material and responses to accommodate, this book required an organizational device, with the layout responding to the collected content, not simply squeezing everything into a one-size box. To impose a 'control', more in the sense of a scientific experiment than a restriction, the editorial and design team set another prerequisite at the beginning of this project. We decided to call in the actual objects, the paper versions, the real things, and photograph them, in order to glean a sense of a project's effectiveness. We would, literally, be on the receiving end of the design solution, just as someone receiving a letter or promotional item would be. These photographs have given designer Nathan Gale an opportunity to impose consistency on the content, and signal the beginning of each contributor's section, while still allowing flexibility in the layout. We couldn't photograph each element of every designer's identity, or even all the pieces supplied, so we've mixed in supplied images too. And, of course, some designers don't use hard copy at all.

This process alone marks out *Designers' Identities* from much contemporary publishing and journalism. More usually, content is only collected over the wire, with file transfer protocol and portable document format putting paid to the joy of receiving (hopefully) expertly packaged parcels, containing truly surprising combinations of paper, ink and special treatments.

Being able to examine the actual paper stationery items (which is what I fell into calling them) gave me much more information than any hi-res image could. Unsurprisingly, the captions and descriptions have become more detailed, and I hope the reader finds them useful. I combined information supplied with my own 'reading' of the objects, but there are inconsistencies and gaps. Sometimes even designers who have happily used a stationery system for years have forgotten the 'spec', and printing being a process with so many variables and possible means to ends, it's not wise to guess. I've noted the printing method only in instances where it is more exotic than offset litho, or where one item comprises a combination of methods.

Why all the explanation? Because a comprehensive study of designers' identities is beyond the remit of this one book, which can only highlight some of the choices and solutions currently being explored by the graphic designers who kindly contributed. But there is so much more to say on the subject. From minimal means to maximum impact; from experimenting with technically advanced systems to rediscovering traditional methods, from selecting the finest, pristine materials to reusing discarded ephemera, from collective endeavours to the most personal insights; the options are endless, and this book can only provide a snapshot.

When it comes to a designer's own corporate identity, there is freedom to explore. To start with, what constitutes 'promotion'? Books and exhibitions, limited-edition prints, tote bags, T-shirts, mugs and more; self-instigated projects that get the designer's name out there, earn some press, perhaps generate income and a sense of achievement; these constitute the widest definition of corporate identity. Then add the details – the hundreds of choices to be made when designing stationery, brochures, websites, online newsletters and more.

Underlying so many of these design decisions is the grid, which dictates not only where the organizing devices will appear but how a page or screen may be used. There's the bold step to go landscape or adopt the more informal notepaper size. The weight of paper selected dictates how something may be folded, which affects the tone of communications.

Manuel Krebs of Norm told me; '…it's like hairdressers cutting their own hair; designers can redesign their identity whenever they feel like it.' All these solutions are essentially temporary, as the designer is apt to change their mind, their company name, their city, their working method. All these identities have a limited lifespan; some will evolve, others will be discarded.

Believe it or not, graphic designers aren't the best archivists. One designer who has carefully conserved examples of her company's letterheads throughout a career spanning three decades is Nancy Skolos of Skolos-Wedell; she shares them here. Nancy suggests that the golden days of letterhead design may be gone, as commercial printers are no longer able to finely detail a 12-colour job. She's not apportioning blame but, rather, recognizes that ways and means for promotion and communication have changed. Designers are still expending their time, energy and consideration on the subject of stationery, though. By way of extreme contrast, Hans Gremmen offers a highly personalized, one-off, low-impact means of communicating information, via a blank sheet of paper. As a designer who works closely with fine artists, Hans adopts a conceptual approach to his promotional identity.

Many designers have demonstrated a commitment to sustainable practices, which has led to ecologically sensitive solutions. While some celebrate the materiality of print, others are revelling in the freedom of, literally, deconstructing the means.

The cover design for this book
functions as an abstract logo. It is a
representation of the letters 'd' and 'i',
referencing the three main elements
of a stationery system: the letterhead,
compliments slip and business card, as
shown here.

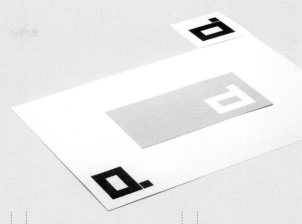

Ultimately, this book aims to reveal diversity of
definition and application in the name of corporate
identity, by focusing on many different approaches,
aesthetics, materials and solutions. Go a step further,
into the realm of collaboration, and many more options
may be added to an identity. Bunch show how it's done on
a grand scale; literally hundreds of fellow designers have
contributed ideas and logos to the Made in Bunch project,
which in turn has became an identity system applied
across multiple media.

Creating an archive of designers' promotional
material and stationery (not to mention websites) would
be one way of growing this project. For confirmation
of the worth of such an exercise, look to Elaine Lustig
Cohen's collection of letterheads. Featuring the great
practitioners of the Modernist era, she amassed
an archive via her business, Ex Libris, a bookstore
specializing in avant-garde printed matter. She notes that
letterheads rarely sold, so she gladly added them to her
collection, which in turn inspired the book *Letters from
the Avant Garde: Modern Graphic Design* (Princeton
Architectural Press, 1996), co-authored with Ellen
Lupton. Showcased are the personal graphic languages
and aesthetic choices of such luminaries as Alvin Lustig,
E. McKnight Kauffer, Sonia Delaunay and Jan Tschichold,
among many others. Without that book, how would we,
mere mortals, see such things?

My colleague, Michael Dorrian, started collecting
business cards, and borrowing examples from my desk,
about a decade ago. His magpie tendency inspired three
books about business cards (*Business Cards: The Art
of Saying Hello* (2004); *Business Cards 2: More Ways
of Saying Hello* (2006); *Business Cards 3: Designs on
Saying Hello* (2009) all published by Laurence King.
These exist as an archive, not only of those cards, but
of the contributors too, those designers and creative
businesses from around the world who sent us their
business cards. That project prompted me to look further,
to consider the complete system of corporate identity.
The idea was hatched of focusing on designers' own
identities, keeping it personal and aiming for the most
inspired and innovative examples.

Today, fewer and fewer paper solutions are being
produced. Designers still revel in print, but many have
discarded the professionally produced letterhead
for an in-house digitally printed version or a PDF.
Thanks to technology, it's also easier to create multiple
personalities. Stage an event and build a micro-site,
link it to your main site, give it a logo and identity, but
relate it to your umbrella identity. You might read such
an evolution as dispersal, watering down, viral or niche.
Identity systems these days have become more scattered
and more pervasive, more flexible and more controlled;
networks allow for digression, but they may effectively
deliver a stronger message.

A project starts with just an email address. Perhaps
that's the first shoot of an identity; it was for this
book. Then it was Nathan Gale's task to design a more
permanent incarnation; and he took the opportunity to
design a corporate identity too. It shares characteristics
with his company's, Intercity, in its spare organization
of bold but discrete elements. For *Designers' Identities*,
the system needed a logotype and stationery that would
combine the project's communications, the book's cover
and internal layout, and the publisher's marketing needs.

This project has been a revelation. I've been privy to
so many designers' personal visions, in the form of such
varied elements of corporate identity, of which I wouldn't
ordinarily be the recipient. These are, perhaps, the most
honest and personal iteration of their practice – and
perhaps the projects they have the most fun with, too.

three forty four design   101 n. grand avenue, suite 7   pasadena, ca 91103
tel/fax: 626.796.5148   e-mail: three44@earthlink.net

344 Design   Stefan G. Bucher   Pasadena, CA, USA   www.344design.com

Originally from Germany, Stefan G. Bucher ran a thriving illustration business while still at school; he travelled to the United States to study design, and after stints in both advertising and the record industry, set up his studio. 'Since then it's been word of mouth,' he says. That said, Stefan has created both online and editorial projects that have brought him to the attention of his peers, the media and the public; and he has staged launches, exhibitions and lectures to promote his various published projects.

With a hint of his off-the-wall logic, Stefan explains why his company is called 344 Design: 'A few years ago, I realized that the 344th day of a non-leap year is 10 December, the day I moved from Germany to California. And that's a good enough reason. Nobody in the United States can pronounce my name, so 344 is more "neutral"; and my little "seal" looks good on a funny drawing but also great on an elegant catalogue. An identity should be the signature, not an entire letter.'

Back in 2006, Stefan dreamt up a blog featuring a speeded-up movie of him drawing a monster, a different one every day. With a book (*100 Days of Monsters*, 2008), and his creations featuring on a popular television show, he'd like the project to hit the big screen. 'I'm giving myself ten years to achieve that with the Monsters. And I'll probably tack on another ten; I'm nothing if not persistent.'

Asked what his original motivation was for creating a daily blog, he cites a number of reasons: 'I love to draw, but I wasn't drawing. Committing myself to a project is how I get it done, so I make little lists of what I'd like to make happen. The Post-it said:

Concrete goals for 2006:
Make enough money to live comfortably.
Have faith that I won't go broke.
Do more drawings.
Develop one piece of original content and get it out
     under my own name.
Get one piece of work in the *New York Times*.

'That last one took a while, but everything else started happening.'

Maximizing that impetus, Stefan regularly attends design industry events which he often helps to organize, as well as staging his own. How does he get the most out of these promotional opportunities? 'It's an extension of my business philosophy, such as it is: make the best stuff I can and have fun doing it. I see each event as a chance to create something entertaining. For talks I might film a new Monster, make a video montage, or remodel all my slides. When I host an event I like to have projections (because I did that at bossa:nova, a club I worked with), and create a stage-set where people can have their photo taken (by my friend, graphic designer Tim Moraitis).'

Bespoke, interactive sculptures of monsters; giant foamboard book covers and playful signs are all on hand as photo backdrops, with the hope that they'll make it on to blogs and networking sites too. 'These are gifts, a thank you for the support people give me, so I don't brand those elements, just add a 344 seal.'

Letterhead (opposite page)
2/0, yellow and black, on
white stock.

Business Cards
Seal card: 2/1, blue, black and grey,
on white stock. Featuring the 344 seal.

Face card: Four-colour CMYK,
on white stock. Featuring a stylized
self-portrait.

three forty four design   101 n.grand avenue, suite 7   pasadena, ca 91103.3576
Stefan G. Bucher   telephone: 626.796.5148   e-mail: stefan@344design.com

344 DESIGN
STEFAN G. BUCHER
PASADENA
CALIFORNIA

626 796 5148
stefan@344design.com

1

2

3

4

5

6

7

8

9

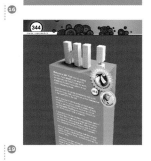

10

11

12

13

14

15

16

17

18

19

20

21

22

Magazine Column
(opposite page, 1–3)
'ink & circumstance' published in
STEP magazine. Stefan was a regular
contributor, producing these illustrated
advice columns for this well-regarded,
US-based design magazine.

Live Projection (opposite page, 4)
Featured at events and lectures.

Books
(opposite page, 5 and 6)
*All Access: the making of thirty
extraordinary graphic designers*,
Rockport, 2004.

(opposite page, 7 and 15)
100 Days of Monsters, How Books,
2008.

(opposite page, 8)
*The Graphic Eye: photographs by
international graphic designers*,
RotoVision and Chronicle Books, 2009.

Event Posters
(opposite page, 9 and 10)
For a talk in Chicago, Stefan poses in
front of a list of 344 'things you might
not know about me'.

(opposite page, 11 and 12)
'The Principal Navigations, Voyages
and Discoveries of the 344 Empire',
front and back. Here Stefan assumes
the persona of a Victorian explorer for a
talk in Washington, D.C.

Websites
(opposite page, 13, 16–22)
www.344design.com
(opposite page, 14)
www.dailymonster.com
Stefan's various websites (see also
www.stefangbucher.com) promote
interactivity, with layers of content and
mini-movies accessed via animated
illustrations, accompanied by surprising
sound effects. The 344 seal (18) also
appears on the homepage. The Daily
Monster blog (14) opens with a desktop
facsimile featuring tools of the trade.

Stickers (below)
The 344 'seal', realized in
eye-searing glitter.

Julian Morey
Studio 116
31
Clerkenwell Close
London EC1R OAT
Telephone 0171
336 8970
Facsimile 0171
490 2718

Having bought his first Apple Macintosh, Julian Morey began publishing typefaces, an option he initially adopted to recoup for time spent designing them but, he adds, 'I found that making my work available to a wider audience gave my name extra exposure.'

Launching his own foundry, Club-21, followed. 'I didn't set out to make typefaces commercially, but it came about due to interest from other designers...and there were very few alternative fonts back then. I remember wanting to use a stencil font for a project, but there were only two available and I didn't like them. So, I used Fontographer to make PostScript fonts for my own work. It was more personal, and I enjoyed the process of making typefaces. However, there's a lot of time involved, so making the fonts available to buy seemed a natural process.'

Both Club-21 and Julian's studio, abc–xyz, provide him with opportunities to design a range of promotional material, which when viewed together have many elements in common: the use of uncoated stock and the integration of his various logos and typefaces, all printed in strong colours on a white ground. The end result is a continuously evolving corporate identity.

Not satisfied with two companies, Julian has also launched Editions Eklektic, for '...anything that I might publish as an edition. I refer to it as "work that falls outside graphic design". It's a continuation of my promotional work, but "for sale"; just like Club-21, making these items commercial helps to cover the production costs.'

Letterhead (opposite page)
Digital, in-house, black, on white stock.

Promotional Card (below left)
2/1, black and grey, on white card.
To announce the website launch.

Business Card (middle and
middle right)
1/1, black and grey, on white card.

Website (bottom)
www.abc-xyz.co.uk
The website opens with Julian's three-
colour logo, which morphs his name into
his company's logotype.

Catalogue (top right)
Available from Editions Eklektic,
this 18-page, one-colour catalogue
wrapped in a three-colour cover,
contains a selection of Julian's work as
abc–xyz; this and all his promotional
and stationery elements use custom-
designed typefaces.

abc-xyz.co.uk

Julian Morey

11J Peabody Buildings
Dufferin Street
London EC1Y 8SA

T. +44 (0)7775 863 321
julian@abc-xyz.co.uk

http://www.abc-xyz.co.uk

Club-21
Julian created a logo and 'quite a
bit of marketing material' to promote
his type foundry, including a two-colour
catalogue and three posters, all
of which include a full listing of
available typefaces.

Catalogue (top right)
Two-colour, square format, simle and
spare, this type sampler is a welcome
antithesis to the often over-complicated
type specimen.

Posters (below)
Featuring an illustrated letterform
on the front and font information on
the reverse.

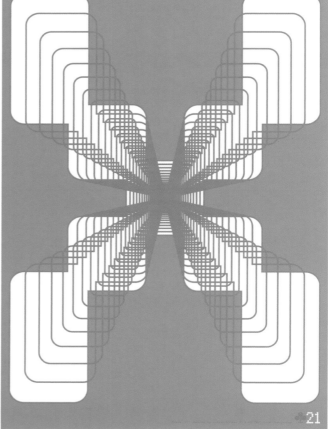

Editions Eklektic
Each of Julian's graphic products is identified by his 'double e' logo, printed on the reverse of all cards and posters.

Business Cards, two versions
(top right)
1/1, orange, on white card.
2/1, black and grey, on white card.
'I dropped the logo in favour of using Plantin for the identity.'

Magazine Advertising (below)
Appears in selected design publications, featuring abstracted fragments from various products.

EDITIONS EKLEKTIC | Limited Edition Prints | www.eklektic.co.uk

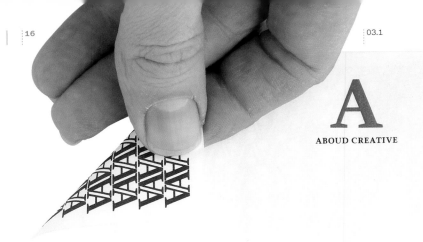

A

ABOUD CREATIVE

| Aboud Creative | Alan Aboud | London, UK | www.aboud-creative.com |

With one of the longest-running creative collaborations in fashion and retailing, Alan Aboud has designed for Paul Smith since being spotted by the fashion maven at his St. Martin's degree show. Working with his partner photographer, Sandro Sodano, Alan has created identities for Paul Smith's many brands, with an emphasis on using dynamic imagery.

But when Alan launched his new company, Aboud Creative, he decided to take a different route. 'I wanted to create a simple, dignified corporate identity that would last. For months, the studio's designers and myself looked at various options, but nothing worked,' he recalls. 'A while later, in Tokyo, I came across a book, *Vita Activa*, showing work by the typographer Georg Trump. The cover was a repeat pattern of the capital "T" from his typeface Trump Mediaeval, designed in 1954 for Linotype.'

That's when Alan decided to use a mix of typography and materials '...to convey the simplicity and luxury of our work.' Although trained in typography, Alan admits, 'I'm not a craftsman,' and so collaborated with someone who, he says, 'knows letter shapes expertly.' Julian Morey is a college friend whom Alan has worked with over the years. 'I showed him the book, and my ideas, and we set to work; Julian crafted the font and suggested the spacing and size of the elements.'

'The repeat "A" pattern came first, then the playing-card idea for the business card evolved from that. The monogram "A" was a strategic choice because sometime in the future I may want to migrate "Aboud Creative" to "A Creative", thus allowing for more democracy in the company. I'm not an egotist, like some designers who author all of their agency's work as their own. I give credit where credit is due; it's much fairer.'

STUDIO 26   PALL MALL DEPOSIT   124–128 BARLBY ROAD   LONDON W10 6BL
TELEPHONE +44 20 8968 6142   FACSIMILE +44 20 8968 6143   MAIL@ABOUD-CREATIVE.COM   WWW.ABOUD-CREATIVE.COM
Aboud Creative Limited. VAT registration No. 911 9979 86. Registered in England No. 06357926. Registered address as above.

Logotype and font
Julian Morey, abc–xyz (see page 12).

Letterhead (opposite page) **and
Compliments Slip** (below)
Litho, 1/2, red and black, die-stamp,
2/0, red and black logotype on front,
on white Cranes Crest Fluorescent,
105gsm, die-cut round corners.
A certain amount of show-through
brings a subtle version of the repeat
'A' pattern to the front surface.

Business Card (bottom)
Litho, 1/2, red and black, die-stamp,
2/0, red and black logotype on front,
on white Cranes Crest Fluorescent,
365gsm, die-cut round corners.

A
ABOUD CREATIVE

STUDIO 26   PALL MALL DEPOSIT   124–128 BARLBY ROAD   LONDON W10 6BL
TELEPHONE +44 20 8968 6142   FACSIMILE +44 20 8968 6143   WWW.ABOUD-CREATIVE.COM

ALAN ABOUD
CREATIVE DIRECTOR

A
ABOUD CREATIVE

STUDIO 26
PALL MALL DEPOSIT
124–128 BARLBY ROAD
LONDON W10 6BL

TELEPHONE +44 20 8968 6142
FACSIMILE +44 20 8968 6143

ALAN@ABOUD-CREATIVE.COM
WWW.ABOUD-CREATIVE.COM

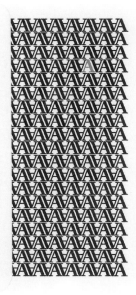

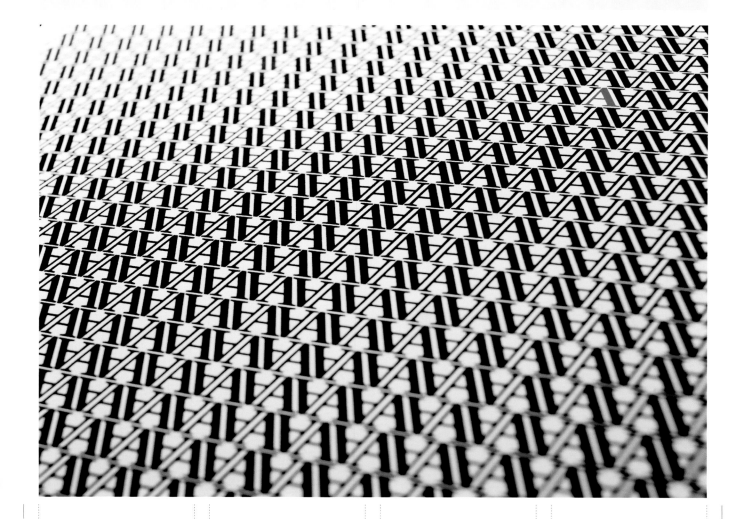

Letterhead (opposite page)
Spec. as on page 16.

Note Card (top right)
Die-stamp, 2/0, red and black, on white
Cranes Crest Fluorescent, 600gsm,
duplexed, die-cut round corners with
gold flat edge.

Website
www.aboud-creative.com
Roll the mouse over the single red 'A' to
reveal the pattern, and discover a site
that is easy to navigate, realized in a
neat red, white and black palette.

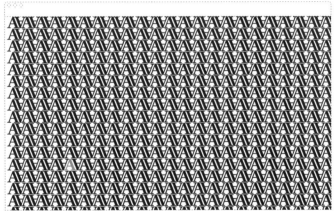

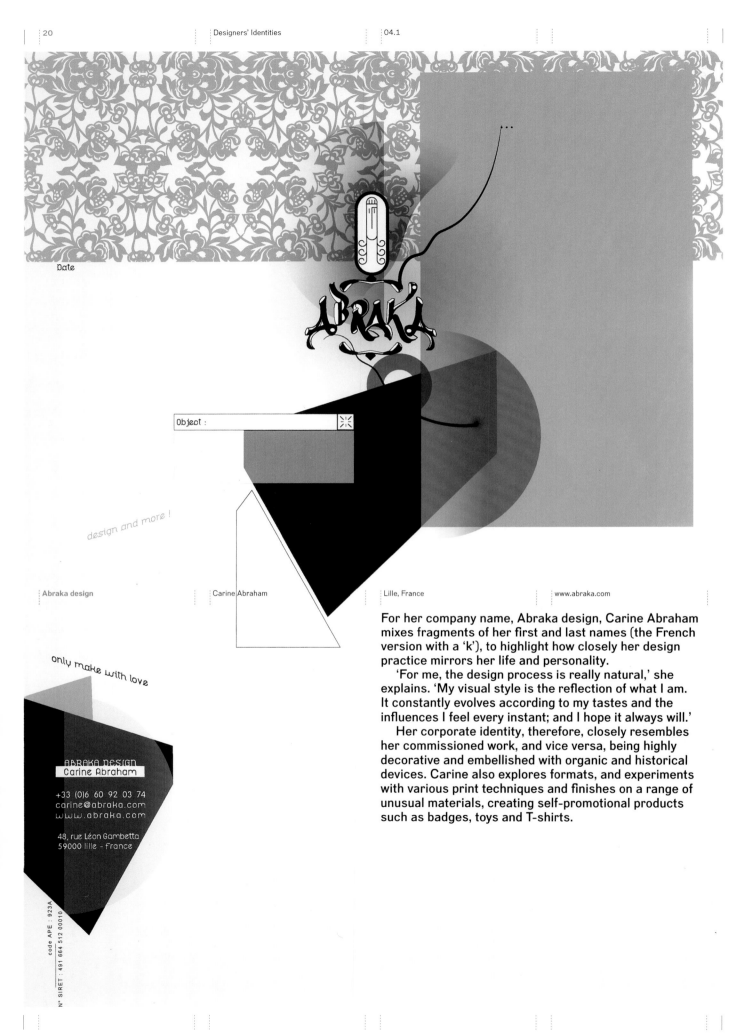

Date

design and more !

only make with love

ABRAKA DESIGN
Carine Abraham

+33 (0)6 60 92 03 74
carine@abraka.com
www.abraka.com

48, rue Léon Gambetta
59000 lille - france

code APE : 923A

N° SIRET : 491 664 512 00010

Object :

Abraka design   Carine Abraham   Lille, France   www.abraka.com

For her company name, Abraka design, Carine Abraham mixes fragments of her first and last names (the French version with a 'k'), to highlight how closely her design practice mirrors her life and personality.

'For me, the design process is really natural,' she explains. 'My visual style is the reflection of what I am. It constantly evolves according to my tastes and the influences I feel every instant; and I hope it always will.'

Her corporate identity, therefore, closely resembles her commissioned work, and vice versa, being highly decorative and embellished with organic and historical devices. Carine also explores formats, and experiments with various print techniques and finishes on a range of unusual materials, creating self-promotional products such as badges, toys and T-shirts.

Letterhead (opposite page)
Digital, in-house, on white stock.
Features a panoply of devices favoured
by Carine, including a stylized self-
portrait (line-drawing in lozenge,
upper middle).

Postcard Pack (below and bottom left)
Cartacarine
Digital, in-house, on iridescent stock.
Limited edition of 50, series of ten
self-promotional postcards, presented
in a folded cover.

Badges (bottom middle)
Limited edition, series of ten badges.

T-shirts (bottom right)
Screenprinted, series of three self-
promotional T-shirts.

Business Cards (top right)
Digital, in-house, on iridescent stock.
A series of four cards presents
elements from Carine's personal
design language.

absolutezero°   Address   Telephone

www.absolutezerodegrees.com   Absolute Zero Degrees ltd   +44 (0)20 77376767
reg. address   10 Empress Mews
unit 13   Kenbury Street
Empress Mews   London
Kenbury Street   SE5 9BT
London
SE5 9BT
reg. in england no. 4287568

Absolute Zero Degrees   Merryl Catlow, Mark Hampshire, Keith Stephenson   London, UK   www.absolutezerodegrees.com

A multi-skilled partnership, Absolute Zero Degrees (AZD) mix it up: they run their own interiors accessories label, author and design books, and create branding and communications solutions from a logo to a brochure, packaging to print design.

'We think the process from idea to artwork should be seamless...and our collective experience allows us to work in a number of disciplines across a variety of sectors,' explains Keith Stephenson. Additional services include trend analysis, copywriting and retail design.

When it comes to their own corporate identity, AZD aim to communicate a no-nonsense approach tinged with a sense of humour, citing influences as diverse as 'science labels, old technology and mix tapes'. The results are both practical and eccentric.

Another means of professional promotion, and one that constantly informs their identity, is their work as pattern designers, which forms the basis of their product ranges, including their own brand, Mini Moderns.

Keith explains, 'We set up Absolute Zero Degrees because of the constraints we felt working in larger agencies, where our experience wasn't being utilized. I'm from a fashion retail background; Mark is from furniture design and broadcast marketing. So, with AZD we could be as expansive as our talents and interests allowed.'

Commissioned to design a range of wallpapers, right at the resurgence of that trend, AZD gave it a contemporary twist while using traditional production methods. Their collection won awards and press coverage and was cited as influential by the decorating world.

'Having that success early on raised the profile of our branding agency and led to more pattern-based branding work,' recalls Keith.

Their own brand, Mini Moderns, is discretely hived off from AZD, with its own website. Their interior design products for kids and kidults, including wallpapers, sell in Europe, the United States and Australia, and are manufactured in the UK. Using this brand as a PR tool, they run extensive campaigns that raise their profile and win new clients. 'Our own interior accessories company demonstrates that we can create and deliver a brand from concept through production to marketing.'

Letterhead (opposite page)
Four-colour CMYK, on white Oxygen 50:50, 110gsm.
The reverse features a camouflage pattern created from maps of various countries, and a close-up detail of a wallpaper design. The stock, Oxygen 50:50, is made using 50 per cent recycled fibre and 50 per cent FSC virgin fibre.

Business Cards (below)
Four-colour CMYK, on white Oxygen 50:50, 350gsm, handwritten.
Quoting the graphic language of both the science label and the mix tape, the business cards feature space for a personalizing signature. The reverse showcases various AZD patterns.

CD and Sleeve (top right)
1/0, black, on white sticker stock, handwritten.
Disks feature screenprinted images of AZD's shelves, showcasing their books and collectables. The CD sleeves are recycled floppy disks, found at a flea market and re-purposed with a printed sticker.

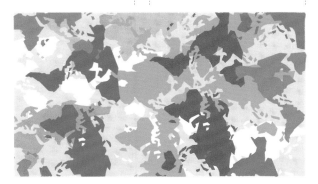

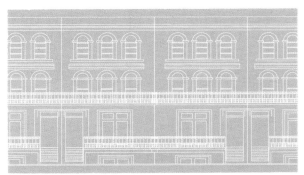

absolutezero° ISSUE#01

Make it Mine
Accessories

Putting the boot in
Dr Martens Dept Store

**Who lives in
a house like this?**
Mass Market Classics

The cure
Pharmacy freeride

Street Life
Red or Dead

Trans Urban
T.U.T.C

...and an unexpected Japanese cult!

absolutezero° ISSUE#02

Get Stuffed!
White Stuff

Playing Away!
Gola

Me gusta Mine!
Mine Successories

and *Styled Counsel*
HSBC's Open Line Services

...including late breaking news!

absolutezero° ISSUE#05

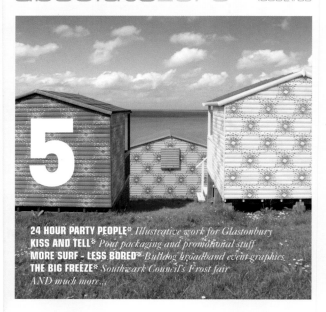

24 HOUR PARTY PEOPLE* *Illustrative work for Glastonbury*
KISS AND TELL* *Pout packaging and promotional stuff*
MORE SURF - LESS BORED* *Bulldog broadband event graphics*
THE BIG FREEZE* *Southwark Council's Frost fair*
AND much more...

absolutezero° ISSUE#06

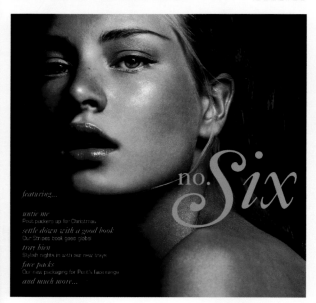

featuring...

untie me
Pout puckers up for Christmas

settle down with a good book
Our Stripes book goes global

tray bien
Stylish nights in with our new trays

face packs
Our new packaging for Pout's face range

and much more...

absolutezero°   ISSUE#03

3

NEW WORK
featuring
Art of the matter **Spectrum Fine Art** *See here* **Southwark Council**
Dream Building **Dwell Developments** *Exposure!* **DMP Media**
...including late breaking news and
Dossier a-z° archive

absolutezero°   ISSUE#04

FOUR

NEW WORK *including...*
Cuddle up with the results
of the absolute zero degrees
field trip to Portmeirion **STEEL TOWN** *Illustrative work for a revamped*
housing development **HUE & SATURATION** *Colormatch by Ali Hanan*
ROAD TRIP *New identity work with an illustrative bent*
THE BUG! *The new DAB radio from hemingwaydesign and Pure*
Digital...and so much more!

absolutezero°   ISSUE#07

lucky

7

NEW WORK
featuring
mini moderns **Our new range of wallpaper and crockery**
festival! **Better Bankside**
the perfect gift **Chosen One** *pot lucky* **World Snooker**
...including late breaking news and
press appearances

absolutezero°   ISSUE#08

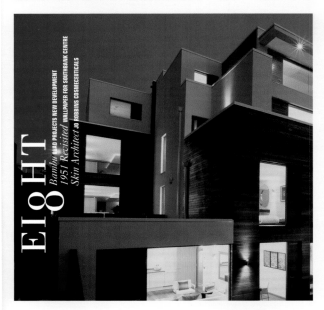

EI8HT

Bamba **QUAD PROJECTS NEW DEVELOPMENT**
1951 Revisited **WALLPAPER FOR SOUTHBANK CENTRE**
Skin Architect **JO ROBBINS COSMECEUTICALS**

Magazines
(previous spread)
Digital, in-house, four-colour CMYK,
on Era Silk, 130gsm.
Taking inspiration from zines, and
produced in short runs using recycled
stock, these self-promotional
magazines featured news and
projects, and proved very popular
with clients. The website now fulfils
this promotional function.

Tote Bag
Do you live in a town?
Screenprinted, 10oz canvas.
Made in the UK.

Christmas Card
Turning AZD's signature camouflage
pattern back into a tree.

Website
www.absolutezerodegrees.com
Launched in the early 1990s, AZD's
site pre-empted blogging culture,
offering a mix of projects, news,
press and a 'boutique'. Designed
and programmed with a content-
management system, it's easy to update
and has 'the right amount of basic
aesthetics, which we like,' says Keith.
Avoiding Flash and adopting a small
'window view', it is easily accessed from
a mobile device, for fans on the move.
'In our Fieldtrip section we add places
to see, shop, eat and stay, all with links.'

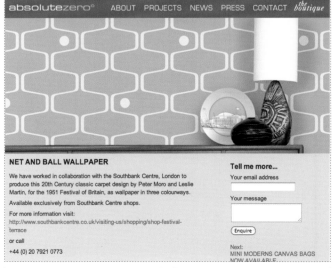

AdamsMorioka, Inc.
8484 Wilshire Boulevard, Suite 600
Beverly Hills, California 90211-3227

adamsmorioka.com
323 966 5990 telephone
323 966 5994 facsimile

AdamsMorioka

AdamsMorioka, Inc.   Sean Adams and Noreen Morioka   Beverly Hills, CA, and New York City, NY, USA   www.adamsmorioka.com

'We're not IBM, so we took liberties with the identity programme,' admits Sean Adams, one half of the partnership that likes to borrow references from *The Sound of Music* and make overblown claims, such as 'America's Favorite'! Their stationery features a hometown Hollywood hero and a Japanese anime character, 'referring to the firm's egotistical owners', explains Sean.

Meanwhile, their primary mark, a two-colour, two-name tag, with Sputnik detail, appears on all stationery, presentations and correspondence. Extra logos pop up on individual promotions, including postcards, lecture posters, notebooks, a shopping bag, and even a home-movie that gets shown at conferences and exhibitions; the aim being to reinforce the firm's attitude of 'playful, energetic optimism'.

Humour is a major part of AdamsMorioka's studio culture, and both partners are regular and popular speakers at AIGA events and at universities. For these events, they have designed an archive's-worth of inspirational, promotional posters, all tailored to the location and the partners' connection to that particular town or state.

Letterhead (opposite page and this page, below)
2/2, PMS (various and fluorescent) on Strathmore Writing Wove, Ultimate White, 24# Writing.
'Our colour palette is intentionally vibrant, using fluorescents whenever possible. If you get an invoice from us, at least you'll be happy for a couple of minutes.' The reverse of the letterhead features stylised alter-egos of the two principals.

Logos (top right)
Playful 'add-on' logos, loosely based on mid-20th-century branding.

Business Cards (below right)
PMS (various) on Strathmore Writing Wove, Ultimate White, 110# Cover Bristol.

Envelope (bottom left)
2/2 PMS (various) on Strathmore Writing Wove, Ultimate White, 24# Envelope.

Sticker (bottom right)
PMS (various) on sticker stock.

Sean Adams
8484 Wilshire Boulevard, Suite 600
Beverly Hills, California 90211-3227
323 966 5990 telephone
323 966 5994 facsimile
sean_a@adamsmorioka.com

AdamsMorioka, Inc.
8484 Wilshire Boulevard, Suite 600
Beverly Hills, California 90211-3227

AdamsMorioka

AdamsMorioka, Inc.
8484 Wilshire Boulevard, Suite 600
Beverly Hills, California 90211-3227

Holiday Gift (opposite page, top)
Every year the studio creates a
giveaway. Past gifts have included
a series of blank notebooks and an
eco-friendly shopping bag.

Postcards (opposite page, middle)
'When we started in 1994, we didn't
have any work, so we put ourselves
on the postcard. It created a lot of
controversy: some people loved it, some
hated it, and we got back versions with
all sorts of additions. When we got too
old for dressing up, we switched to
iconic images.'

AdamsMorioka: The Early Years
(opposite page, bottom)
To the theme from *The Way We Were*,
this video functions as a tongue-
in-cheek retrospective to entertain
conference audiences.

Posters
Each poster acts as a lecture invitation
and an opportunity to maintain and
widen the AdamsMorioka presence.
The posters are typically entertaining,
and personal – one featured Sean's
family tree.

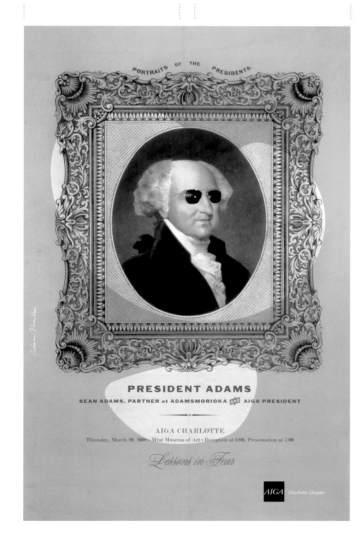

339 Upper Street
London N1 0PB
www.airside.co.uk

T: +44 (0)20 7354 9912
E: studio@airside.co.uk

Airside   London, UK   www.airside.co.uk

Creating animation, illustration, graphic design and branding, the colourful, characterful Airside approach has been closely associated with vector-style graphics. 'With our 10th anniversary in 2008, we decided that it was time to evolve a new visual aesthetic for our branding,' says Anne Brassier.

This major rebrand set out to communicate Airside's multi-disciplinary offering, in all formats, physical and digital. A bespoke typeface was the first building block, guaranteeing ease of identification across every element. A series of animated and static logos were developed from the typeface, which appear frozen in a moment of time and motion. Rather than sticking the logo discreetly in a corner, it's used for maximum impact with the design of each element derived from the logo itself.

One of Airside's founders, Nat Hunter, is also involved with Three Trees Don't Make a Forest, offering advice to the design and advertising industries on how to improve environmental sustainability. That commitment is also part of Airside's approach. 'We tried to make the branding have the smallest possible impact on the environment,' explains Elliot Hammer. 'All of Airside's branding is printed on one sheet, to minimize wastage; the DVD packaging may be reused and includes an indicator to say when it was made. Everything is printed with soya inks too.'

VAT No. 740 2403 78
Company No. 3814850

Letterhead (opposite page)
PDF, digital, in-house.
'We print them out as we need them.'

Disk Labels and Envelopes
(below left)
CD labels are white, and so
differentiated from the black
DVD labels.

Postcard (below right)
Postcards feature colour images
and information about key projects.

Sticker (below middle)
Four-colour CMYK, on white
sticker stock.

**Showreel Boxes and
DVD Labels** (top right)
Can be reused and updated; a black
label is used to differentiate the DVD
from the CD.

339 Upper Street
London N1 0PB

www.airside.co.uk

Anne Brassier
PR & New Business

T: +44 (0)20 7354 9912
E: anne@airside.co.uk

339 Upper Street
London N1 0PB

www.airside.co.uk

T: +44 (0)20 7354 9912
E: studio@airside.co.uk

Vitsœ.com

Launched in February 2009, Airside's
redesign of Vitsœ's website introduces
a new audience to this unique
shelving company. Combining
accessible design with digital
interaction and moving image, the
site provides a simple planning and
ordering system as well as detailing
Vitsœ's rich history and values.

Airside: No. 2 Digital Agency - Design
Week Creative Survey

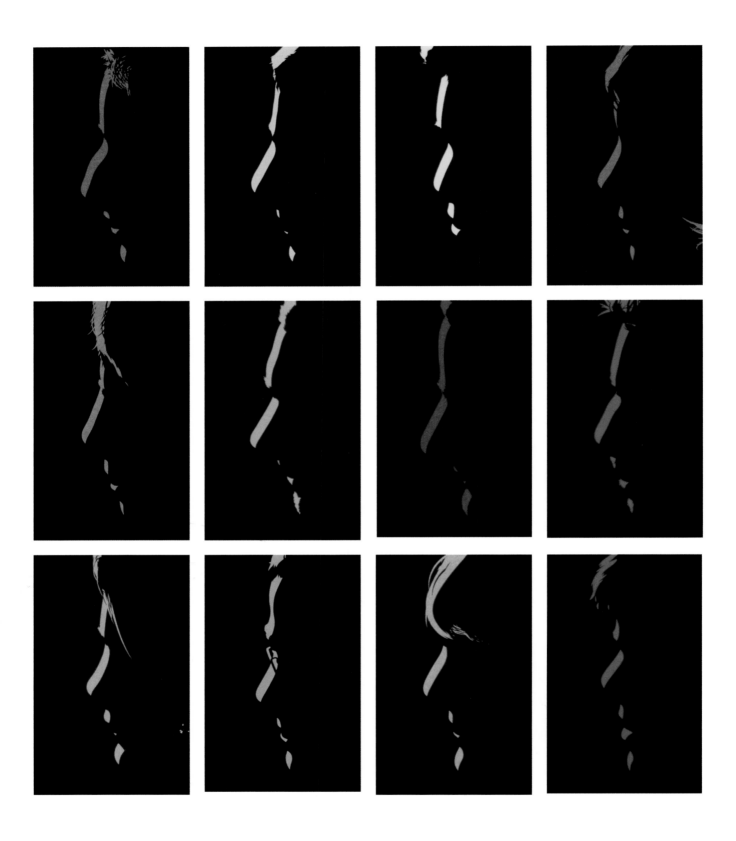

Business Cards (opposite page)
Four-colour CMYK, on Revive
Uncoated, 350gsm.
Business cards feature a subtle profile
of each studio member teamed with a
signature colour.

Logo (below left)
Two iterations from a series of
animated logos developed from the
bespoke typeface. These appear as if in
suspended motion, and demonstrate the
logo's flexibility.

Folded Poster (below right)
1/1, blue, on white stock.
Mailed to clients and colleagues when
Airside relocated their studio.

Website (bottom)
www.airside.co.uk
On a low-energy black ground, Airside
displays its showreel, work, blog,
environmental projects and shop,
which presents a range of creative
products by Airside members,
colleagues and friends.

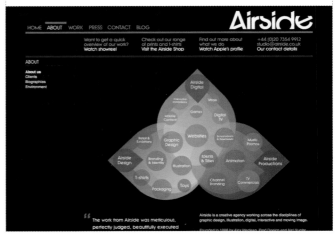

AKATRE, DESIGN GRAPHIQUE
JULIEN, SÉBASTIEN, VALENTIN
1, RUE CHARLES GARNIER
93400 SAINT OUEN
+33 (0) 9 50 42 49 19
AKATRE@AKATRE.COM
WWW.AKATRE.COM

Akatre

Valentin Abad, Julien Dhivert, Sébastien Riveron

Saint-Ouen, France

www.akatre.com

Working with media and cultural clients, including magazines, theatres and choreographers, the Akatre partners often turn themselves into 'artworks'. Performance is a key part of their practice, and of their corporate identity.

'When we want to communicate using images, we use the human triangle,' they explain. 'We wanted a strong, iconic image for our homepage, but we didn't want to show our faces, so we decided to represent Akatre by its first letter.' So they created a 'living logo' of the three of them linked together, which they refresh each year with a new pose.

To further emphasize their partnership, Akatre designed a bespoke typeface, Aspirateur, to use as a signature. Featuring a notch device, the blocky letterforms knit together into lines of decorative, almost textural type.

And, if you look closely at their work you'll find them, disguised with costumes and special effects, appearing in a number of projects. 'We often use ourselves as models; it's more convenient and it forces us to adopt "subterfuge", to not be recognized.'

SIRET 499 931 632 00016 | APE 923A

Letterhead (opposite page)
Digital, in-house, black on
recycled paper.

Business Card (far right)
1/0, black foil, on Sirio Black, 380gsm.

Website
www.akatre.com
Features various performance and
type-based animations. 'We make
movies to present our atelier because
we don't want to simply include text on
our website.' In one movie (bottom), the
unseen partners scribble the company
name on to an opaque screen, as the
voiceover repeats, 'English Version',
over an eerie, insect-like noise, 'which is
the sound of us talking, speeded up.'

oostkousdijk 12a   +31(0)10 477 18 19
3024 cm rotterdam   almostmodern.com
the netherlands   mail@almostmodern.com

almost Modern   btw: NL8510.59.528.B01
    giro: 1290997

aan: betreft:

almost Modern   Jorn de Vries and Markus Rummens   Rotterdam, the Netherlands   www.almostmodern.com

A section header of their website, 'printed matter', hints at this duo's love of words, and sits amid thumbnail details of various poster and publication projects, located within an editorialized grid. A proliferation of silkscreen-printed posters reveals Jorn de Vries and Markus Rummens's consistent exploration of the technique, using the minimum of means, one- and two-colours, and with an emphasis on legibility by means of a choice of simple but bold typography.

That directness of communication is reiterated in almost Modern's graphic identity, their name shortened to an emphatic 'aM'. Stationery items are based on a well-defined grid and stickers are used to heighten awareness. 'We came up with the idea of stickers because we wanted to brand our name and our logo; the sticker is part of every mailing, an extra "present",' they explain.

het bovenstaande factuur bedrag geld uitsluitend voor de omschreven werkzaamheden. De geleverde ontwerpen worden beschermd door de Auteurswet en blijven eigendom van Almost Modern. De geleverde ontwerpen mogen zonder toestemming van Almost Modern op geen enkele andere wijze gebruikt worden dan in de opdrachts omschrijving vermeld staat, of op andere wijze dan door Almost Modern toegestaan. Mocht Almost Modern toch ontdekken dat een ontwerp zonder toestemming is uitgelekt of aangepast en gepubliceerd, stelt Almost Modern de opdrachtgever vernoemd in deze factuur aansprakelijk en zal mogelijk een gerechtelijk procedure in gang worden gezet. Door betaling van deze factuur geeft de opdrachtgever aan akkoord te gaan met deze voorwaarden.

Letterhead (opposite page)
Digital, in-house, 1/0, black, on white
stock, 90gsm.

Business Card (top left)
1/1, black, on white card.

Poster for Event (middle left)
Plastic Cups Party.
'We organize parties.'

Limited Edition T-shirt (middle right)
'We asked people to choose a number
between 0 and 9999.'

Website (bottom left)
www.almostmodern.com
The site uses a five-column grid to
create an editorial format, with strong
black and white identity elements to
the fore.

Blog site (bottom right)
www.letmeholdyoutight.com
A new venture, in studied contrast to
the 'studio' site, this four-column blog
aims to 'discover things that have
already happened', and provide a
contemporary history lesson.

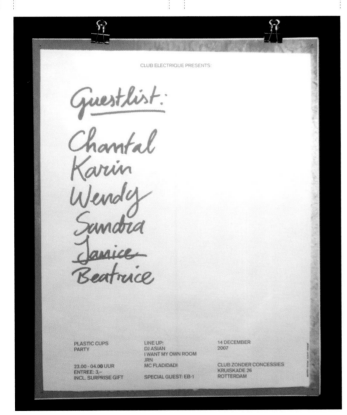

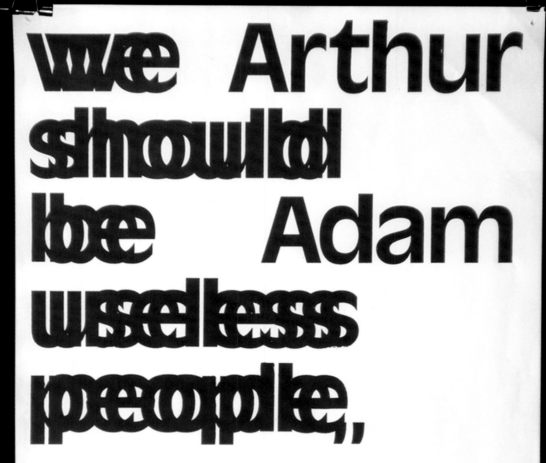

we Arthur
should
be   Adam
useless
people,

baby

in a cabin with

graphic design: almost modern

Posters (opposite page and
this page, main picture)
Screenprint on various stock.
'We send these to people who we're
interested in.'

Sticker (top left)
One-colour vinyl sticker.

Alter   Jonathan Wallace and Dan Whitford   Windsor, Australia   www.alter.com.au

Alter is a design studio founded by Jonathan Wallace
and Dan Whitford; while Jonathan guest-lectures at
Monash University in Melbourne, Dan is frontman of the
band Cut Copy. With a diverse list of clients, from record
labels to furniture manufacturers, and a liking for staging
exhibitions and events, Alter have developed a corporate
identity that favours neon brights, is entertaining and
experimental, and continues to evolve through a number
of self-instigated projects.

Jonathan explains: 'The non-commercial projects
aren't planned or strategic. They're not so much
marketing, more just an opportunity to focus little
moments on our own expression. These projects reflect
our personalities and interests, and keep us inspired and
informed, so in that sense they're fundamental to building
our design practice.'

He adds that these projects aim to be provocative,
but realizes that their reception is beyond his control.
'Among our many motivations is a desire to explore the
absurdity of our profession, which is a veritable goldmine
for anyone observing behaviour. We're a part of this
sometimes ridiculous posturing, pitching and positioning,
and we're conscious enough of our role within it to reflect
on it. We don't have a "masterplan" though, we're more
like skeptical, but happy, disciples.'

Alter...
151 Union Street
Windsor 3181
Victoria Australia
Phone +61 3 9533 2200
Facsimile +61 3 9533 2299
Email alter@alter.com.au
www.alter.com.au

Letterhead, two versions
(opposite page and below)
1/1, black and pink PMS, on Saxton
Brilliant White Smooth, 100gsm.
2/2, black, red PMS, orange PMS,
on Saxton Brilliant White Smooth,
100gsm.
The tagline 'things change' is circled
on the reverse; some sheets have
the addition of an action photo of the
founding partners.

Business Cards
Dan and Jono piano card (bottom right)
Black and orange PMS, and silver foil
block, on Elements Bright White Lines,
298gsm.

T-shirt Business Card (bottom left)
2/2, black and red PMS and orange
PMS on white card.
More action-packed imagery hints at
Alter's dynamic energy.

Compliments Slip, two versions
(below right)
2/0, black and pink PMS, on white
stock.
2/1, pink PMS and green PMS, on
white card.

Poster (top right)
Black on grey stock, folded.
Identikit images of the design team.

Installation (main picture),
Card and Folded Leaflet
(below and right)
Lost and Found

Booklets (below and middle)
Perpection is everything
Man: Past Presents Future
Black, on white stock and coloured
cover stock.

Website (bottom)
www.alter.com.au
A tongue-in-cheek 'Always Pro' logo
references a 'print shop' attitude. The
Other Stuff section provides a blog-
space for Alter-organized design events
and initiatives in and around Melbourne,
Australia's design capital.

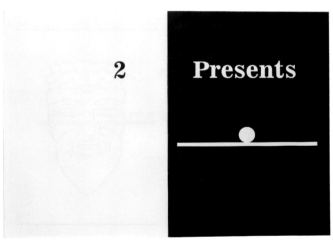

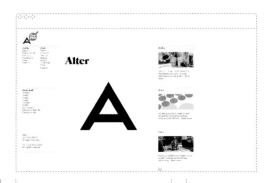

172 JOHN STREET, TORONTO ON CANADA M5T 1X5
TELEPHONE 416.599.2699   FACSIMILE 416.599.2391
WEBSITE AMOEBACORP.COM

AmoebaCorp   Mike Kelar and Mikey Richardson   Toronto, ON, Canada   www.amoebacorp.com

A 14-strong team, AmoebaCorp was founded by Mike Kelar and Mikey Richardson in 1996, with a commitment to change the ways in which the design industry works with commercial clients. Mike Kelar explains: 'We create work that is sustainable and ecological, based on our daily observations of how natural resources have been abused. Since designers have compounded the problem, through our own business practices, we need to take some responsibility for fixing it or at least lessening the impact. Trying to do "the right thing" usually takes time and money, so we look for opportunities to deliver against a core value of sustainability.'

Leading by example, through the creative reuse of reclaimed materials, AmoebaCorp's comprehensive and eye-catching corporate identity and stationery system offers a creative and unique solution.

'We use billboard material that is headed for landfill; cropped in tight it's impossible for the "ads" to be recognized,' Mike explains. Up close, these giant images are revealed as a series of overlapping dots, printed in various colours through wide-gauge screens. When seen from a distance, the coloured dots merge to create legible images; the macro view, however, creates an ever-changing, colour-saturated backdrop for AmoebaCorp's correspondence and presentations. 'Each piece is unique,' he says, 'the tricky bit is parting with them.'

♻ THIS WAS PRINTED ON RECLAIMED BILLBOARD MATERIAL.

Letterheads (opposite page and below)
1/1, black and opaque white, on reclaimed billboard stock.

Envelopes (bottom left)
1/0, opaque white, on reclaimed billboard stock, die-cut, hand-finished.

**Presentation Covers with
Mailing Label** (bottom right)
Reclaimed corrugated paper duplexed with reclaimed billboard stock, die-cut; 2/0, embossed, die-cut on MACtac sticker stock, hand-finished.

Business Cards (top right)
1/0 on FSC card stock, duplexed with reclaimed billboard stock, die-cut; 2/0, embossed, die-cut on MACtac sticker stock, hand-finished.

Notebook
The Medium Was the Message
Front cover: screenprinted, 2/0, 100%
post-consumer pressboard.
Back cover: screenprinted, 1/0, 100%
post-consumer pressboard duplexed
with reclaimed billboard stock; punched,
spiral bound.
Inside pages: reclaimed billboard stock,
french folded, punched.
Printed tag attached with metal chain.

Website (main pictures)
www.amoebacorp.com
'For our site, we wanted navigation and updating to be user-friendly, while also creating a dynamic experience,' explains Mike. Several devices are employed: a revolving library of thought-provoking images foregrounds 'change'; a main navigation menu presents equally weighted categories of commercial and personal work alongside biographies of AmoebaCorp personnel; projects are viewed as images at various scales; PDFs and video may be downloaded, and quick arrow navigation brings you to their blog, featuring work, play and finds.

Disk Envelopes (top right)
1/0, opaque white, on FSC card stock, duplexed with reclaimed billboard stock, die-cut.

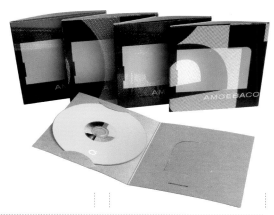

Richard Ardagh   Richard Ardagh   London, UK   www.elephantsgraveyard.co.uk

On graduating from Central Saint Martins College of Art and Design, Richard Ardagh admits to feeling 'quite dismal about the prospect of being released into the "real world", among thousands of other young designers. It seemed as though putting up a website was a bit like throwing a needle into a haystack.' So, he chose a name for his website that was a little out of the ordinary.

'It refers to a mythical place to which elephants are instinctively drawn during their final days. Legend has it that the elephants' graveyard holds a book, containing incantations, which could bring peace or destruction. So trackers have followed elephants that were near death, only to be led in circles.'

Unlike that legendary place, Richard's website actually exists, and 'people seem to remember the elephant connection'. A compulsive image-gatherer, Richard acknowledges a propensity for elephant imagery, and recalls that Peter Beard's photograph, *The End of the Game*, 'triggered my imagination'.

Letterhead (opposite page)
Digital, in-house, black, on white stock, hand-stamped.

Poster (below)
Elephant Man
2006
Letterpress, on newsprint, limited edition of 300.
Produced for a 'Victorian Freak Show' during the London Design Festival, and featuring a poem used by Joseph Merrick (the Elephant Man) on all correspondence. 'I'm interested in nineteenth-century type, and it suits some projects. I get commissions from people who've seen my graphic identity and the letterpress posters (which I print with Graham Bignell).'

Business Card (bottom right)
How Do You Do?
'I stumbled upon this image deep in a pile of dusty volumes some years before, and when I founded my own studio, I thought it summed up my new professional approach.'

Plectrum (below, far right)
2003
'Sort of an alternative business card, and an attempt to appeal to an audience I could relate to.'

Rubber Stamps
Inspired by trips to Japan, where stamps and seals are used everywhere, by families, at temples and at train stations, Richard regularly has stamps cut from his own designs, as 'they're a great way of personalizing correspondence.'

**Join me for tea and
Best wishes for 2008** (top right)
'I'd moved studio, and received part-payment for a branding job in tea bags; so one thing led to another.'

ATTAK

—　　　　　　　　　　　　　　　　—

| ATTAK Powergestaltung | Casper Herselman and Peter Korsman | 's-Hertogenbosch, the Netherlands | www.attakweb.com |

With commercial and personal projects ranging across graphics, illustration, art and type design, and eager to distance themselves from a homogeneous design industry, Casper Herselman and Peter Korsman attempted a redefinition. 'When we started out, we wanted to create a word/term/statement/ name that would differentiate us. So, we came up with Powergestaltung, adding "power" to the German word for "design". Some people think we're German, but they remember it, simply because of the odd word.' The name is used big and bold in the stationery elements of their corporate identity, while their website underlines their no-nonsense approach, archiving projects for a range of international clients.

——　Oude Vlijmenseweg 190c　　T　+31 (0) 73 6230 950　　KvK　1717 2432
　　　5223 GT 's-Hertogenbosch　　E　attak@attakweb.com　　BTW　NL 8138.84.111.B01
　　　The Netherlands　　　　　　W　www.attakweb.com　　RABO　1033 82895

POWERGESTALTUNG

Letterhead (opposite page)
1/0, PMS 295, on yellow stock.
'Like the Yellow Pages.'

Invoice (below)
1/0, PMS 295, on pink stock.
'Like financial newspapers.'

Business Card (below right)
1/1, PMS 295, on white Chromolux.
'A chic hello, with one side shiny and
one side matte.'

T-shirt Swingtags (top right)
Screenprinted, 2/2, black and
fluorescent yellow, on white card,
die-cut.
Attached to an ever-changing range of
T-shirts available from the website.

ATTAK

ATTAK

— Casper Herselman

Oude Vlijmenseweg 190c
5223 GT 's-Hertogenbosch
The Netherlands

T   +31 (0) 73 6230 950
E   attak@attakweb.com
W   www.attakweb.com

POWERGESTALTUNG

— Oude Vlijmenseweg 190c   T +31 (0) 73 6230 950   KvK   1717 2432
5223 GT 's-Hertogenbosch   E attak@attakweb.com   BTW   NL 8138.84.111.B01
The Netherlands   W www.attakweb.com   RABO 1033 82895

POWERGESTALTUNG

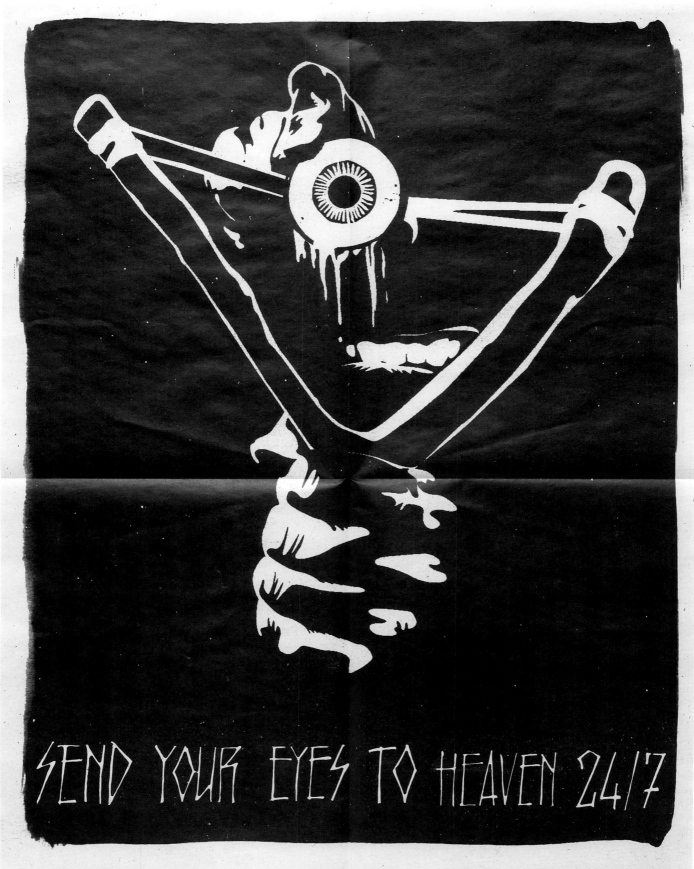

SEND YOUR EYES TO HEAVEN 24/7

WWW.ATTAKWEB.COM
13/2/2009 AT 13:13 CET
WEBSITE RELAUNCH

NO PRESALE, NO FREE DRINKS
JUST LOTS OF FRESH GRAPHIC
DESIGN & POWERGESTALTUNG

ATTAK | Powergestaltung
CASPER HERSELMAN
PETER KORSMAN

Vinyl Stickers (top left)
Various designs.
'Stickers are perfect for trashing around the globe, the best giveaway, and great advertising.'

Posters (opposite page and bottom, shown in situ)
'We sticker a lot and we glue posters around the city, just to make people aware of graphic design,' says Casper. 'The best thing is seeing your wet poster being ripped off a wall because somebody likes it, or hates it. We're doing the opposite of street artists, though; we're turning graphic design into street art by using it in the streets.

Postcards (below, main picture)
These are used as compliments slips, and sent out on request from the website, mailed in numbered envelopes, for free.

BANK™

MEGASOLUTIONS TO MICROPROBLEMS

| BANK™ | Sebastian Bissinger and Laure Boer | Berlin, Germany | www.bankassociates.de |

It's important for this German and French couple, Sebastian Bissinger and Laure Boer, to keep their business small and retain the freedom to select only the assignments that allow for maximum creative freedom. So, they collaborate with a network of practitioners on projects ranging across identity, illustration, editorial and promotion, for a client list that includes record labels, publishers, fashion companies and nightclubs, and organizations as diverse as Adidas and UNESCO.

That said, their own corporate identity plays with perceptions of power and scale; by calling themselves BANK™, adopting a 'hard-sell' tagline, and creating a promotional image of a fictitious, gigantic headquarters building, Sebastian and Laure have subtly subverted corporate culture.

–
BANK™ / Rungestraße 22—24 / 10179 Berlin / Germany
T +49 (0)30 24 04 75 -70 / F -71
tellme@bankassociates.de / www.bankassociates.de
–

© BANK™ / Megasolutions to Microproblems

Letterhead (opposite page)
1/1, black, on white stock.
The tagline, 'Megasolutions to
Microproblems', features on all
stationery, along with a series of
'rules' that underline an orderly,
business-like attitude.

Business Cards (top left and below)
1/1, black, on white card.
Two sizes of business card: one for
convenience, one for maximum impact.

Website (bottom)
www.bankassociates.de
With a strong black and white
aesthetic and generous use of rules,
the site closely echoes BANK™'s
printed identity.

BANK™

MEGASOLUTIONS TO MICROPROBLEMS

–

Rungestraße 22 – 24 / 10179 Berlin / Germany
T +49 (0)30 24 04 75 -70 / F -71
tellme@bankassociates.de
www.bankassociates.de

–

BANK™

MEGASOLUTIONS TO MICROPROBLEMS

–

Rungestraße 22 – 24 / 10179 Berlin / Germany
T +49 (0)30 24 04 75 -70 / F -71
tellme@bankassociates.de
www.bankassociates.de

–

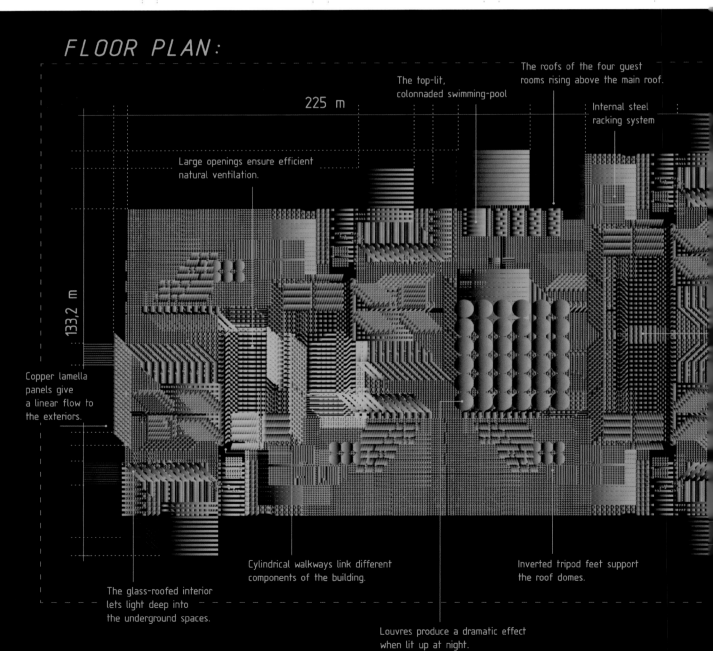

FLOOR PLAN:

225 m

133,2 m

The top-lit,
colonnaded swimming-pool

The roofs of the four guest
rooms rising above the main roof.

Internal steel
racking system

Large openings ensure efficient
natural ventilation.

Copper lamella
panels give
a linear flow to
the exteriors.

The glass-roofed interior
lets light deep into
the underground spaces.

Cylindrical walkways link different
components of the building.

Inverted tripod feet support
the roof domes.

Louvres produce a dramatic effect
when lit up at night.

Folder and Project Sheets
(opposite page, top)
1/0, black, on greyboard; digital,
in-house, black, on white stock.
A selection of projects are presented to
new clients and the press in the form of
single sheets building into a portfolio,
housed in a customized folder.

Limited Edition Poster
Promotional image, featuring a
'blueprint' of BANK™'s fictitious
headquarters, on a larger-than-life
scale. This edition was distributed via
their website.

SECTION:

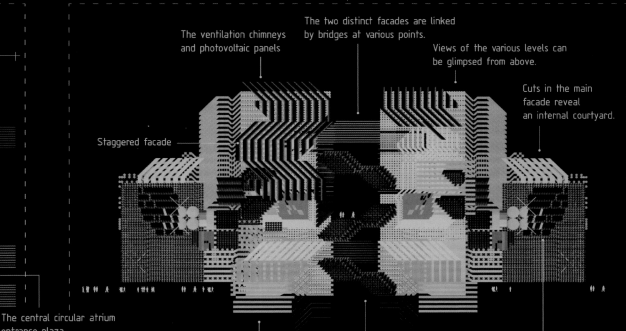

The ventilation chimneys
and photovoltaic panels

The two distinct facades are linked
by bridges at various points.

Views of the various levels can
be glimpsed from above.

Cuts in the main
facade reveal
an internal courtyard.

Staggered facade

The central circular atrium
entrance plaza

Ribbed concrete entrance and glazed entrance
structure both located on a central axis.

A dynamic geometry of elements
characterizes the external stair towers.

Adjustable screens animate
the facade.

PROJECT: BANK™ HEADQUARTERS
PLANNING: BANK™
AREA: 22000 SQM/236720 SQFT
COST: CONFIDENTIAL

BANK™
HEADQUARTERS
2008

1:2250

| Fabien Barral | Fabien Barral | St Bonnet Près Orcival, France | www.fabienbarral.com |

Having access to printing technology, Fabien Barral saw an opportunity to expand his graphics studio by designing, manufacturing and selling interior design products through his company Harmonie intérieure. 'I've always thought that graphic design can be used differently than simply a client-based, business-to-business project,' he explains.

Fabien's range of large-scale, vinyl stickers and posters transform his decorative illustrations into instant wall art, deliverable by post. Fabien created the corporate identity for this project in collaboration with his wife, Frédérique Barral: 'she paints watercolour backgrounds and textures and I scan them, and mix in old papers and textures from antique books that I buy at second-hand markets.'

The resulting images appear on packaging, brochures and the website. But while Fabien's signature style is layered and densely decorative, by contrast his personal business card is monochrome, the textural interest created by embossing.

Business Card (opposite page)
Letterpress, 1/0, black, on cream card, blind emboss.
The circular design is intended as a ripple effect, demonstrating that actions have consequences. Fabien uses his card as a mini-portfolio, to demonstrate the possibilities of business card design.

Business Card, Brochure, Labels, Packaging
Harmonie intérieure
2/2, duotone, on white card.
The aesthetic language of Frédérique and Fabien's graphic products is demonstrated in this corporate identity, promotional material and packaging.

Website (bottom)
www.graphic-exchange.com
Fabien has developed an international network of contacts and colleagues via his extensive blog, which also features a wide range of personal projects.

bezoekadres
Cingelstraat 30
4811 MC Breda

postadres
Postbus 1168
4801 BD Breda

telefoon
076 520 51 20
fax
076 520 52 20

email
battery@battery.nl
website
www.battery.nl

rabobank breda
18.24.09.708
kvk breda
20074061

btw nummer
NL 8159.98.451.B.01

aan

betreft

breda

| Battery Battery | Yurrian Rozenberg | Breda, the Netherlands | www.battery.nl |

Having developed a design process that stresses the virtues of flexibility and change, updating Battery Battery's corporate identity provided an opportunity to showcase the team's unconventional methods.

Yurrian Rozenberg explains: 'In 2006 we needed to take Battery Battery to the next level. The existing identity had been a big change, and had done its job. We still liked the idea, which built up using specially selected elements, so why not recycle it?'

That first lateral thought led to a pattern-making method that married computing with a chance moment. 'We cut and pasted shapes from our previous stationery, then dropped it on the floor!' Tempering chaos with a classical element, they adopted Linotype's Bulmer (originally designed by William Martin in the eighteenth century) for all correspondence. '...We wanted our house style to be a bit more sophisticated,' adds Yurrian, 'but we also wanted to experiment with different types of fluorescent and metallic ink.' Once again, they reined in the random by imposing control mechanisms, using rules and grids to define various text areas and usage; even providing guide-markers for your hole punch.

That mix of approaches and methods is typical of Battery Battery. 'We combine creativity with strategy, and search for the best technical solution,' explains Yurrian. Asked what he thinks this bold identity says about Battery Battery, Yurrian is clear: 'That we're a company with the courage to stand out from the crowd because we aim to inspire.'

Leading by example paid off, as the new identity earned Battery Battery an assignment for a printers' sample book, *NPN Proef*, a comprehensive guide on how to achieve a range of effects, using various techniques and inks on four different paper stocks.

On a lighter note, the story behind their name reveals just how fundamentally Battery Battery embrace the random. 'It has to do with a little note that we discovered during a photoshoot; it fell from a device, a certain toy for women.'

grafisch ontwerpbureau

Battery Battery

Printing: Koninklijke Broese
and Peereboom

Letterhead (opposite page)
1/2, PMS 876 copper and PMS 805
fluorescent red, on Conqueror CX 22
High White, 100gsm.

Process Images
These images document Battery
Battery's pattern-making process,
whereby elements from the previous
identity system were cut up and
scattered, then photographed, to
provide a new geometry for the
second, evolved system.

Brief (opposite page)
1/2, PMS 876 copper and PMS 805 fluorescent red, on Conqueror CX 22 High White, 100gsm.

Document Folder (below left),
Note Card (below right),
Disk Envelope (top right),
and Business Cards (bottom),
1/2, PMS 876 copper and PMS 802 neon green, on Conqueror CX 22 High White, 250gsm.

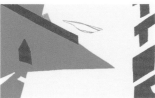

Alexandre Bettler   Alexandre Bettler   London, UK   www.aalex.info

Alexandre Bettler has created a range of books, posters, T-shirts and products, often utilizing unorthodox recycling methods to make new products from old. He also re-purposes standard, mass-produced objects, through subtle additions and handmade alterations; he has adapted materials and objects as diverse as workmen's reflective jackets, twigs, bread, seashells, envelopes and street signs. His archival website is crammed with all sorts of projects, across different media and disciplines, most of which are self-instigated and therefore, to a degree, self-promotional.

Alexandre's own corporate identity is far from corporate; instead, he uses the need to communicate basic information as an opportunity to explore visual language. By comparing business cards designed and produced by print shops from around the world, he reveals how, by default, they create different, very local identities. Here he explains the project.

'My business cards are part of a personal project that started a few years ago. The aim is not to design my own business card, but to get other people to do it. So each time I visit a new country, I find a printer and ask him to make a business card for me, as I believe his design and final object will accurately reflect that country's "trend" for business cards, at that moment in time, as well as revealing part of its "history".

'About ten years ago, I visited my brother in Ecuador and found a printer using letterpress; it was easy to explain that I just wanted an email address on the card, along with the latitude/longitude of Ecuador, and I had about 300 cards made.

'I repeated the process in Sri Lanka and got some great cards with rounded corners and gold edges, and then again in Belarus when I was giving a workshop there. The "Nueva Dirección" sticker came from Barcelona in Spain, where many locksmiths and other traders use this cheap medium to advertise their services on shop shutters.

'I loved the idea of the high-visibility, cheap and mobile medium, so I found a printer in the suburbs and wrote down the information that I needed on the sticker; the minimum order quantity was 3,000. The tagline "Nueva Dirección" must have been a standard text or left over from the previous sticker printed; it means "New Address."

'I use these stickers as business cards because I like the idea that if people don't want to keep one, they can stick it somewhere else. It's also a perfect way to "reuse" other people's business cards. Also, the sticker creates an odd situation, as nobody really knows how to use them or where to put them. Most people end up putting them on their mobile phone, I'm not sure why...

'The latest card comes from New York, where I found a Jewish printer who chose a logo to represent my work even though it wasn't clear to him what graphic design was. And he refused to make the card if I wouldn't have my full address on it! It just didn't make sense to him to have a business card without an address, "How can you do business without an address on it?" he said. After a few visits to his shop I also managed to get my name written in Hebrew. Tough work, but a great card!

'I like the fact that each of these cards represents, in a way, a stereotype or "classic" version of each country's business cards, because the printers have created a "basic" or "undesigned" version of a standard business card, one that would suit anybody.

'I also really like the concept of being naïve and this is something I try to push and question; but I've also noticed that it is difficult to explain what I understand by 'naïve'. For me, it is a positive notion. It helps to reach a wider audience by using other people's design language and means of communication.'

Barcelona 'Nueva Dirección' Stickers
On a roll (opposite page, top) and in situ,
on a shop shutter and a mobile phone
(opposite page, bottom).

New York Business Card
(below left)

Belarus Business Card
(below right)

Sri Lanka Business Card
(bottom left)

New Website Business Card
(bottom right)

Alexandre Bettler

AALEX.INFO

Website WWW.ALEX.INFO
E.mail   HELLO@AALEX.INFO

19 Warburton Road
E8 3RT London
Tel # 44 (0) 7743699430

БЕЗ ВИЗИТКИ НЕТ ПРОБЛЕМ,
ЛИШЬ БЫ НЕ БЫЛО ВОЙНЫ

Alexandre Bettler

olaaalex@hotmail.com
+44(0)77 43699430

Minsk-05

නැවත පැමිණෙන්න
PLEASE COME AGAIN
மீண்டும் வருக

olaaalex@hotmail.com

each page of my new website has two sides
www.and-or.org *(finissage 27.09.04)*
now on paper only

alexandre bettler
17a kingsland road e2 8aa london
+44 77 436 99 430 olaaalex at hotmail.com

Bunch Ltd
27 Phipp Street
London EC2A 4NP
United Kingdom

+44/0/207/168 2539
info@bunchdesign.com
www.bunchdesign.com
www.madeinbunch.com

Registration Number 4440786
VAT Number 853 6117 26

Bunch   London, UK and Zagreb, Croatia   www.bunchdesign.com

The black silhouette of a bold capital 'B' was the starting point for a project that brought collaboration, in a big way, into the corporate identity of Bunch. This team of long-time friends, with studios in London and Zagreb, reached out to a network of contacts and beyond, asking other designers to embellish their logo. 'The ultimate aim was to extract a new playful identity,' they explain. 'However, we weren't sure how the project would be received or if we'd ever get our ID!'

After six months, there were more than 200 contributions from around the world. Called 'Bunchisms' and displayed on an additional micro-site, they come not only from invited guests, but from a wide range of designers, as anyone is free to post. In effect, each Bunchism is a combination logo, showing off the preferred aesthetic of the collaborator, while playing with Bunch's 'B'. Unexpected results abound from, among others, such famous names as Build, Paul Davis, Julian Morey, Si Scott and Thirst.

Many have been incorporated into the stationery system, which includes 127 different business cards. Each staff member is treated to a set of 32, featuring their favourites.

Letterhead (opposite page)
1/0, black, on white stock.

Identity Range
The full identity system consists
of a vast number of elements and
objects: letterheads, business cards,
compliments slips, postcards, poster,
CD envelopes, stickers, rubber stamps,
packing tape, mug, T-shirt, tote bag,
murals and signage.

T-shirt (bottom left)
Featuring Paul Davis's Bunchism.

Vinyl wall motif (bottom right)
This Bunchism features a reversed-out
white B.

Book
Bastardised: 289 Selected Bunchisms
by Made in Bunch, 2008.
Self-published in a hand-numbered
limited edition of 1,500 and featuring
covers in various colourways.

Website (bottom right)
Bunch's commercial website (www.
bunchdesign.com) links to the project's
micro-site, www.madeinbunch.com.
An index of contributors makes for
easy access to hundreds of logos or
'Bunchisms'.

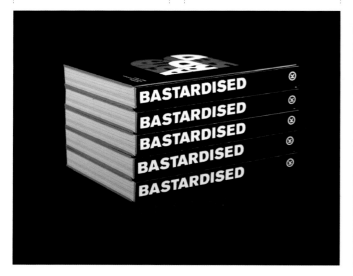

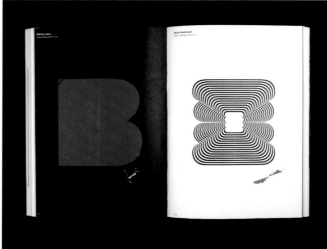

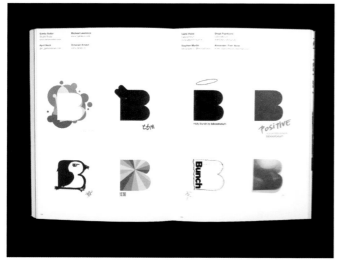

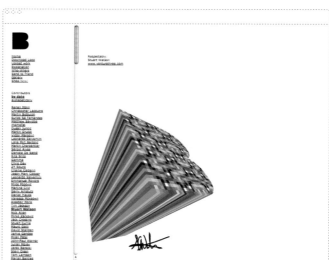

Business Card
Letterpress, 2/1 black and magenta,
on Brilliant White, Conqueror Sleek,
300gsm.
Typographer: Birte Ludwig
Letterpress Printer: Martin Z. Schröder
Letterpress Studio: Druckerey, Berlin
'I keep it simple: business cards only.'

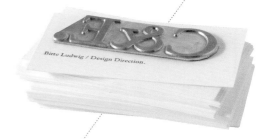

Bureau Ludwig   Birte Ludwig   Berlin, Germany   www.bureau-ludwig.com

'I wanted my card to have a clear motto and came up with two letters: "C" stands for Career – my successful work; "E" stands for Ego – my ambition to constantly refine. It's a very personal statement, so I decided to hand-make the business cards on a lead typesetting machine, and found a small print shop in East Berlin that still practices lead typesetting. The two big letters weren't available in an appropriate size or typeface, so I had to create a "cliché". When printed they look elegant because they are a little embossed, and the result is quite tactile.'

Birte Ludwig's chosen print method introduced another element to the mix: chance. 'The printer mentioned that there would be some "failures" on the way to achieving the right colour from the mix of blue and red ink, as the colour wouldn't always spread evenly across the surface. Out came a moiré effect, which I liked a lot,' says Birte. Each card is therefore unique, something Birte admits was a surprise, but which he is happy with.

C&E.

Bureau Ludwig / Concept, Strategy, Design /
inform@bureau-ludwig.com / www.bureau-ludwig.com /
+49 (0) 177 72 74 854

C&E.

Bureau Ludwig / Concept, Strategy, Design /
inform@bureau-ludwig.com / www.bureau-ludwig.com /
+49 (0) 177 72 74 854

C&E.

Bureau Ludwig / Concept, Strategy, Design /
inform@bureau-ludwig.com / www.bureau-ludwig.com /
+49 (0) 177 72 74 854

BURNEVERYTHING
STUDIO 3.6. 27 PARLIAMENT STREET
LIVERPOOL, UNITED KINGDOM. L8 5RN
TEL 0151 707 6707
INFO@BURNEVERYTHING.CO.UK
BURNEVERYTHING.CO.UK

Burneverything | David Hand, Matt Lewis, Sam Wiehl | Liverpool, UK | www.burneverything.co.uk

This three-strong partnership designs books, bars, logos, posters, T-shirts and identities for organizations as diverse as Tate Liverpool, the Shanghai Biennale and every other cool venue in their hometown. So how did they get started? 'Burneverything was born out of far too many glasses of ale and a purposeful feeling of wanting to change where we were "at" at the time,' they explain.

Their logo features three figures riding a horse: 'We've been reluctant to walk most of our lives and having rode on the back of fire engines and polar bears decided it was time to mount a thoroughbred.'

With projects that foreground drawing alongside their art direction skills, and an identity that mixes up a layered aesthetic and a healthy dose of humour, do they ever get typecast? 'We seemed to go through a period of being known as illustrators and then interior designers, but we've worked on so many different projects, and our clients are aware of that; the studio has a strong personality that we try to express in our work, when it's appropriate.'

So what sort of reaction does the corporate identity get? 'A good one; hopefully people appreciate the craft, but they probably like it because it's shiny. Most people have a bit of magpie in them!'

Letterhead (opposite page)
1/0, gold foil block, on natural uncoated stock, 190gsm.

Greetings Card (below, main picture)
2/1, yellow and black, gold foil block, on natural stock, duplexed, 500gsm.

Business Card (below right)
1/0, gold foil block, on natural board, duplexed, 700gsm.

Website (bottom)
www.burneverything.co.uk
Gold caps introduce an archive with a side-scrolling slideshow.

HELLO AGAIN

WWW.BURNEVERYTHING.CO.UK

We are an experienced award winning design studio. We work across a broad range of disciplines including branding / identity, print and multimedia design, interior design, exhibition design, environmental graphics and surface decoration.

We would be good together.

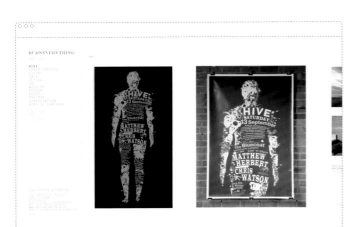

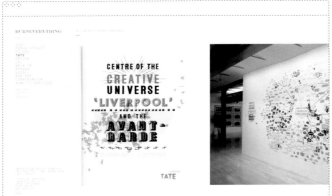

```
COBOI
Grafik Design
Katharina Reidy
PROGR/Atelier 359
Postfach 145
3000 Bern 7

T 031 311 33 36
T 077 451 02 56
katharina@coboi.ch
```

Coboi   Katharina Reidy   Bern, Switzerland   www.coboi.ch

Katharina Reidy runs her own studio, and collaborates with local designers on projects that often employ hand-drawn type, illustrations and quirky found images. Her corporate identity is also distinctly uncorporate: 'The word "coboi" is the pronunciation of "cowboy" in Swiss German,' Katharina explains. 'It's a nice word that reminds me of my childhood...even if I always played the Indian.' An old tin badge of a cowboy has become part of the Coboi identity, and is now officially the studio mascot.

Letterhead and Invoice
(opposite page)
Digital, in-house, 1/0, black, on Fischer
Papier Marina.
Katharina uses Akkurat Mono from
Lineto, designed by Laurenz Brunner,
for her stationery. It is legible but quirky,
with distinctive Swiss roots.

Business Cards (below, top)
Digital, in-house, 1/1, black, on Fischer
Papier Marina.
'The shapes on the cards are
characters of the typeface Naht Sans,
made in collaboration with Krispin Heé
at Koi. Naht means "seam"; you can use
the shapes as patterns for sewing, to
make letterforms. So, these are letters
but not as we are used to seeing them;
you have to look closely and search for
the real shape of each character.'

Website (below, middle)
www.coboi.ch
An engaging opening page contains an
array of graphic images in a unifying
monotone; use the mouse to roll over
and reveal the colour versions.

Agendas and Postcards
(bottom)
Announcing the range of agendas for
2009, designer in partnership with KOI.

Studio Mascot
Found item that inspired the company
name; tin cowboy badge.

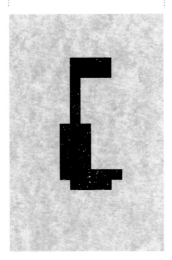
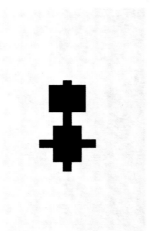
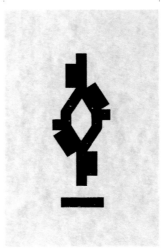

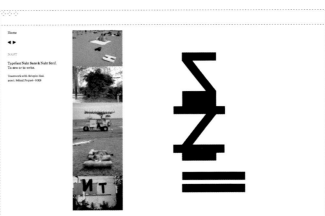

Deanne Cheuk Design   Deanne Cheuk

New York City, NY, USA   www.deannecheuk.com

Originally from Perth, Australia, Deanne Cheuk is a renowned illustrator, designer and magazine art director. She has also designed, edited and published her own magazine, *Neomu*, featuring cross-media creativity from a wide range of contributors.

'My own branding never seems to be a priority,' Deanne admits. 'This letterhead was designed years ago, and I've only had one other that I used for nearly ten years,' adding that her influences shifted from Art Nouveau to Art Deco for her business card. Her current logo is pared down and ultra-fine, featuring some signature organic flourishes.

Recently, she's launched her first personal website, 'another self-promotional project that was always on the backburner, but I finally decided to focus on it.' Time went into gathering files from her vast archive of projects, 'but I built it quite quickly.' Categories showcase work by genre: from print, to pattern (for textiles and fashion), type, products and more, each page of thumbnails opening into a click-forward slideshow.

'The reaction has been great; most comments are in regard to the volume of work, and the funny thing is that I haven't put everything up yet....'

Before the website, Deanne gained international recognition through her magazine *Neomu*. There's been a publishing gap of a few years, so she doesn't consider it to be a current promotional tool. 'I was funding the entire project,' she says, explaining that other obligations, including her own book (*Mushroom Girls Virus*, 2005), put it further down her list of priorities. 'I would like to publish two more issues, to make it ten in total. When it was in circulation, it gathered a lot of press and a lot of contributors earned freelance commissions from it too.'

Letterhead
(opposite page, main picture)
Digital, in-house, on white stock.

Business Card (opposite page, bottom)
Digital, in-house, on white stock.

Website
www.deannecheuk.com
Designer and programmer: Deanne
Cheuk
The website features Deanne's current
logo (top).

Postcards
2004
Four-colour CMYK, on white matte
stock, packaged in drawstring canvas
pouch with mailing label (opposite page,
top). The reverse of the cards feature
ornate line-drawings indicating the
stamp position (bottom). This attention
to detail is typical of Deanne's approach
to both commissioned work and her
self-promotional projects.

designjune
1bis avenue de la folie   +33 (0)9 53 83 96 01
95160 montmorency   designjune.com
france

urssaf   750 9692101835 756
siret   414176032 00038
ape   744B0

designjune   Julien Crouïgneau   Montmorency, France   www.designjune.com

Principal of designjune, Julien Crouïgneau, describes the corporate identity. 'The blue of the sky is our corporate support, to which we add different illustrations; we try to be as light as we can.' Pinning down that blue, Julien says, 'it's inspired by the deep blue of a sky with no clouds, and the month of June, when winter is furthest away. There's also a lighter shade of blue on the horizon: it's Pantone 306.' This blue is generously applied throughout designjune's world, from stationery, to the workplace and portfolio. With an illustrative logo that offers a 'vision of technology mixed with romanticism' and a bespoke typeface, 'june', the identity presents an elegant reinterpretation of natural inspiration, which is wholly contemporary and wilfully sophisticated.

julien crouïgneau
julien@designjune.com
+33 (0)6 81 43 34 83

designjune
1bis avenue de la folie   +33 (0)9 53 83 96 01
95160 montmorency   designjune.com
france

Letterhead (opposite page)
1/0, PMS 306, on white stock.

Business Card (opposite page, bottom)
2/2, PMS 306 and UV varnish, on
white card.
Elements of designjune's identity include
a whole host of illustrative icons, which
build into a graphic language; if you
look very hard you'll see some on the
business card, printed in UV varnish.

DVD and Box (below left)
Included with each mailed DVD is a
short company biography.

Portfolio (below right)
More illustrative elements appear
on the studio's portfolio, this time in
sophisticated black on black; complete
with a logo bubble.

Studio (bottom left)
Vinyl stickers bring the illustrative
icons into the real world and the studio.

Website (bottom right)
www.designjune.com
A sophisticated, side-scrolling
movement adds extra dynamism to the
website, with projects sorted by client
and media. A regular newsletter brings
designjune's identity to the user's inbox,
offering audio and video clips along with
the latest news.

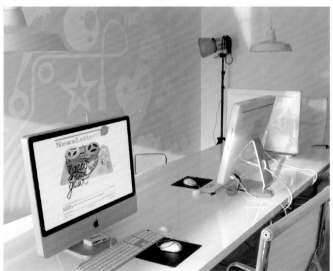

deValence   Alexandre Dimos and Gaël Étienne   Paris, France   www.devalence.net

Primarily collaborating with cultural organizations, this partnership specializes in designing for print and has worked with artists and curators at the Centre Pompidou (*Dada* catalogue, 2005), the Jeu de Paume, the publishers Flammarion (*Cindy Sherman*, 2006), and with the respected Swiss publisher JRP-Ringier. Developing typefaces in tandem with these projects, their typeface, Dada (in which this book is set), is distributed by Swiss company Optimo.

Aficionados of the business card (they don't have a letterhead), deValence frequently update theirs to promote recent work and showcase new fonts. Meanwhile, their tagline, '*Design graphique toutes surfaces*', often appears on the cards (the duo translate it as 'Four-wheel-drive graphic design').

DESIG
GRAPI
TOUTE
SURFA

deValence
Alexandre Dimos & Gaël Étienne

32 rue de Paradis
75010 Paris — France
+33 (0)1 53 34 88 10
everyone@devalence.net
www.devalence.net

DESIGN
GRAPH IIQUE
TOUTE S
SURFA CES

deValence
Alexandre Dimos
& Gaël Étienne

32 rue de Paradis
75010 Paris — France
+33 (0)1 53 34 88 10
everyone@devalence.net
www.devalence.net

Compliments Slip (opposite page)
2/1, blue and black, on white card.
Matches the latest business card with
a wraparound tagline.

Business Cards (opposite page)
2007: Letterpress, 1/0, black, on grey
card (top left).
2007: 2/1, plum and black, on white
card. With a horizontal wraparound
tagline (top right).
Current: 2/1, blue and black, on white
card. With a wraparound tagline
(bottom left).

Notebook used as Business Card
2001: 2/1, red and black, on white
stock. Using their font, Sensa, to spell
out an ironic message, in French (black)
and English (red). The reverse features
notebook rules.

onwees
tarepas
notdesc
oolmecs
guyscoo
ls ×

×devalence
Alexandre Dimos et Gaël Étienne
c/o Mains d'Œuvres 1 rue Charles Garnier 93400 Saint-Ouen
t/f : 01 40 11 82 37   everyone@devalence.net   www.devalence.net

2/1, blue and black, on white card.
A pocket-sized type specimen uses
similar graphic language to the current
stationery, and includes deValence's
contact details.

Notebook used as Business Card
(opposite page, top)
2003: Notebooks used as business
cards, 24 pages, various photographic
covers, contact details on back cover.

Website (opposite page, bottom)
www.devalence.net
With the simplest of means, black
and red 'typewriter' font and scrolling
navigation, deValence produce a blog-
style site with lots of links and stunning
imagery – almost a 'documentary' of
their work.

Dada Grotesk
Une famille de caractères du Light au *Heavy italic.*

Dada Lumière.
Dada Livre.
Dada Support.
Dada Gras.
Dada Lourd.

Dada Grotesk
The whole family from Light to *Heavy italic.*

DADA GROTESK
Un caractère typographique dessiné
par deValence disponible
en cinq graisses chez *www.optimo.ch*
au format Opentype avec
les caractères est-européens.

DADA GROTESK
A font designed by deValence
available in five weights
at www.optimo.ch in Opentype
with extended latin character set.

ABCDEFGHIJKLMNOPQRSTUVWXYZ
abcdefghijklmnopqrstuvwxyz
0123456789¼½¾^{123}+−×±÷≈≠<=>≤≥%‰∞

ÀÁÂÃÄÅĀĂĄÆÆÇĆĈĊČĎĐÈÉÊËĒĔĚĘĖ
ĜĞĠĢĤĦÌÍÎÏĨĪĬĲÌIJĴĶĹĻĽĿŁÑŃŅŇÒÓÔÕÖŒ
ØÖŌŐŔŖŘŚŜŞŠŞŢŤŢÙÚÛÜŨŪŬŮŰŲŴẀ
ŴŴÝŶŸỲŹŻŽÞ

àáâãäåāăąåæǽßçćĉċčďđðèéêëēĕěęėfffifflffifflfl
ĝğġģĥħìíîïĩīĭįıĵķĸĺļľŀłñńņňŋòóôõöōŏőøœǿŕŗř
śŝşšşſťţùúûüũūŭůűųŵẁẃẅ ý ÿ ỳ ŷ ź ż ž þ

#§¬\/Ω∂∆∏∑◊Ωπ√∫ €$¢¥£ƒ¤©®™* º ª ∧ ~
,-.:;!¡?¿…--_'»''»'',"""„«»‹›&@¶°(())[[]]/\{}||
´ ` ¨ ˆ ˇ ˙ ˝ ˛ ˘ ¯ ° ˜ ¸ † ‡ • · · · □

deValence, 32 rue de Paradis 75010 Paris – France – www.devalence.net

deValence

News :

SAÂDANE DEVALENCE

deValence and Saâdane Afif are proud to announce the opening of their common show at GDM, Galerie de Multiples, in Paris, from October 17th to November 18th 2009.

Since 2006, we collaborate regularly with Saâdane Afif (artist). From our Parisian studio, we conceive printed objects for the exhibitions of the artist in Lyon, Carquefou, Caen, Brussels, Antwerp, Margate, Rotterdam, Monaco, Turin, Berlin or Miami. "Saâdane deValence" presents the posters, the books and the cds we created.

deValence et Saâdane Afif sont heureux d'annoncer l'ouverture de leur exposition à GDM, Galerie de Multiples à Paris, du 17 octobre au 18 novembre 2009.

Depuis trois ans, nous collaborons régulièrement avec Saâdane Afif (artiste). Depuis notre studio parisien, nous concevons les objets imprimés pour les expositions de l'artiste à Lyon, Carquefou, Caen, Bruxelles, Anvers, Margate, Rotterdam, Monaco, Turin, Berlin ou Miami. "Saâdane deValence" présente les posters, les livres et les disques issus de cette collaboration.

---

deValence
design graphique toutes surfaces
| Travaux | Fontes | Terrain de jeux | À propos | Liens | Contacts | Crédits |

Travaux
| Réalisations | Références |

Réalisations
| Dada | Saâdane Afif | Tropico-Végétal | Collection Lambert en Avignon | Cindy Sherman | Raphaël Zarka | ENSBA | Thomas Hirschhorn Musée Précaire Albinet | Mains d'Œuvres | Robert Malaval | Le Journal des Laboratoires | Picobello | Magic, revue pop moderne | Gérard Thurnauer | Agnès Thurnauer | Les Inrockuptibles | Art Grandeur Nature | Bad Sound | Art Press | Camabook |

Dada | catalogue d'exposition — Centre Pompidou, Paris, 2005 — 21,5 x 28,5 cm — 1024 pages — sous la direction de Laurent Le Bon — photographies droits réservés

---

deValence
design graphique toutes surfaces
| Travaux | Fontes | Terrain de jeux | À propos | Liens | Contacts | Crédits |

Travaux
| Réalisations | Références |

Réalisations
| Dada | Saâdane Afif | Tropico-Végétal | Collection Lambert en Avignon | Cindy Sherman | Raphaël Zarka | ENSBA | Thomas Hirschhorn Musée Précaire Albinet | Mains d'Œuvres | Robert Malaval | Le Journal des Laboratoires | Picobello | Magic, revue pop moderne | Gérard Thurnauer | Agnès Thurnauer | Les Inrockuptibles | Art Grandeur Nature | Bad Sound | Art Press | Camabook |

Tropico-Végétal | exposition au Palais de Tokyo, 9 juin 2006 au 27 août 2006

Allora & Calzadilla : Land Mark | Palais de Tokyo/Paris Musées, 2006 — 16,5 x 21,7 cm — 64 pages

---

deValence
design graphique toutes surfaces
| Travaux | Fontes | Terrain de jeux | À propos | Liens | Contacts | Crédits |

Fontes

Manuel | 2003

ABCDEFGHIJKLMNOPQRSTUVWXYZ
0123456789 (!É&À➔)

LES STUDIOS ➔
← LE RESTO

Dextro.org   Dextro   Baden, Austria   www.dextro.org

Dextro, in the guise of Dextro.org, creates abstract imagery, which is then applied to graphic design projects, both moving and still. The result of digital experimentation combining interactivity, algorithmic animations and self-generating programs, these densely patterned images may appear on record sleeves, as moving wallpaper on a video monitor or as a magazine illustration.

With such rich visual output, Dextro chose to keep the corporate identity simple. Using a palette of grey, black and white, and a trio of decorative devices, the combination is used sparingly. The website header is echoed in the stationery, but all remains digital, as Dextro decided against producing paper stationery. 'I change the design too often to have it printed; and all correspondence is by email, using PDF attachments,' he explains. Asked if there are any special requirements when designing digital stationery, he replies, 'Sure: the data size, and legibility in low resolution.'

Letterhead (opposite page)
PDF
The black rule denotes the text area.

Business Card , also used as a
Note Card (below right)
PDF

Website (bottom)
www.dextro.org
Tiles of thumbnails invite inspection;
alternatively, a portfolio opens when
you click on the logo.

Imagery (overleaf)
Four examples of the many hundreds of
algorithmic images created by Dextro
that feature on his website, and which
have become his signature output.

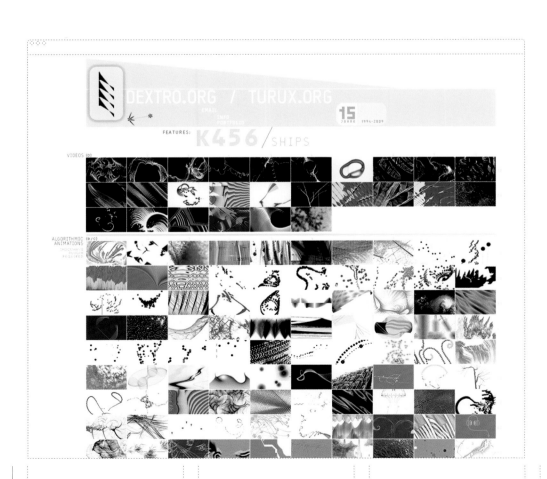

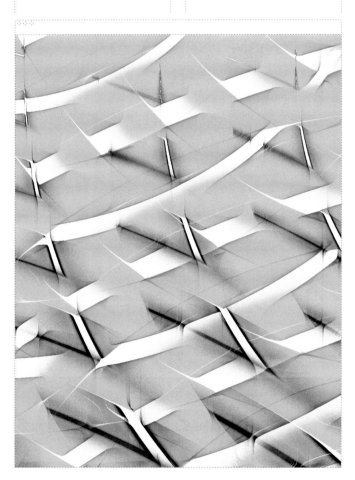

131 ESSEX STREET #5 SOUTH NEW YORK, NEW YORK 10002 P—212.260.5979 E—CASUAL@DRESSCODENY.COM WWW.DRESSCODENY.COM

dress code   G. Dan Covert and Andre Andreev   New York City, NY, USA   www.dresscodeny.com

G. Dan Covert and Andre Andreev met while working at MTV; when they decided to go it alone, coming up with a company name was the first hurdle. Realizing that using their own names would require too much 'spelling', and 'we would seem small', a brainstorming session led them to the bookshelf, and a volume called *Dress Codes*. 'We thought dress code would be a good name, since it means nothing but sounds cool,' explain Dan and Andre.

Settling on a simple logotype using their favourite font, Akzidenz Grotesk (originally released by the H. Bertold AG foundry in 1896), they modified the 'r', 'to make it less generic'. The dotted line looks like stitching but, they admit, it was a happy accident.

Working on projects for a wide range of media clients, many of which are screen- and moving-image-based, dress code's website is central to their corporate identity; plus, it helped raise their profile and attract all-important early clients. 'We designed the website while we still had day jobs, so we would look legit. Slowly this helped us get enough clients to start our own firm for real.'

'We wanted something that would keep changing and be fresh, so people would come back for another look. The homepage tells what each of us is doing at any given time of the day. Trying to write clever copy has become part of our identity, and this was the first time we used that trusty solution.'

Each partner wrote 24 'sayings' about the other. 'It was much easier to write about each other than ourselves, and it became a game to see who could make funnier comments. We think of the most ridiculous things that we obsess about and then make fun of them; they're insider jokes or stupid pop-culture references, the more obscure the better.'

These sayings change every hour, along with the site's background colour. 'When we first launched, the sayings were very X-rated in the middle of the night, talking about sex and drugs, since we figured nobody would be checking the website then.' When friends and students mentioned these activities, the duo refined their strategy.

And how does it go down with clients? 'It gives clients a sense of what they're getting into before they hire us – our rather quirky humour. We always try solutions that make people smile, so this is an insight into our personalities.'

Letterhead (opposite page)
Digital, in-house, 1/0, blue, on white stock.
'We use whatever nice paper is lying around; and on the first page of our presentations we write something funny.'

Business Cards
2006: Kinkos Card
Printer: Kinko's
Colour xerox, on white card.
'For the longest time we didn't have cards because we were too lazy to design them. Then we got our first speaking gig and realized that someone would probably ask us for one. We put it off until the night before, and decided to make them at Kinko's. This inspired the card's design, which features our logo with the Kinko's icon. We were nervous; Kinko's might not think it was funny that their name was on our card, but the people in the store didn't even notice. We expected tons of laughs when we gave the cards out but nobody "got" the joke, so we explained it – with lacklustre results.'

2007: Man With A Van Card
Printer: East Side Copy
1/1, black, on white card.
'Since nobody "got" our first card and we had just quit our day jobs, we wanted a fresh version. We had a card from when we moved, "A Man With A Van", the dude who helps you bring stuff home from Ikea. We thought it would be funny if we just stole the design and added our info. To make sure it was a joke we included different animals; Dan got a cat, Andre a dog, and the intern a penguin. To take it up a notch we printed this card with thermography, which is a very cheesy process that lots of dry cleaners use for their cards. Again we had to explain the joke every time we handed it out, and definitely lost work because people didn't take us seriously. To top it off, we got a call asking to help with an apartment move.'

Current: High Class Card
Printer: Coeur Noir
Letterpress, 1/1, blue, on white card, duplexed.
'After two failed joke cards we decided to make a very "class" card that might actually impress people and get us business; using double-thick stock to look official. We were sick of our logo so we used Akzidenz Grotesk, and added personality with icons, fist bumping for Dan and a crest from his Grandpa's watch for Andre.'

kinkos!

68 RICHARDSON STREET ROOM 504 · BROOKLYN, NEW YORK 11211
415.336.5961 · CASUAL@DRESSCODENY.COM · DRESSCODENY.COM

212-260-5979 INTERN@DRESSCODENY.COM

A MAN WITH A VAN
Specializing in Light Moving
Merchandise Pickup and Delivery For Major Stores
Transport to All Major Airports
At An Affordable Rate

dress code

DAN@DRESSCODENY.COM
P 212.260.5979 M 646.334.0805

dress code

ANDRE@DRESSCODENY.COM
P 212.260.5979 M 646.334.1723

Neon Sign (opposite page)
'We made a book called *Never Sleep* and the phrase has become a motto, so we decided to get a neon sign made of it. A lady in Chinatown designed it in Microsoft Word while we waited. It is super-bright and you can see the glow from blocks away. There are tons of neon signs in the Lower East Side, and we admit we stole the idea from Paul Sahre (one of our favourite designers), who also has one in his window.'

Website
www.dresscodeny.com
Programmer: Jon Dacuag
'A lot of people think the homepage is updated in real time, so they expect us to literally be doing what the site says!'

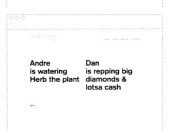

Andre is watering Herb the plant
Dan is repping big diamonds & lotsa cash

Andre is drinking the coffee
Dan is fighting dyslexia

Andre is preparing to take it up a big notch
Dan is talking to robocop 3D guy thing

Andre is wondering beard or no beard
Dan is aligning his shampoos

Andre is training for FC Bulgaria
Dan is chewing on Andre's pen

Andre is digesting vegetables
Dan is trapped between two dreams

Andre is breaking up a soccer brawl
Dan is dropping science

Andre is not having a cigarette
Dan is talking to sprinkles

Andre is "working" in his room.
Dan is beating off to Suicide Girls.

Andre is experiencing teenwolf envy
Dan is cursing his late 90's computer

We could not think of anything funny to put up here.

EightHourDay | Katie Kirk and Nathan Strandberg | Minneapolis, MN, USA | www.eighthourday.com

EightHourDay set out to attract design-savvy clients, and by employing the simplest of means for their own corporate identity, successfully demonstrate their inventiveness. Challenging themselves to create a high-profile system in budget-conscious black and white was the start of EightHourDay's journey into plaid.

Katie Kirk, one half of the partnership, explains, 'We were really striving for elements that felt modern but timeless, sophisticated yet edgy. With the plaids, the logo and icons, we wanted to reference a number of cultural "graphic" elements, and create our own.'

By formulating their own symbology, which quotes time passing, the seasons, their location, calligraphy, pattern, print and pixels, the end result is a lively riot of detail. Eye-catching though it is, the identity rests on a firm foundation of elegant typography, while the black and white scheme keeps the whole balanced and coherent.

The identity has brought the studio a lot of attention. 'Immediately, it began showing up on blogs and forums,' says Katie, '...and people came to visit our online portfolio, framed by this brand, so our site stats climbed too.'

718 North Washington Avenue
Suite 210 (SoHo Lofts)
Minneapolis Minnesota 55401

Phone: 612 788 9098
Email: hello@eighthourday.com
Nathan Strandberg & Katie Kirk

EightHourDay

www.eighthourday.com

Art direction and design: Katie Kirk
and Nathan Strandberg

Letterhead (opposite page)
1/1, black, on Cougar Opaque
Smooth Cover White.

Icons Sticker Sheet (top right)
1/0, black, on white sticker stock.

Envelope with Icon Stickers (below),
Package Label (below middle),
Postcard (bottom right) **and**
Business Card (bottom left)
1/1, black, on Cougar Opaque
Smooth Cover White.

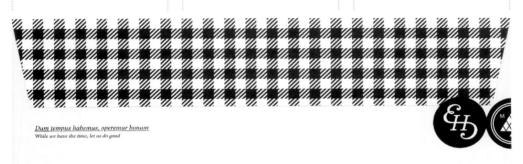

Dum tempus habemus, operemur bonum
While we have the time, let us do good

718 North Washington Avenue
Suite 210 (SoHo Lofts)
Minneapolis Minnesota 55401

Mail to:

EightHourDay

online: www.eighthourday.com

    www.eighthourday.com

718 North Washington Avenue   Phone: 612 788 9098
Suite 210 (SoHo Lofts)   Email: hello@eighthourday.com
Minneapolis Minnesota 55401   Nathan Strandberg & Katie Kirk

Dum tempus habemus, operemur bonum
While we have the time, let us do good

EMMI

address
3rd Floor, Unit 17
310 Kingsland Road
London E8 4DB
United Kingdom

tel / web / email
+44 (0) 7752 001 311
www.emmi.co.uk
hello@emmi.co.uk

EMMI   Emmi Salonen   London, UK   www.emmi.co.uk

Finnish-born designer Emmi Salonen works with clients from the worlds of art, academia and commerce, creating print and web-based solutions with an emphasis on sustainability. 'Luckily, with most projects it makes sense to be eco, and adds value to the concept of the design,' explains Emmi, 'but it's not always practical.'

An eye-catching element of her own graphic identity is the 'branded' packing tape. 'We post a lot of stuff and receive a lot of packages too. It felt a bit cheap reusing the envelopes sent to us, but chucking them away wasn't a solution either. So the tape was designed to brand the envelopes, and say, "yes, this is reused material, and it's better for it!"'

Letterhead (opposite page)
Digital, in-house, 1/0, black, on
Kaskad paper.

Business Card (bottom)
Four-colour CMYK, vegetable-based
ink, recycled stock, hand-finished,
die-cut.

Promotional Items
Quirkily packaged badges and
mugs featuring graphic icons, for
sale online alongside EMMI's self-
published brochures.

EMMI SALONEN
Graphic Designer
www.emmi.co.uk
hello@emmi.co.uk
+44 (0) 77 5200 1311

Studio Brochure #1 (top right)
and Studio Brochure #2 (below)
Vegetable inks on various stock,
hand-finished, die-cut.
Clever use of unconventional stocks
and bindings, including elastic bands
and die-cut slits, showcase EMMI's
work in the tangible form of inventive
publishing solutions.

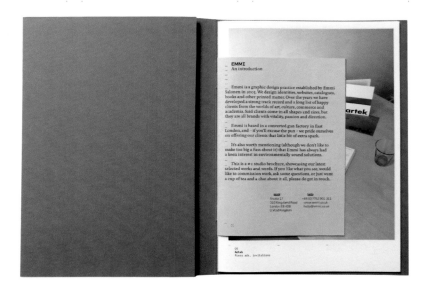

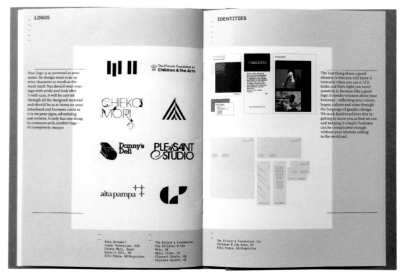

Packing Tape (below left)
For branding reused envelopes.

Rubber Stamps (right)
A 'With Love' heart icon, and an
address label complete with paper clip,
to personalize correspondence.

Website (bottom)
www.emmi.co.uk
Elements from the stationery, rubber
stamps and the studio brochures are
featured. The Shop uses the lined-
notepaper detailing from EMMI's
business card, while the Newsletter
resembles a notebook.

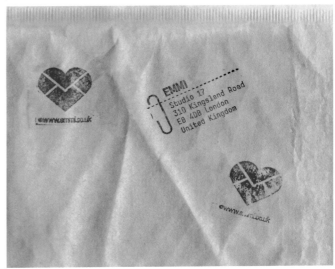

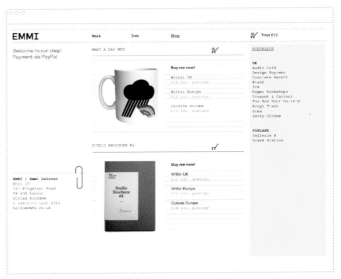

Mario ~~Esquenazi~~ ~~Esquenaci~~ ~~Eskinazy~~ ~~Esquinasi~~ ~~Eskinaze~~ ~~Eskenaci~~ ~~Eskineazy~~ ~~Esquenasi~~ ~~Esquinazi~~ ~~Esquezani~~
Eskenazi Plaza Berenguer el Gran 1 4°1ª 08002 Barcelona Teléfono 933 192 369 Fax 933 192 228 m-eskenazi@m-eskenazi.com

Mario Eskenazi   Mario Eskenazi   Barcelona, Spain   www.m-eskenazi.com

Mario Eskenazi Boverman NIF. 35 087 866 D

With a diverse portfolio of projects ranging across identity, signage, editorial and packaging, for clients including cultural institutions, banks, airports and FMCG (fast-moving consumer goods) brands, Mario Eskenazi is a well-known and respected member of Spain's design scene; it doesn't stop people spelling his name wrong, though. So, instead of letting it get to him, he's embraced the annoyance and used this in-joke as a witty identity. 'Diego Feijoo and I were thinking about what would be a good way to represent my studio. My surname is often misspelt in correspondence, and we thought we could make a virtue out of that. So we incorporated all the myriad ways in which my name had been incorrectly written over the years,' explains Mario.

The stationery system is also notable for a dynamic use of colour. Mario continues, 'this idea could work in black and white as it isn't dependent on colour. But my previous stationery had been black and white, and people often teased me, saying I made it more affordable to print by not using colour. So I responded to that playfully, and went for the most striking colours available; each one of us at the studio can choose a different fluorescent.'

Design: Mario Eskenazi and
Diego Feijoo

Letterhead (opposite page)
1/1, black and fluorescent, on white
Conqueror Connoisseur, 110gsm.

Business Cards (top)
2/1, black and fluorescent, on white
Conqueror Connoisseur, 300gsm.

Envelope (middle right)
2/0, black and fluorescent, on white
Conqueror Connoisseur, 110gsm.

Stickers and Disk Labels
(below left and bottom)
2/0, black and fluorescent, on
label stock, die-cut.

Mario Esquenazi Esquenasi Esquinasi Eskinatzi Eskenaci
Esquonnasi Eskinezi Esquenasi Eskenasi Esquinazi Eskenazi
Gemma Capdevila Plaza Berenguer el Gran 1 4°1ª 08002 Barcelona
Teléfono 933 192 369 Fax 933 192 228 E: gemma@m-eskenazi.com

FL@33 multi-disciplinary design studio for visual communication

contact@flat33.com

59 Britton Street
London EC1M 5UU
United Kingdom

Studio +44 (0)20 7168 7990
Mobile +44 (0)7801 950 195

http://www.
flat33.com
stereohype.com
bzzzpeek.com
postcard-book.info
madeandsold.com

FL@33   Agathe Jacquillat and Tomi Vollauschek   London, UK   www.flat33.com

FL@33 is a multilingual, multiple-media design studio founded by Agathe Jacquillat, originally from Paris, and Tomi Vollauschek, who is Austrian. They met at London's Royal College of Art, and set up in 2001, opening Stereohype, their 'graphics boutique', in 2004.

Aiming to balance commissioned and self-initiated projects while also creating publications, FL@33's work philosophy is based on a 'Power of Three' theory: the combination of intellect, skill and emotion.

As far as their corporate identity goes, the duo has adopted a flexible approach and earned worldwide recognition from both peers and the public by way of their self-initiated projects. 'We've never actually printed letterheads as we send out all correspondence as PDFs by email, and we use postcards as business cards,' explains Tomi.

Self-initiated projects range from an online sound collection (bzzzpeek.com), to the award-winning magazine *trans-form*, and three books, including *Postcard* (2008) and *Made & Sold* (2009) for Laurence King Publishing. The second book features 'product sidelines' by graphic designers, illustrators and artists, tapping into FL@33's network of contributors and colleagues, while also showcasing their own offerings.

Tomi comments: 'Self-initiated projects play an important role and inform our commissioned work. Plus we try to avoid being associated with one particular style, method or activity, as that keeps it interesting for us and for our clients.'

Keeping that in mind, it makes perfect sense not to construct a rigid identity system, but to keep developing their various logos and images.

Under the label Stereohype, the duo designs and produces a clothing range, books and magazines, prints, posters and badges, which they distribute to a global audience. They created a standalone brand (rather than simply trading under their studio name) so as to invite in 'people whose work we admire or consider inspirational,' whether well known or up-and-coming. Under the banner of 'B.I.O. (by invitation only)', they run a button badge initiative, alongside an annual button badge design competition, which is open to all. FL@33 contributes artworks to the B.I.O. series, alongside designers such as Vaughan Oliver, Genevieve Gauckler and Vault49.

Founding Directors:
Agathe Jacquillat MA (RCA)
Tomi Vollauschek MA (RCA)

FL@33 Ltd is registered in England.
Company No: 5250153

Letterhead (opposite page)
PDF.

Logos (left to right, top to bottom)
FL@33: 2001, 2002, 2004
and current.
Stereohype: 2004
bzzzpeek.com: 2002
A playful attitude to FL@33's corporate
identity has resulted in a fluid approach,
highlighted by the development and
use of multiple logos both for the main
company and the various adjunct
companies and websites.

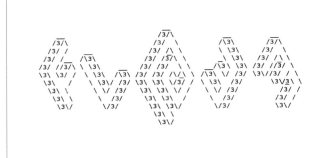

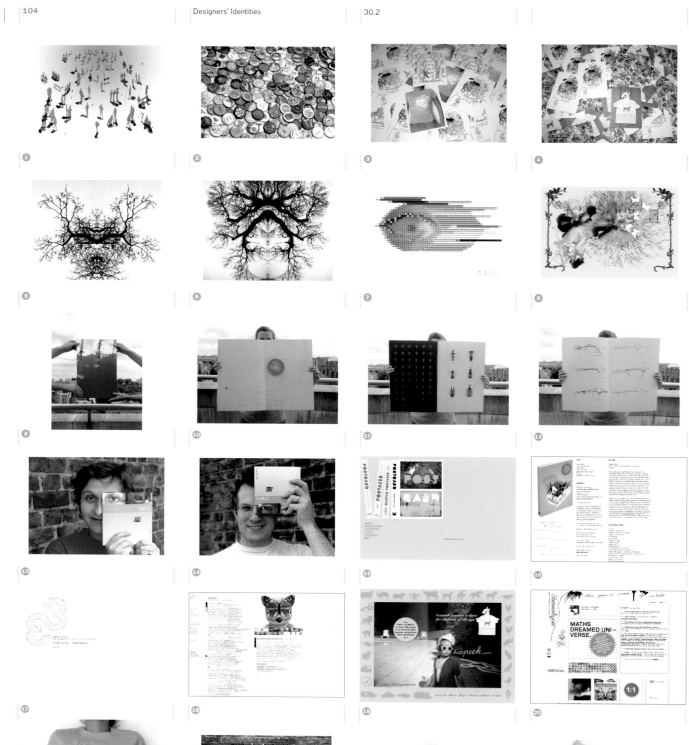

Postcards (1–4)
All postcard sets are produced in limited editions and printed on matte uncoated 100% recycled stock. Stereohype orders are sent with a free postcard, while others are distributed at trade shows and exhibitions.

Posters
Deer (5), 2003
Hibernation (6), 2003
Eye Sculpture (7), 2002
Spring #1 (8), 2003

Magazine (9–12)
trans-form, 2002.

Books
FL@33: design and designer (13 and 14)
Pyramyd Editions, 2003.

Postcard (15)
Laurence King Publishing, 2008.

Made & Sold (16)
Laurence King Publishing, 2009.

Websites
www.flat33.com (17 and 18)
www.bzzzpeek.com (19)
www.stereohype.com (20)
www.postcard-book.info (15)
www.madeandsold.com (16)
Various activities are grouped around a number of micro-sites that may be accessed from the main website. They all share distinctive, hand-rendered and colour-coded elements that build into a unique FL@33 graphic language.

T-shirts (21 and 22)
FL@33 also design the labels and tags and add a postcard to every mailed order.

Button badges and packs (23 and 24)
FL@33 and their invited contributors have produced hundreds of button badge designs.

Poster (this page)
Butterfly Sculpture Contains 818 Pencils
2002
Exhibited at Magma Gallery, London.

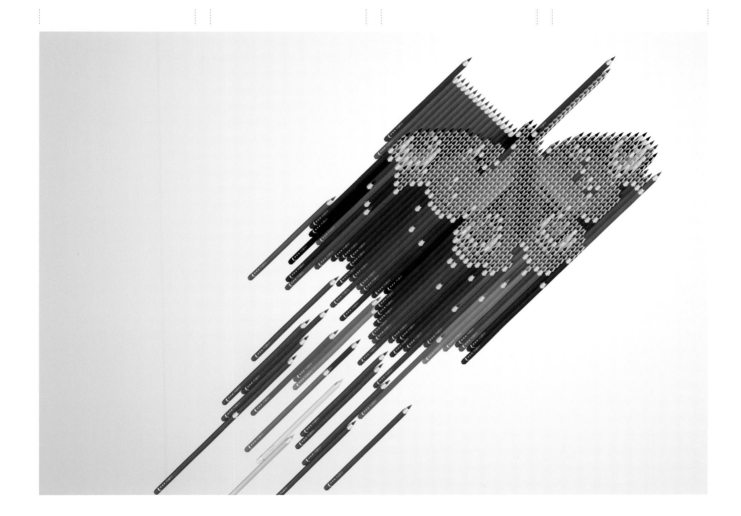

Form®

47 Tabernacle Street
London EC2A 4AA, UK

Telephone: +44 (0)20 7014 1430
Fax: +44 (0)20 7014 1431
ISDN: +44 (0)20 7014 1432

Email: studio@form.uk.com
Web: www.form.uk.com

Form   Paula Benson and Paul West   London, UK   www.form.uk.com

Long associated with the UK's vibrant indie and dance music scenes, Form's tagline, 'We will amplify your message,' proclaims their energetic approach to design, communication and branding. Partners Paula Benson and Paul West have grown the company into a busy studio that handles commissions from cultural, educational, publishing and media clients, many of which are household names: think Depeche Mode and Ministry of Sound, Goldsmiths College, Damien Hirst, Knoll and Formula 1.

Unsurprisingly, Form's corporate identity, stationery system and promotional items dress to impress. Maximum impact is guaranteed through a consistently experimental approach to materials and delivery methods, from their stainless steel business card to being an early adopter of web-based newsletters. 'We're glad you noticed we were one of the first!' declares Paula. 'The newsletters remind people we are here, and that we work in many areas for a wide variety of clients, because it's easy to get pigeonholed in the design industry.'

Producing photogenic projects for high-profile clients often earns Form column inches, especially for their celebrity-endorsed commissions, 'so our e-mailers keep clients in touch with all areas, from branding major organizations, to websites and moving image,' explains Paula. 'Music clients see our corporate work and vice versa. Some clients might have been receiving our newsletters for a couple of years before they approach us with a project they think we're right for, but without the newsletters they may well have forgotten us.'

Paula offers some advice for aspiring self-promoters: 'Newsletters need to be something more than just "about us". We inject other bits of information and cultural news, so that it really communicates who we are.'

As pro-active members of the London design community, Form frequently organize events, including the 'InForm' studio talks by guest artists and designers, plus they run myriad discussions via their busy blog. And yes, they still have time to run a clothing brand too. UniForm utilizes their band merchandising chops (learnt from producing tour tees and the like for their musician clients): '...so we thought we'd do it for ourselves.' The resulting urban-wear label, sold via a linked e-commerce site, has been getting Form artwork out on to the streets for more than a decade.

Partners: Paula Benson/Paul West
VAT No: 523 4071 79

Letterhead (opposite page and below)
Folded Letterhead (below right)
1/1, grey and lime green, on Courier
Super Wove Super White, 104gsm,
die-cut.
'We wanted the letterhead to create
a tactile experience,' explains Paula.
The holes spell FORM in the old ticker
typesetting code. When folded to fit
into a DL envelope, the dots printed on
the reverse appear through the die-
cut holes. The continuation sheet also
features perfectly aligned green dots.

Compliments Slip (bottom)
2/0, grey and lime green, on Courier
Super Wove Super White, 104gsm,
die-cut.

Business Card (top right)
Stainless Steel, etched and
die-stamped.
'Because people pay little attention to
business cards these days, we wanted
to make a lasting impression.'

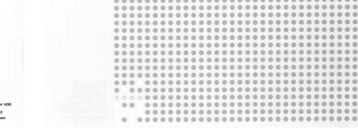

Email Newsletter
Form News sent as a jpeg mailer that may be saved and archived. 'The newsletter format tells us how many people view it, or follow the links, so we can track results and adjust accordingly.'

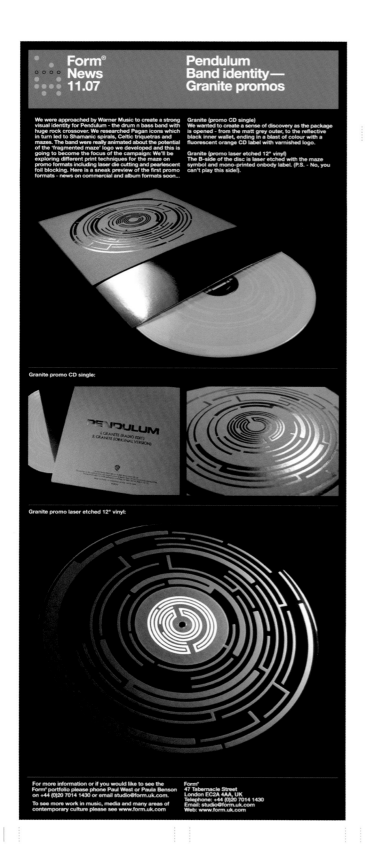

Form® News 11.07

Pendulum Band identity— Granite promos

We were approached by Warner Music to create a strong visual identity for Pendulum - the drum n bass band with huge rock crossover. We researched Pagan icons which in turn led to Shamanic spirals, Celtic triquetras and mazes. The band were really animated about the potential of the 'fragmented maze' logo we developed and this is going to become the focus of the campaign: We'll be exploring different print techniques for the maze on promo formats including laser die cutting and pearlescent foil blocking. Here is a sneak preview of the first promo formats - news on commercial and album formats soon...

Granite (promo CD single)
We wanted to create a sense of discovery as the package is opened - from the matt grey outer, to the reflective black inner wallet, ending in a blast of colour with a fluorescent orange CD label with varnished logo.

Granite (promo laser etched 12" vinyl)
The B-side of the disc is laser etched with the maze symbol and mono-printed onbody label. (P.S. - No, you can't play this side!).

Granite promo CD single:

Granite promo laser etched 12" vinyl:

For more information or if you would like to see the Form® portfolio please phone Paul West or Paula Benson on +44 (0)20 7014 1430 or email studio@form.uk.com.

To see more work in music, media and many areas of contemporary culture please see www.form.uk.com

Form®
47 Tabernacle Street
London EC2A 4AA, UK
Telephone: +44 (0)20 7014 1430
Email: studio@form.uk.com
Web: www.form.uk.com

Form® New Work: 02.09

Your ideas are the future: Form® rebrand ©CEDIM, Mexico

Time flies! To think, this time last year we were preparing a major trip to Mexico to give lectures and workshops to aspiring designers and image makers in Guadalajara and Mexico City. En route we visited our friends at ©CEDIM, the highly regarded and innovative college in Monterrey to discuss a rebrand of their '08/09 college identity.

In August we spent four days art directing a photoshoot to capture the sense of open space, activity and talent that bursts from the college, and we reflected this openly in all elements of the brochure and marketing materials as featured in our summary below.

"Form is the most enthusiastic and professional team of designers I have ever worked with. They take the time to understand who you are before attempting to communicate it. They are well organised, meet every deadline and are passionate about their work. They amplify your message". Michael Garcia Novak, Director General, ©CEDIM.

Brochure front and back covers

Brochure spreads

"Tip-in" sections

Promotional poster

Press adverts   Website

Flyers

Other Stuff:

— We have recently won the commission to work with UBM on the branding of The Sleep Event 09. Watch this space.
— Partner, Paul West's talk on mentoring in design at a recent D&AD event (mentioned in our last newsletter) is now online: see link at bottom of page.
— Our ©CEDIM work has been included in Design Week magazine and also in the Mexican magazine P400 together with other Form key projects.
— The British Embassy, Mexico are showcasing Form® as a case study and will be filming us for a piece highlighting the successful exporting of UK creativity.

We will amplify your message
To see more examples of our work in music, media, entertainment and youth-orientated education and culture see www.form.uk.com
Phone Paul West or Paula Benson on +44 (0)20 7014 1430 or email studio@form.uk.com

Form®
47 Tabernacle Street,
London EC2A 4AA, UK.
Telephone: +44 (0)20 7014 1430
Email: studio@form.uk.com
Web: www.form.uk.com

Mailer (top)
This snail-mailer makes an intriguingly shaped package that won't get lost in a pile of post.

Studio (middle left)
Bringing their love of experimentation with materials to their own workplace, Form create more branded messages in glass and metal.

Poster (middle right)
LongLunch
Paul and Paula were guest speakers at this prestigious event.

Brochure (bottom)
Acting as an updateable portfolio, this plastic ring-binder, die-cut with the Form logo, contains case study pamphlets; new projects are regularly mailed out.

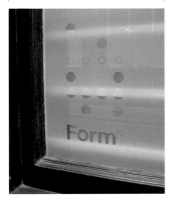

LongLunch
Presents Form®

27th May 2004. Doors 7.30pm
Warm-up: Phillip Lockwood-Holmes
Venue: NMS Royal Museum Lecture
Theatre (was The Lumiére) Edinburgh

Christmas/New Year Campaigns
2008/09
A month of beautiful tree images
greeted visitors to the Form website
throughout December, higlighting a
tree-planting scheme, while seasonal
homepages also featured.

Websites
www.form.uk.com (main picutres)
Being technology-friendly has won Form
many media clients, and helped bring
their own message to a large fanbase,
via a multi-layered website. The opening
image is forever changing, acting as an
emotive shop window into Form's world.

UniForm (bottom)
www.uniform.uk.com
Urban-wear clothing label, featuring
Form graphics.

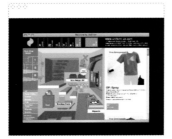

FoUR PAcK
ONTWERPERS

FoURPAcK ontwerpers

grafisch ontwerpstudio

Veemarktkade 8

5222 AE 's-Hertogenbosch

t 073 612 44 43

f 084 876 65 19

www.fourpack.nl

post@fourpack.nl

/NIEUWS	/E-MAIL	/LINKS	/PROJECTEN	/INFO	/VOORWAARDEN
/GRAFISCH	/ILLUSTRATIEF	/WEB	/WEBONDERHOUD	/CLIENTELE	/ROUTE

FoURPAcK   Tessa Hofman and Richard Pijs   's-Hertogenbosch, the Netherlands   www.fourpack.nl

This energetic design company grew out of a self-publishing experiment. Co-founder Richard Pijs describes the process, which began with the aim of keeping in touch with fellow students after graduation. 'We started a monthly booklet. Creatives were invited to submit their work on a specific theme, each of which was a four-letter word because we thought that a short title would be easily remembered.'

After negative feedback about the ever-changing name, Richard decided to stick with PAKK, 'which is Dutch for "get". It was pointed out that this booklet was something you must "get and read".'

Four regular contributors became friends and each month worked on the little magazine. When a gallery suggested an exhibition, they came up with a name, 'FOR PAKK', jokingly calling it FOuR PAcK. 'For aesthetic reasons we switched the cases, and FoURPAcK was born!'

Combining upper- and lowercase in their name also creates a strong type mark, providing recognition without the use of a logo. 'We hope that copywriters and administrators use this format, so our name makes a statement, even in plain text,' explains Richard.

Along with their distinctive name and commitment to working with cultural clients, FoURPAcK are avid fans of print, which is well showcased in a corporate identity that includes virtuoso stationery and promotional projects.

Richard explains the corporate colours of the identity system, which stem from his fascination with print technologies, having interned with a printer. 'Creating the whole spectrum of colours from four inks seemed like a magic trick. I realized that it was very rare to print in cyan and magenta, and this fascination led to using cyan in our corporate identity – to show that we love graphic work and as an ode to the printing press. Our second colour is red, in two forms (we prefer the fluorescent version but sometimes we must be practical); fluorescent ink reflects its colour back three times stronger than regular ink.'

Alongside the vibrant colour is a tightly constructed grid, with space for playful interventions. 'When developing an identity for FoURPAcK, the timeless designs from Piet Zwart (Dutch National Post Company, PTT) and Karel Martens (known for his simplicity and repeating shapes) were a welcome inspiration. At FoURPAcK, we're very fond of repeating systems, numbers and grids, and which project deals with this better than corporate identity? Plus, we didn't want to worry about the design once it was finished.'

After nine years, the identity not only reflects the history of Dutch graphic design, which Richard loves, but it still looks fresh and timeless: 'it works!'

'To translate all these concerns into graphic design was a blast,' he admits. 'Plus, the identity also leaves room for pleasure; the grid provides a stage to display icons, which we print on each correspondence, and which relate to the subject matter. This playfulness is important; it shows our involvement in our work. And if the recipient reacts to that, it's mission accomplished.'

Letterhead (opposite page and
in use overleaf)
3/0, cyan, fluorescent red PMS
824 (two hits), on white, Olin, 70gsm,
hand-stamped plus digital icon.
'We search our massive image library
for the right icon to match the nature of
the letter. We then place it in the grid,
and print it beautifully with our laser
printer,' explains Richard.

Invoice (below left)
1/0, cyan, on white, Olin, 70gsm.
'This visual treat is a gesture to our
customers, to soften the need to pay our
fee; printed purely in cyan.'

Compliments Card (middle, right)
3/3, cyan and fluorescent
red PMS 824 (two hits), on white
card, hand-stamped.
A face is added to the blank circle
using a rubber stamp.

Business Card (below, top right)
3/3, cyan and fluorescent red
PMS 824 (two hits), on white card,
hand-stamped.
This version tells FoURPAcK's client
how they can best meet their needs; the
icons hint at specialities. 'Our personal
passion is visualized; Tessa loves
printed matter, and Richard loves the
Macintosh (since 1984).'

Envelope (bottom left)
3/0, cyan and fluorescent red PMS
824 (two hits), on white stock.

Envelope Sticker (bottom right)
3/0, cyan and fluorescent red PMS
824 (two hits), on white sticker stock.
Intended for oversized packages,
the cyan bar folds over the edge of
the envelope.

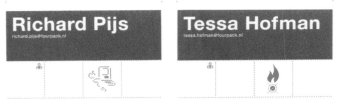

BRIEF

FoURPAcK ontwerpers
grafisch ontwerpstudio
Veemarktkade 8
5222 AE 's-Hertogenbosch
t 073 612 44 43
f 084 876 65 19
www.fourpack.nl
post@fourpack.nl

| /NIEUWS | /E-MAIL | /LINKS | /PROJECTEN | /INFO | /VOORWAARDEN |
| /GRAFISCH | /ILLUSTRATIEF | /WEB | /WEBONDERHOUD | /CLIENTELE | /ROUTE |

FoUR PAcK ONTWERPERS

's-Hertogenbosch, 29.03.2008 ★ ★ ★ offertenummer 4444-10-08

Dear Liz,

This is an example of our letterhead. We search our massive icon library for the right icon to match the narure of the letter. We then place it in the grid and print it beautifully with our laserprinter.

In the left upper corner we manually stamp the right word that indicates the nature of our letterhead. This is often the word 'brief' which is Dutch for 'Letter'.

Kind regards,
Richard Pijs

FoURPAcK ontwerpers

Other examples of our stamps are:

Fax Paper (below)
Programmed, not printed. Black.

Icons (below right)
EPS, added to stationery to indicate the
nature of the correspondence.

Business Card Duo Pack (bottom)
3/3, cyan and fluorescent red
PMS 824 (two hits), on white card,
hand-stamped, die-cut perforations.
Do-it-yourself version of the business
card, which can be ripped into several
versions: 'we stamp our faces on
the back.'

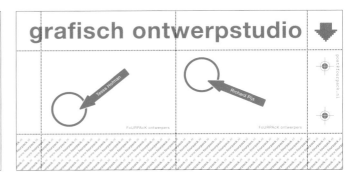

Moving Card (below left)
3/3, cyan and fluorescent red PMS
824 (two hits), on white card.

Stickers (below right)
Digital, in-house, 3/0, cyan, red and
black, on white sticker stock.
Enriches all posted material with
FoURPAcK's corporate identity.

Vinyl Stickers (top right)
Screenprinted, 1/0, red PMS 021,
on self-adhesive vinyl.

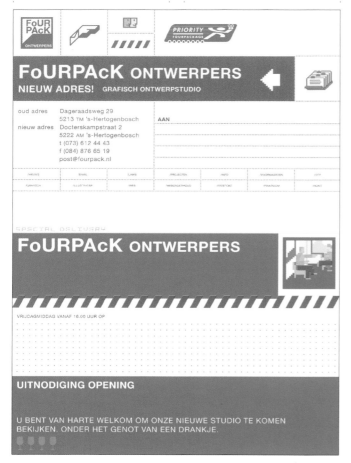

Website
www.fourpack.nl
Closely following the grid and colour-
scheme of the printed stationery, this
website neatly completes FoURPAcK's
corporate identity, right down to the
'hand-stamped' labelling.

FoURPAck Bike
Customized bike, featuring stickers
and licence plate in corporate colours.
'The best way to travel in the
Netherlands, and the best way for
FoURPAcK to be seen on the streets.'

**Screengrabs of email
correspondence**

Malcolm Goldie   Malcolm Goldie   Kingston, UK   www.malcolmgoldie.com

Having trained as a graphic designer, Malcolm Goldie has
expanded his creative remit to include multiple-media; he
works with drawn imagery and electronic sounds, often
in collaboration, and showcases his output through a
website, exhibitions and events. Paper-based stationery
doesn't figure, though. He explains, 'my corporate identity
has long been reduced to nothing more than putting
pathetic jokes (meaning miserably inadequate) at the
bottom of my emails.' He also describes these as 'tiny
efforts to liven up my day.'

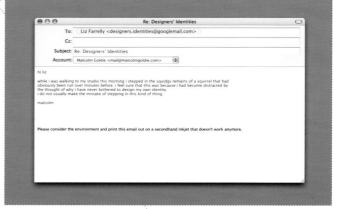

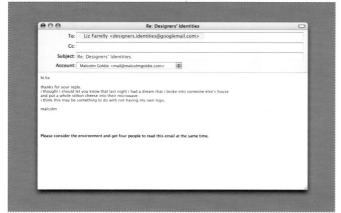

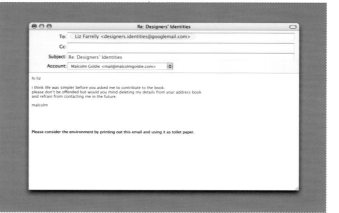

Hans Gremmen   Hans Gremmen   Amsterdam, the Netherlands   www.hansgremmen.nl

An identity as a white sheet of paper

'If you make a work, book or newspaper, it has to be as pure as possible, a good designer is not afraid to be totally invisible in the final product.'
Dutch Resource: Collaborative Exercises in Graphic Design, by Maxine Kopsa and Paul Elliman (Valiz, Amsterdam, 2005).

Hans Gremmen explains: 'This quote from Mark Manders, a visual artist from the Netherlands and co-founder of Roma Publications, got stuck in the back of my mind. Manders suggests that a designer should never put his own visual ideas (read: ego) up front. Design is not about showing your capacity to reinvent the wheel over and over again. It is about creating the perfect circumstances in which content may achieve its own form.

'Design should not showcase designers; it is a tool for artists, writers and photographers to tell their story. Therefore, as a designer, my visual identity is a white sheet of paper, because it does not exist. In my work, I want to apply an approach, not a style, and a visual identity creates visual expectations of the designer. Instead, I try to get to the core of the content, by way of having an open dialogue with the client. It is very important that this dialogue starts in the abstract, and at the beginning consists only of words and ideas; no images or visual expectations are allowed at this stage.

'Then the building starts: images, colours and typefaces are slowly added to create a system. Later, these elements may be used to emphasize certain details of the content. The visual outcome of that dialogue is what you could call a design. For me, this is the only way to do what I do.

'If I have to write an invoice or an estimate, I do it on a blank sheet of paper. The same goes for a business card; I simply write down my information on a sheet of paper, or in an agenda, or onto a Blackberry; every time it's different and appropriate to the occasion. It's like the books I design, where I find a solution for every situation. My website also works like that, only more random. Out of a database of over 500 images, eight images are randomly selected that represent my work; a simple card is as important as a complex book project. I use this random, custom, default identity because it's practical.'

Grundini

Peter Grundy
+44 (0)20 8384 1076
peter@grundini.com
www.grundini.com

Studio 69
1 Town Meadow
Brentford
Middlesex TW8 0BQ
United Kingdom

Grundini Limited
6205154

Director
Peter Grundy

Registered
in England
33a Milton Road
Hampton
Middlesex TW12 2LL

Vat number
871 3734 15

Grundini   Peter Grundy   Brentford, UK   www.grundini.com

Adapting his nickname and a self-portrait into a corporate identity, the renowned illustrator and information designer, Peter Grundy, launched his new company, Grundini. Peter created his emoticon logo while a student at London's Royal College of Art in 1979, 'and it's stuck with me ever since...Grundini is a long-time nickname simply waiting for the opportune moment to become my company name. Somehow it seems to encapsulate everything about me, and my work; don't ask why.'

Bringing a decidedly left-field approach to the discipline of information design, Peter creates bold, colourful and entertaining solutions that also deliver facts, figures and statistics.

In 1980, he and his then partner, Tilly Northedge, an RCA colleague, set up Grundy & Northedge. 'Information design became our mission. Firstly, because it was a totally unglamorous area of the industry, which we thought we could change, and secondly, because it was less about selling things and more about explaining things, which seemed a lot more interesting.'

Tilly left the studio in 2006, and Peter renamed the business Grundini: 'I wanted to define my new work for clients, customers, friends and myself by way of a bold printed statement; something that went beyond a commercial brochure and was free from compromise.' A self-published book set the scene – *Grundini: Very graphic work by Peter Grundy*, is a large-format square, perfect-bound, printed on coated and uncoated stock and coloured acetates, using foil block, embossing and debossing. It's a fine example of what can be achieved in the medium of print; and it's the first of a series of books Peter is planning '...to keep refreshing my personal, creative direction.'

Letterhead, two versions (opposite
page and below)
2/3, PMS 032 red, PMS 012 yellow,
black and silver foil block, on white
stock.
1/2, PMS 032 red and PMS 012
yellow and silver foil block, on
white stock.
A rare thing, this letterhead may be
used portrait or landscape. A cropped
version is used as a compliments slip.

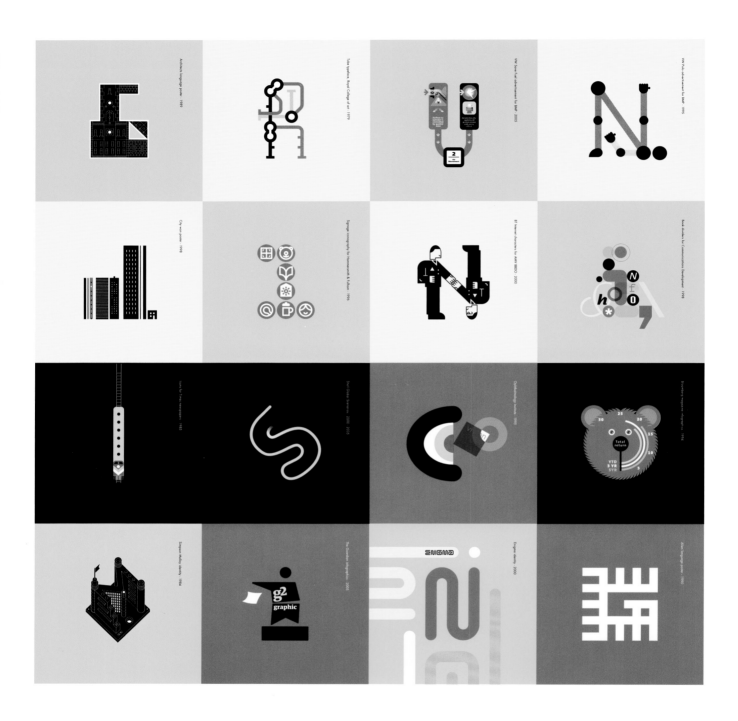

Poster (opposite page)
Peter rearranges his favourite images from the book and leaflet into a large, square-format poster, which is mailed to interested parties.

Booklet (right)
Red, yellow, black and silver foil block, on white card, concertina fold. Used as a business card and mailer, this mini-portfolio announced the new company via a series of arresting images, and remains a popular hand-out.

Book (below)
Grundini: Very graphic work by Peter Grundy, 2008.

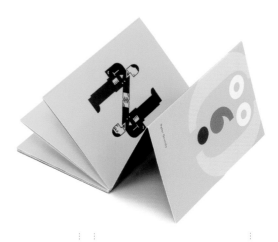

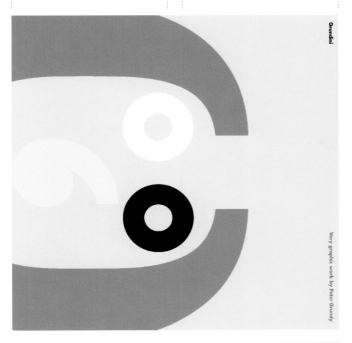

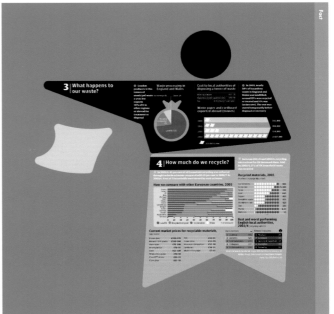

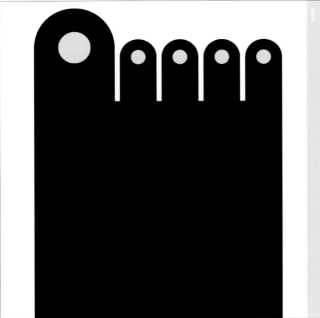

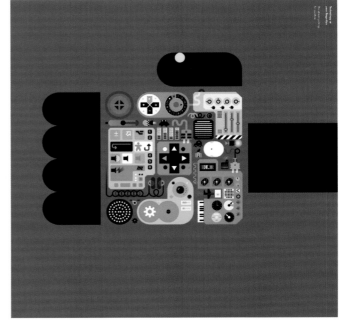

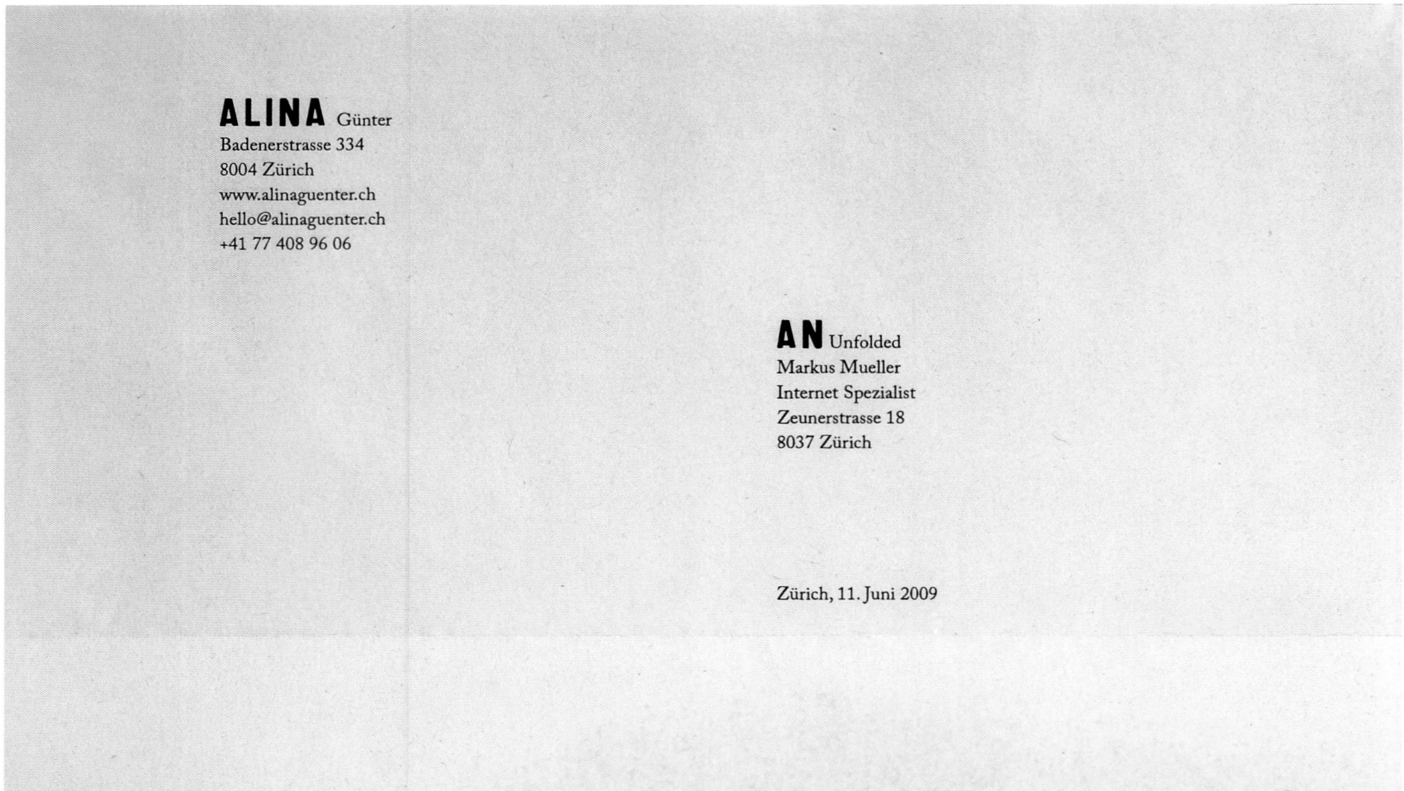

ALINA Günter
Badenerstrasse 334
8004 Zürich
www.alinaguenter.ch
hello@alinaguenter.ch
+41 77 408 96 06

AN Unfolded
Markus Mueller
Internet Spezialist
Zeunerstrasse 18
8037 Zürich

Zürich, 11. Juni 2009

Alina Günter   Alina Günter   Zurich, Switzerland   www.alinaguenter.ch

'The most important aspect of my stationery is that it is
easy to make and low-cost,' explains Alina Günter. 'I use
a rubber stamp for the envelope, and print the letterhead
in-house, choosing different coloured paper that I find in
stationery shops, to detract from the cheap printer.'
    Her current business cards showcase Alina's
graduation project, featuring drawn portraits of people
she's previously photographed; a business card
accompanies each piece of correspondence. 'They
symbolize the character of my work,' she explains.

Letterhead (opposite page)
Digital, in-house, 1/0, black, on various
colour stock.

Business Cards (below)
4/1, four-colour CMYK and black, on
white card.

HELLO@
ALINAGUENTER.CH
077 408 96 06

HarrimanSteel   Julian Dickinson and Nick Steel   London, UK   www.harrimansteel.co.uk

HARRIMAN⅃ƎƎ⊥S

This busy cross-platform studio, with clients from the worlds of fashion, retail, media and culture, is as happy creating broadcast advertising and websites as it is designing for print. Their favoured approach is to provide conceptual thinking for a campaign, and implement it across online, print, guerrilla techniques and viral films. 'We like to use all our skills in one job,' declares founding partner Nick Steel. HarrimanSteel take a similar approach when it comes to self-promotion projects, developing solutions in various media.

'We want to demonstrate our sense of humour, and say something about the unique people who work here – and shooting a viral is a bonding experience for the whole team,' Nick explains. 'This is a serious industry, but we don't want to be too precious, so, especially with our Christmas Virals, we like to be as odd as possible, and dress up, and hope we don't offend too many people.'

Not only do they send their promotional projects to advertising agencies, current clients, and an extensive database, but they also distribute them to blogs and via YouTube. 'One client saw a viral while eating breakfast and rang up to tell us, "you guys are strange".'

Intended to raise a smile, these projects also ensure that any prospective client 'gets' HarrimanSteel before they start working together.

Art Direction and Design:
HarrimanSteel

Letterhead (opposite page)
1/1, fluorescent pink and black, on
white stock.

Business Card (bottom)
1/1, fluorescent pink and black, on
white card.

Booklets and Packaging
(top right and middle)
A set of four 16-page self-promotional
booklets, the size of a business card,
featuring HarrimanSteel's signature
fluorescent pink, alongside images from
projects. Each booklet was dispatched
in a numbered, stencilled package, to be
torn open, one a week for four weeks.

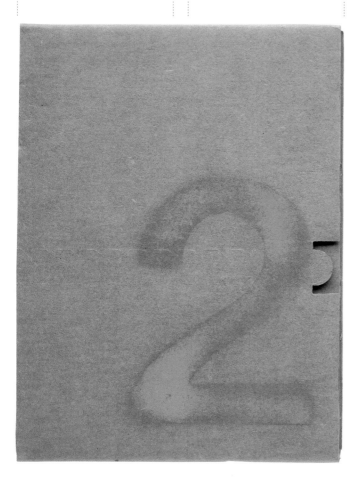

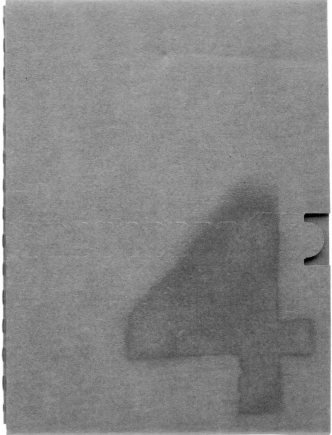

HARRIMANSTEEL
2 ACADEMY BUILDINGS, FANSHAW STREET, LONDON N1 6LQ.
T: +44 (0)20 7324 7530. F: +44 (0)20 7324 7531.
E: MAIL@HARRIMANSTEEL.CO.UK URL: WWW.HARRIMANSTEEL.CO.UK

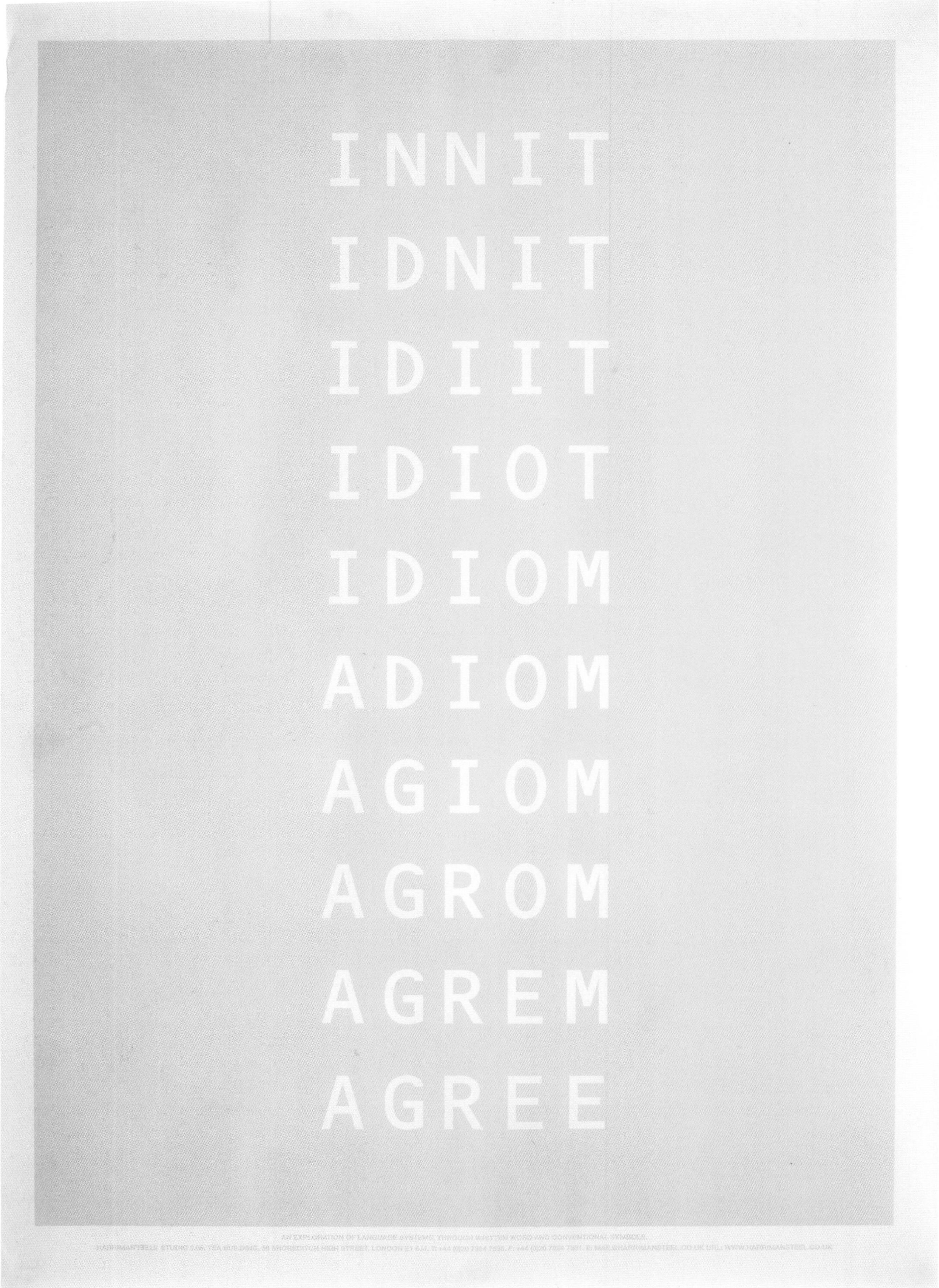

INNIT

IDNIT

IDIIT

IDIOT

IDIOM

ADIOM

AGIOM

AGROM

AGREM

AGREE

AN EXPLORATION OF LANGUAGE SYSTEMS, THROUGH WRITTEN WORD AND CONVENTIONAL SYMBOLS.

HARRIMANSTEELE STUDIO 2.05, TEA BUILDING, 56 SHOREDITCH HIGH STREET, LONDON E1 6JJ. T. +44 (0)20 7324 7530. F. +44 (0)20 7324 7531. E.MAIL @HARRIMANSTEEL.CO.UK URL: WWW.HARRIMANSTEEL.CO.UK

Poster Series

Language Poster (opposite page)
For over a decade HarrimanSteel have
experimented with this ongoing personal
and promotional project. Frustrated by
the fact that most promotional material
simply features commissioned work,
they have created a series of limited-
edition pieces (150 of each, hand-
numbered), 'to make people stop and
think, if only for a second; they're about
ideas and observations.' The posters
examine different communication
systems, drawn from spoken, written
and visual language. Posters comment
on a range of issues, from products that
are sexually stereotyped, to the modern
phenomenon of text speak; subliminal
advertising; misunderstanding plain
English; the wordless speech bubble;
colloquialisms and slang, and calorific
temptation (printed with scratch-and-
sniff inks). A number of the posters
are in the permanent collection of the
Victoria and Albert Museum, London.

Limited-edition Moleskine Notebook
(top right)
100 numbered notebooks; the cover is
based on a Language Poster. These are
given to clients and friends.

HarrimanSteel Newspaper
The newspaper showcases recent
projects and case studies, and includes
ten new Language Posters. This is
mailed out, handed out and passed on
to all interested parties, and anyone
the partners would like to work with in
the future.

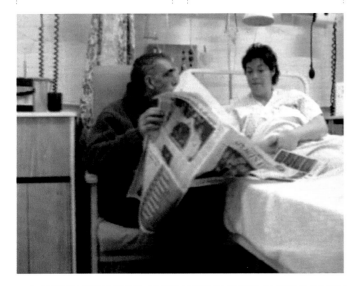

Christmas Viral 1 (opposite page)
Two 30-second films
'Congratulations it's a boy'
HarrimanSteel's aim was to help
people remember the real reason
behind Christmas; a newborn Jesus,
with full beard, appears in a modern
maternity ward.

'Happy Birthday'
A four-year-old Jesus, with full beard,
at his birthday party.

Christmas Viral 2 (below)
Three 45-second films
Highlighting the seasonal proliferation
of what Nick calls 'vacuous'
perfume and aftershave advertising,
HarrimanSteel examined the different
genres, from esoteric/obscure to macho
and romantic/seductive. Studio staffers
play all parts (including drag), and these
provocative movies are well viewed on
YouTube.

**Limited Edition Perfume and
Aftershave Packaging** (right)
Select clients received these luxury
branded gifts, spectacular for their
attention to detail.

   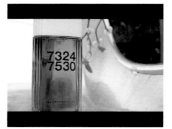

Hexaplex   Micha Bakker and Cheryl Gallaway   Amsterdam, the Netherlands   www.hexaplex.nl

Hexaplex don't have a logo or a letterhead, instead, they explain, 'the Hexaplex identity is like the internet – dynamic, fluid and connected. The content is the foundation and the Internet is the network.'

Using HTML and the Hexadecimal colour system, Hexaplex treat their name to a Red (#FF0000) and Green (#00FF00) colour scheme that 'quite simply reflects our two personalities and tastes.' Secondary colours are used as highlights, while the typographic identity is 'utilitarian and web-safe': a serif and a sans serif, Times New Roman and Helvetica.

'Our "non-design" approach is a result of using the RGB colour palette as it exists on screen,' they explain. Invoices and communications are emailed, personalized by their 'email signature', which indicates the sender by highlighting their names in red and green.

But has adopting such a rigorous and conceptual approach paid off when it comes to attracting clients? Hexaplex are clear about their motives: 'We like to create design that takes advantage of all opportunities in web communication. So by creating an identity that reflects how we like to work with the medium, we can attract clients and projects that are open to our way of thinking.' And, they add, 'it's a good starting point for discussion.'

hexaplex.nl
info@hexaplex.nl

Zaanhof 57
1013 XW
Amsterdam

Micha Bakker
micha@hexaplex.nl
+31(0)6-24900661

Cheryl Gallaway
cheryl@hexaplex.nl
+31(0)6-13555381

hexaplex.nl
info@hexaplex.nl

Zaanhof 57
1013 XW
Amsterdam

Micha Bakker
micha@hexaplex.nl
+31(0)6-24900661

Cheryl Gallaway
cheryl@hexaplex.nl
+31(0)6-13555381

hexaplex.nl
info@hexaplex.nl

Zaanhof 57
1013 XW
Amsterdam

Micha Bakker
micha@hexaplex.nl
+31(0)6-24900661

Cheryl Gallaway
cheryl@hexaplex.nl
+31(0)6-13555381

Business Cards (opposite page)
1/0, black, on white, sticker and hand-drawn highlighter.
'We customize and personalize business cards using our colour system.'

Website (below)
www.hexaplex.nl
Hexaplex's website is their main promotional portal, and features some interesting devices that enliven the interface. Each page refresh is treated to a new combination of the colour scheme, while the typography actually aids navigation: as a user moves towards specific content, the type size increases, so information is continually compressed and decompressed.

Promotional Publication (top right)
Print Screen, Screenprint
Digital, on various colour stock.
'For our offline PR, we developed *Print Screen, Screenprint,* which is an "Unlimited Edition". A webpage gathers content from our site/database and arranges it via a template that is designed using web style sheets (CSS) for the printed page; then it is output as an A5 booklet.'

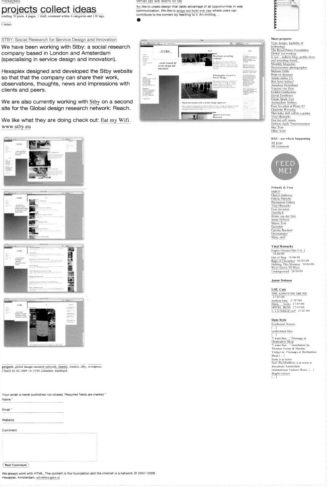

Ian Lynam Creative Direction & Graphic Design   Ian Lynam   Tokyo, Japan   www.ianlynam.com

After studying in the United States, Ian Lynam relocated to Japan. Creating a corporate identity that functions not only in two languages but also in different alphabets was the challenge – it's a lot of information to organize. Ian explains his solution: 'I use a set of hand embossers for all stationery items apart from business cards so that if additional information is needed, in English or Japanese, I can custom-print the necessary items and then emboss them.' The blind embosser enables Ian to include twice as much legible information as usual, but in a super-subtle method that doesn't crowd the page. There are also cultural issues about mixing the two alphabets/languages; to an extent, Ian's English information is considered decorative, so it needs to look good.

'In Japan, English is most often used to create an "image", the elusive combination of *funiki* (atmosphere), emotion and sensation,' he explains. 'A Japanese audience will classify any English text longer than a few words as decoration, to be felt, rather than read, especially if equivalent Japanese text is included.'

IAN LYNAM
ライナム イエン

CREATIVE DIRECTION   GRAPHIC DESIGN
創造的演出家／グラフィックデザイン

080 5527 8090 (日本)
661 373 3045 (US)

WWW.IANLYNAM.COM
IAN@IANLYNAM.COM

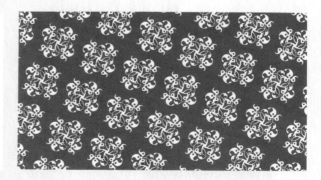

Letterhead (opposite page)
White antique laid stock, blind deboss.
All stationery for the studio uses the
same type treatment.

Business Card (opposite page, on top
of letterhead)
2/1, purple, black, silver foil, on white
card, blind deboss.
'The *meishi* (business card) is the
cornerstone of my corporate identity,'
explains Ian. 'In Japan, there are
two primary means of initial contact
between designers and clients:
business cards and websites. Both
must be highly memorable in Tokyo's
competitive design community. So I
designed a subtly indulgent card using
a number of printing processes and
quality materials, and paired a fine
book face, Dolly Small Caps, designed
by Underware, with a nuanced and
sophisticated book *mincho* (a Japanese
font) Ryumin Pro. Neither is given
preference, so they play off each other.'

Envelopes (below)
White and brown envelopes, four sizes,
blind deboss.

Disk Envelope (below right)
Brown card, blind deboss.
The studio DVD reel of motion graphic
work is housed in a custom die-cut
cardboard sleeve, packed in a debossed
envelope.

Postcard (bottom left)
2/1, black, PMS 231, PMS 375, on
White Monadnock Astrolite 130# Card,
chamfered corners.
Published by Pinball Publishing.
A two-colour promotional postcard
is included with each piece of printed
communication. 'It's a real attention-
getter, showing two sides of the
studio's work; the head-clobbering,
pop obsession that cohabits with fine
typography and attention to detail.'

Website (bottom right)
An embellished portfolio site, Ian
includes extras, such as client
testimonials and a selection of his
own writing on graphic design; there
are also links to current projects,
'and heaps of work shot by a
professional photographer.'

Japanese Survival Tool (top right)
3/0, green, pink, grey, on white card.
This phonetic reference guide to the
Japanese syllabary families (*hiragana*
and *katakana*) uses the Dolly and
Ryumin type pairing to communicate
and differentiate the building blocks of
the Japanese language; the colours
intimate Ian's pop sensibility.

Inkahoots   Robyn McDonald, Jason Grant, Ben Mangan, Joel Booj, Mathew Johnson, Kate Booj   South Brisbane, Australia   www.inkahoots.com.au

Inkahoots doesn't sell products for clients; communicating ideas is what they do. On their website, they present a coherent argument and eloquent description of themselves, in their own words: 'Inkahoots doesn't quite fit into any of the usual industry moulds. Sometimes this helps the business, sometimes it harms it. But it's what we are. Over 15 years we've evolved from a collective of rebel community artists, screenprinting political posters in a Union basement, into a multi-disciplined design studio that continues to hustle for social change through visual communication.'

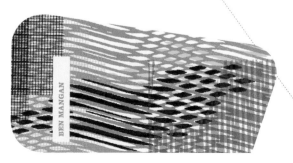

Business Cards (opposite page)
4/2, spot colour, metallic
and fluorescent inks, on uncoated
recycled stock.
The cards feature insightful copy: Public
x Private, Chaos x Calm, Sacred x
Profane. Jason Grant describes them
as 'little visual bombs'.

Exhibition Kit
Unsettled Posters, 2007: Brisbane,
Dirty 3, Bob Dylan, Rosalie Gascoigne,
Jesus Christ, Karl Marx, Redback, Sex.
Packaged in 1/0, black, on brown
board, die-cut, hand-torn.
Clients: Inkahoots and Red Connect.
Inkahoots created a portable version
of their window display space, with
the 'exhibition in a box'. This grew
into a larger exhibition in Brisbane
and London that included video work,
furniture and interactive installations.
'The posters were initially prompted
by participation in Anja Lutz and Anna
Gerber's book, *Influences: A Lexicon
of Contemporary Graphic Design*',
explains Jason. 'We had to nominate
ten influences; with a studio of people
of different ages, backgrounds and
sensibilities, we thought it would
be interesting to agree on shared
influences and inspiration that have
shaped our practice. The posters

consider ways in which personal
inspiration engages with cultural
identity, and attempts to visualize that.'

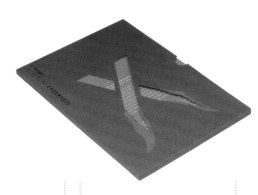

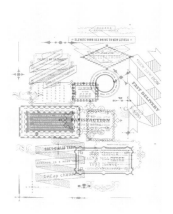

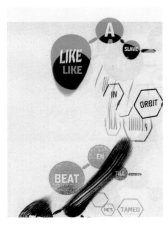

Posters
For a number of years, Inkahoots
used their studio window as a street-
level gallery, displaying a rotating
selection of posters 'as a means of
engaging with the local community
about current issues'.

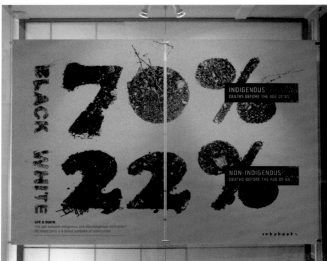

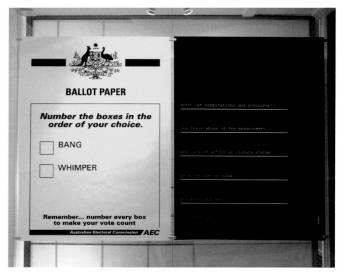

Website
www.inkahoots.com.au
On the homepage a kinetic word game
realized in a custom-designed typeface
randomly generates more than 8,000
poems and statements with a roll of
the mouse.

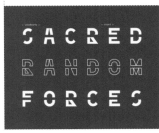

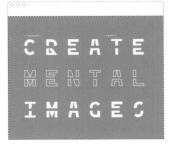

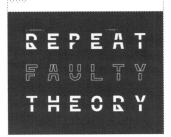

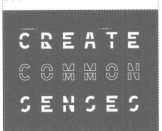

KAPITZA

Kapitza   Nicole Kapitza and Petra Kapitza   London, UK   www.kapitza.com

Sisters Nicole and Petra Kapitza, in their own words, '...share a passion for everyday life, minimalism, patterns and colour.' This they have parlayed into a dynamic, design-led business, the crux of which is an online shop.

Mixing their technical expertise with visual curiosity, they've built a comprehensive, commercial website, offering an inventory of unique graphic products. 'We both have more than ten years' experience in website design, and set up our online shop in 2006 as a platform to release our picture fonts and illustrations. Our objective is to create a source of inspiration, a continually growing resource of high-resolution picture fonts and illustrations for designers to use in their own work.'

Grouped by subject, these geometric patterns and quirky silhouetted figures can be manipulated via a computer keyboard; the sisters describe them as 'lying somewhere between image resource and art project.'

It's such a unique use of the 'font' format – where did the idea come from? 'Originally, from an artwork we did for an exhibition, "Death is Part of the Process", at Void Gallery in Derry, Ireland in 2005. Entitled *Cycle*, we created hundreds of illustrations of people, animals and plants, as a contemporary memento mori, and these illustrations were the starting point for our picture fonts.'

The raw material for the fonts come from the sisters' own photography; so environmental observation and travel is part of the process. Originally from Germany, Kapitza are now based in east London. 'It's a vibrant and dynamic area that provides inspiration for our work, along with nature, people and software.'

Building on such a dynamic retail and product offering, Kapitza's corporate identity is rooted in their website design, which showcases the products against a white ground, framed by abstracted photographic and graphic images; but even amid the abundance of imagery, a clean, uncluttered order prevails. Attention to detail is paramount; colour and drawing spills over onto the stationery system, while their 'font folder' icons are also embellished with tiny snippets of pattern.

Letterhead (opposite page and below left) **and Invoice** (below right)
Four-colour CMYK, on Natural White Munken Lynx.

Business Cards (bottom)
Four-colour CMYK, on Natural White Munken Lynx.

Envelope (top right)
Pink stock.

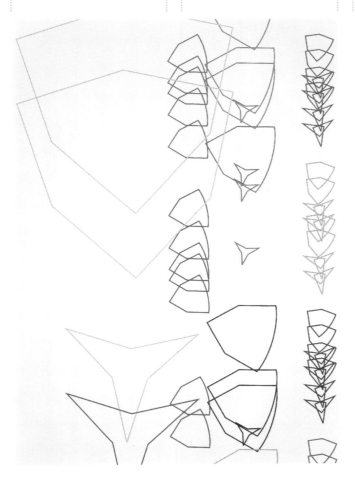

KAPITZA

Petra Kapitza
petra@kapitza.com
0044 0 7791 260314
www.kapitza.com

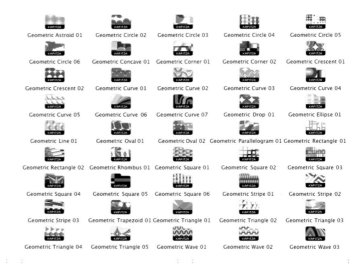

Geometric Astroid 01 | Geometric Circle 02 | Geometric Circle 03 | Geometric Circle 04 | Geometric Circle 05

Geometric Circle 06 | Geometric Concave 01 | Geometric Corner 01 | Geometric Corner 02 | Geometric Crescent 01

Geometric Crescent 02 | Geometric Curve 01 | Geometric Curve 02 | Geometric Curve 03 | Geometric Curve 04

Geometric Curve 05 | Geometric Curve 06 | Geometric Curve 07 | Geometric Drop 01 | Geometric Ellipse 01

Geometric Line 01 | Geometric Oval 01 | Geometric Oval 02 | Geometric Parallelogram 01 | Geometric Rectangle 01

Geometric Rectangle 02 | Geometric Rhombus 01 | Geometric Square 01 | Geometric Square 02 | Geometric Square 03

Geometric Square 04 | Geometric Square 05 | Geometric Square 06 | Geometric Stripe 01 | Geometric Stripe 02

Geometric Stripe 03 | Geometric Trapezoid 01 | Geometric Triangle 01 | Geometric Triangle 02 | Geometric Triangle 03

Geometric Triangle 04 | Geometric Triangle 05 | Geometric Wave 01 | Geometric Wave 02 | Geometric Wave 03

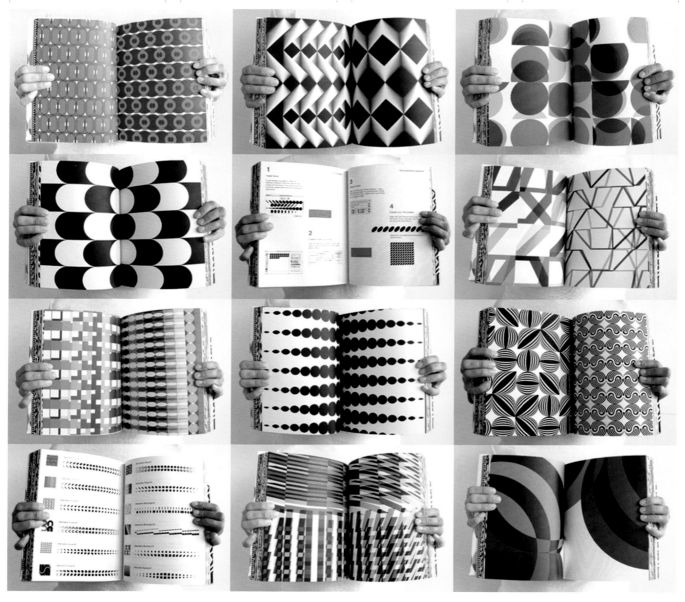

Book (opposite page, top left and
main picture)
*Geometric: graphic art and pattern
fonts*, Verlag Hermann Schmidt,
Mainz, 2008.
Packaged with a poster and DVD.

Font Folders (opposite page, top right)
Each icon offers a snippet of pattern to
enliven your desktop.

Website
www.kapitza.com
A comprehensive and enticing
e-commerce site, bristling with
information and imagery.

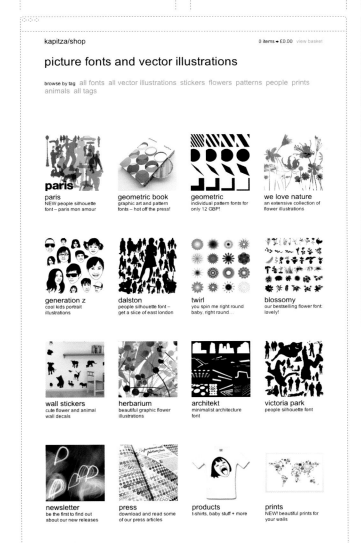

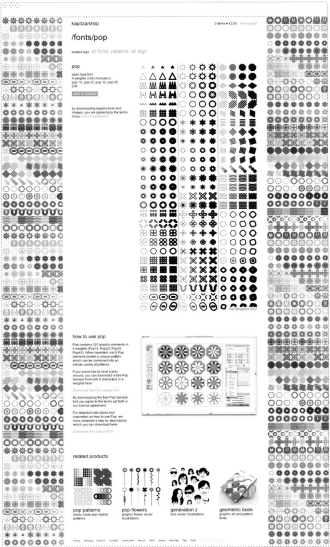

KO.HELLO

KOI   Krispin Heé and Peter Jaeger   Bern, Switzerland   www.koi.li

'The story of the logo is simple,' explains Krispin Heé of KOI. 'We were playing around with the letters K, O and I, and at some point we realized that a mirrored K actually looks like a tailfin; together with the O it becomes a fish, a koi....Then we decided to place the dot of the I next to the logo, and were able to produce all kinds of headings.'

So, a koi is a giant goldfish, but in Japanese it's also a homophone for 'love'. Why choose that word? 'It's a short and catchy term and it stands for beauty, grace and exclusivity; the koi is always the most admired fish in the pond,' says Krispin.

KOI
Aarbergergasse 52
CH-3011 Bern
031 311 00 75
www.koi.li
info@koi.li

Letterhead (opposite page), **Contract,
Offer and Invoice** (below left)
Digital, in-house, 1/0, black, on white,
80gsm.
Koi's house typeface is Dada Grotesk
from Optimo, designed by deValence.
On correspondence, the logo acts as an
arrow, drawing attention to the heading.

Envelope and Stickers (below right)
Digital, in-house, 1/0, black, on white
sticker stock, and on light grey, recycled
envelope.
With the address on one side and
the studio's contact details on the
other, the sticker folds over the edge
of the envelope.

Business Card (top right)
Digital, in-house, 1/0, black, on Fischer
Papier Swissboard GD2, 250gsm.
Carries a clever variation on the
logo, >0.ID.

A5 Postcards (this page, main picture)
Digital, in-house, full colour, on Fischer
Papier Swissboard GD2, 250gsm.
Regarded as 'an important medium for
our customer relations,' KOI frequently
change the front image and add
handwritten messages.

Agenda and Postcards (bottom)
Designed in collaboration with Coboi,
two agendas and a set of postcards
welcome the new year. One features a
menagerie of cute dogs, the other offers
an array of organizing grids.

Website
www.koi.li
Click on a thumbnail image to reveal the
project, more images and the spec.

Screen Icons (below right)
The logo becomes a background image,
combined with the medium: >0.PC,
>0.MAC, >0.TEL.

HKB lehrt und forscht
Plakat
Die Hochschule der Künste publiziert und forscht!
Diese Plakate hängen in den Schaufenstern der
Münstergassbuchhandlung in Bern und machen auf
die ausgelegten Publikationen der HKB aufmerksam.

Auftrag: Hochschule der Künste Bern
17.07.2008

LOS ANGELES
CALIFORNIA 90014

818
SOUTH BROADWAY
SUITE 1000

fax
213 629 1396

APRIL GREIMAN
MADE IN SPACE, INC.

213 629 1380

E-MAIL   : INFO@ MADEINSPACE.LA
WWW   : MADEINSPACE.LA

Made In Space   April Greiman   Los Angeles, CA, USA   www.madeinspace.la

Renowned innovator April Greiman promotes her studio, Made In Space, with, as she explains, 'an identity based on "objects in space" creating visual hierarchies of information. If our work includes some of my specialized "art", my photography in particular, and images that I generate, then I use the name April Greiman Made In Space.'

April was an early adopter of computer technology as an image-making tool and information organizing device. The current Made In Space identity mixes dynamic typography, which breaks through the picture plane, with an investigation of materials, paper stocks, print techniques and finishes, which roots April's experimentation in a real world of infinite possibilities.

'Made In Space is known for a body of work using colour and materials palettes,' says April. 'Therefore, "materials freak to the max" would be a good way to describe our output.'

Letterhead, two versions (opposite page and below)
2/0, green and orange, on Natural White, Cranes Crest, 24#, and various colours ('often the yellow one') Astrobrite, 20#.

Envelope, two versions (bottom)
1/0, black on Curious Gold Leaf, and vellum in various colours. April finds interesting envelopes by hunting through stationery stores.

Slender Business Card (below right)
4/1, green, orange, turquoise, black, on white card.

Holographic Business Card (top right)
2/1, matte gold, turquoise, iridescent silver foil block, on holographic 3D chrome sphere plastic.

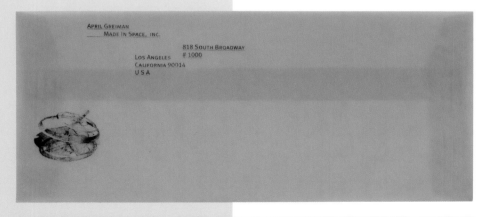

Brochure (below and top right)
Containing several square-format concertina booklets showcasing projects and achievements; packaged in a die-cut folder, and presented with a holographic business card.

Studio (bottom)
Housed on a floor of a downtown loft, the Made In Space studio presents a signature mix of dynamic colour and experimental forms and materials. The building's hard-edged shell remains visible and undisguised, but is softened by a rich blend of elements. Colours (both natural and artificial) and materials (translucent and reflective) are employed to create partitions, furniture, seating and lighting, adding up to a unique working environment. Hanging from a bespoke exhibition system, April's large-scale photography/typography images act as space dividers, evoking a sense of lightness and movement while demarcating quieter spaces.

Website
www.madeinspace.la
A typographic homepage reveals a host
of colour-coded information. Meanwhile,
a deeper interface leads the user into
an alternative space, where the mouse
selects random elements and steers a
multi-dimensional navigation system.

Magpie Studio

Magpie Studio   David Azurdia, Ben Christie, Jamie Ellul   London, UK   www.magpie-studio.com

Magpie Studio's corporate identity sprang from 'an evocative name,' according to Jamie Ellul, 'chosen because we're always on the look-out for visual stimulation, be it scouring blogs or sifting through old stamps at flea markets; we collect shining examples of good design, art, music, writing, fashion.' His more pragmatic explanation includes the fact that two of the three partners have 'unpronounceable surnames', and an amalgam of initials would spell 'ACE, which sounded a bit naff and a lot to live up to.' Jamie admits, 'getting all three partners to agree on the branding was one of the hardest things we've ever done.'

Aiming to mirror their inspiration hunts, they came up with the idea of collecting beautiful 'M's to feature in their branding. 'Magpie also alludes to the fact that we don't have one approach to our work,' Jamie adds, 'every client has a different problem so we hunt for the right solutions, and our brand is a vehicle for showing that eclectic approach.'

The 'M's were photographed (in black and white, naturally) and feature on the reverse of each item of paper stationery. Having so many examples to accommodate, the team decided to create series: two letterheads, three compliments slips, and five business cards for each designer.

They added a hand-drawn logotype, based on the typeface Archer, and use Lexia (designed by Ron Carpenter for Dalton Maag) for all correspondence. 'We wanted a modern typeface with a nod towards the traditional letterpress "M"s,' explains Jamie. 'Lexia's slab serif works for headlines and body copy. It's quirky but legible.'

Hope House
12A Perseverance Works

38 Kingsland Road
London E2 8DD

+44 (0)20 7729 3007
magpie-studio.com

Magpie Studio Limited
Registered in England & Wales — Company Registration № 6415181
Registered Address — Carewell Lodge, Racecourse Road, Lingfield, Surrey RH7 6PP

Letterhead (opposite page and
below left) **and Compliments Slip**
(below right)
1/1, book black, on Mohawk Superfine
Ultrawhite Eggshell, 148gsm.
'The long line of "M"s leant itself
to a landscape letterhead, which
emphasizes that we approach things
differently,' explains Jamie. 'Plus
it's memorable and stands out from
the crowd.'

Business Cards (top right and bottom)
1/1, PMS 877 and book black, on
Curious Skin Black, 270gsm, duplexed
to Curious Skin White, 270gsm.

Website Announcement
Letterpress, 2/0 black, wood block, and silver foil block, on Somerset Book Soft White, 175gsm (poster) and Fedrigoni Tintereto Ceylon Black Pepper, 300gsm (folder), embossed, hand-finished. 'Touches of silver are used to reference the magpie's love of shiny objects' and the edges of the poster are hand-torn, to show how precious this is. The poster can be read either way up, as three 'M's, for the partners, or 'www', for the website.

Website

www.magpie-studio.com
The website reinforces two aspects
of the identity: the collection of 'M's,
and the landscape format, as navigation
is via left-to-right scrolling. The
company tagline, 'Speaking in black
and white but thinking in colour', is also
demonstrated; the site's architecture is
starkly black and white, while the work
is shown in colour.

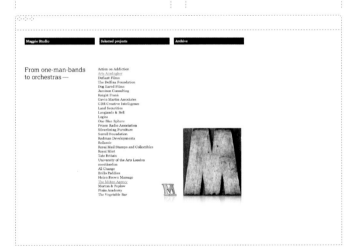

MARC & ANNA
Studio 46
Regent Studios
8 Andrews Road
London E8 4QN

T 020 7249 6111
E hello@marcandanna.co.uk
www.marcandanna.co.uk

MARC&ANNA   Marc Atkinson and Anna Ekelund   London, UK   www.marcandanna.co.uk

Established in 2005, this team is now five-strong; with a belief in collaboration, they aim to supply unique solutions. MARC&ANNA's corporate identity underlines the partnership element with a one-off finishing touch.

It's all in the name... 'We considered all sorts of clever names but agreed that we wanted to come across as small, personal and playful,' they explain. As an antidote to formal surnames, they chose to go on first-name terms, adding an ampersand as a 'symbol of partnership, between us, our clients and the people we like to work with...and because it's one of the nicest characters. We both like to use type playfully, so this allows us the freedom to update and change the identity while maintaining consistency.'

Having built up a collection of ampersands, which are converted into rubber stamps, each studio member is able to personalize every piece of correspondence and mail with a stamp of their choosing. 'We like that there is a personal touch; people we meet can choose a business card, and it's never "perfect" either,' they admit. Describing themselves as 'hands on...we love a bit of drawing, scribbling, spraying and stamping,' they admit that a mass mail-out takes some effort, but 'it's worth it!'

DIRECTORS
Marc Atkinson
Anna Ekelund
REGISTERED OFFICE
52 Great Eastern Street
London EC2A 3EP
COMPANY Nº
5337202
VAT Nº
858 7770 60

MARC&ANNA CREATIVE LIMITED
REGISTERED IN ENGLAND AND WALES

Letterhead (opposite page) **and
Compliment Slip** (below left)
2/2, Pantone silver 877 and black, on
Think White, 115gsm, hand-stamped.

Business Cards (right)
2/2, Pantone silver 877 and black,
(double hit of silver on reverse),
on Think White, 300gsm duplexed
with Colorplan Ebony, 350gsm,
hand-stamped.

MARC & ANNA
Studio 46
Regent Studios
8 Andrews Road
London E8 4QN

T 020 7249 6111
E hello@marcandanna.co.uk
www.marcandanna.co.uk

ANNA EKELUND

MARC & ANNA
Studio 46
Regent Studios
8 Andrews Road
London E8 4QN

T 020 7249 6111
M 07766 202 087
E anna@marcandanna.co.uk
www.marcandanna.co.uk

CONNIE WRIGHT

MARC & ANNA
Studio 46
Regent Studios
8 Andrews Road
London E8 4QN

T 020 7249 6111
E connie@marcandanna.co.uk
www.marcandanna.co.uk

MARC ATKINSON

MARC & ANNA
Studio 46
Regent Studios
8 Andrews Road
London E8 4QN

T 020 7249 6111
M 07766 657 142
E marc@marcandanna.co.uk
www.marcandanna.co.uk

Website and Ampersands
www.marcandanna.co.uk
Programmer: Emiliano Fuksas
With donations of ampersands from
friends and admirers, the collection
is growing. 'We wanted to photograph
them, and thought it would make a
playful homepage for our website.
There is, however, no reason for the
small plastic animals in the picture, we
just like them.' With an ever-changing
ampersand on each page, a chatty
news section and a competition to
nominate and vote on new ampersands,
this website aims to reinforce the core
values of MARC&ANNA, while offering
visitors a means of 'getting to know us'.

Rubber Stamps
MARC&ANNA's extensive collection of ampersand rubber stamps.

Promotional Mailer (right)
1/1, black and four-colour CMYK, on Think White, 115gsm, Regency Gloss and Colorplan Ebony, 350gsm; black envelope, hand-stamped and handwritten.
Sent to prospective clients, this personalized mailer both intrigues and informs. A showcase of recent projects, it mixes and matches stock with handwritten and stamped additions, while promoting unique solutions and collaborations.

this is our **letterhead**™

© MINE™ 190 Putnam St. San Francisco, CA 94110   415 647 6463   minesf.com

MINE™   Christopher Simmons   San Francisco, CA, USA   www.minesf.com

Christopher Simmons of MINE™ took a conceptual route when designing his company's identity, which, he points out, demonstrates his approach to working with clients too. Here he explains the project.

'We set out to express our spare, literate and provocative approach to design; within this seemingly banal system, there are references to poetry, semantics and personal identity,' he says.

'Our aim was to deconstruct each element, examine its function and re-present it in a different (almost opposite) way. Words have become a kind of logo, and extreme obviousness serves to expose some of the subtleties involved in crafting identity. This sets up a discussion about identity, so a client meeting can become an engaging experience.

'Good writing also leaves room for the reader's imagination to contribute to the experience; we frequently write copy for clients...and contribute the most fundamental element of any identity: we name companies, products and organizations. That's a form of writing too, as the name is often supported by taglines or descriptors that we also create.'

Central to MINE™'s stationery range is a deceptively minimal business card, with a hidden message. Hold it up to the light and the owner's name and email address is revealed, buried deep within the fabric of the card. So is it made of some high-tech material, or been subjected to a revolutionary print technology? Christopher reveals the card's secret: 'It's three sheets of paper laminated together. In the centre is a sheet of black 100# stock, which is laser-cut with the copy. Then sheets of white 80# cover stock are laminated front and back. These are printed with our identity and general information. The idea is that when it's handed out, the card appears to lack essential information. Ideally, the card would have been totally blank, but we felt we needed at least some clues that it contained information.'

Working with a printer who was keen to prototype and get it right, the major challenges were the correct registration of the three sheets, using the right amount of glue, and selecting a stock you can actually see through.

Art director and designer:
Christopher Simmons
Designer: Tim Belonax

Letterhead and Proposal (opposite
page and below)
1/0, black, on white stock.

Postcard (below right)
1/1, black, on white card.

CD (middle right)
2/0, black, on white.

Business Card (bottom left)
1/1, black, on white stock, 80#;
laminated with black card, 100#,
laser-cut.

Envelope (bottom right)
1/1, black, on white envelope.
Printed on the reverse with a full-bleed
image featuring the studio's phone
number and a pregnancy scan: another
hidden message.

this is our **proposal**™

this is just to **say:**

this is our **cd**™

this is my **card**™

this is my **card**™

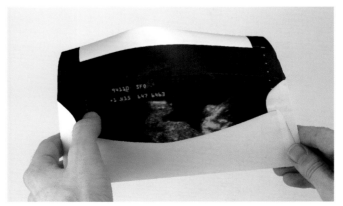

MOJO

MOJO | Jeff Lamont and Michael Kahane | Los Angeles, CA, USA | www.mojohouse.com

MOJO began as a studio creating trailers for the film industry. A large number of screen-based promotional items are needed for every film, and as MOJO were constantly busy, the presentation and packaging was left to the discretion of each staffer. When the partners launched a print division, they decided to develop a cohesive look for their own corporate identity.

It all started with a resin model of the logo. Corey Holms, art director for Theatrical Print, explains: 'MOJO is a coming together of many creative elements and the resin logo depicts the sum of the parts, the company identity, rising out of that creative soup.' The model was photographed and combined with '...a redrawn, tracked-out version of Trajan (originally designed by Carol Twombly for Linotype); it's the movies' typeface!' jokes Corey. The main typeface, however, is Cycles, designed by Sumner Stone for the Stone Type Foundry.

'The identity consists of two parts,' he continues. 'One is refined and clean on uncoated paper, very corporate, for our communications; the other is a "Hollywood" glossy, coated, full-bleed photographic look, used for shipping our product. When we send a trailer, be it a disk or a DVD, it's accompanied by the slick version featuring a crop of a bigger, full-colour image.' Similarly, each poster they send is identified by a sticker on the reverse, in the same fashion.

Corey explains the challenge of creating the new identity: 'We wanted to keep the "heritage", but unify it. It took a lot of organizing and problem-solving to incorporate existing work and pull together those diverse ideas to perform for all aspects of the company.'

MOJO, LLC.
5750 Wilshire Boulevard, Suite 600, Los Angeles, California 90036
323.932.7700 tel 323.932.7701 fax www.mojohouse.com

Creative director: Andrew Percival
Art director: Corey Holms

Letterhead (opposite page)
2/0, blue and grey, on Neenah Paper
Classic Crest Solar White,
24# Writing.

Business Cards (below)
Four-colour CMYK, and blue and grey,
on Neenah Paper Classic Crest Solar
White, 80# Cover, duplexed.
The business card is a hybrid of
MOJO's two aesthetics. An uncoated
side presents the information, while
the coated reverse shows a crop of the
logo. 'We applied the philosophy of the
coming together of creative elements
to the cards, where no single element
or person is MOJO, so no one person's
business card can contain or hold
MOJO,' explains Corey. 'The logo is
spread across a number of cards to
invoke the adage, "the sum of the parts
is greater than the whole". If you get the
right six cards, they come together to
make the complete logo image.'

Compliments Card and Moving Card
Four-colour CMYK, and blue and grey,
on white card, embossed, folded.

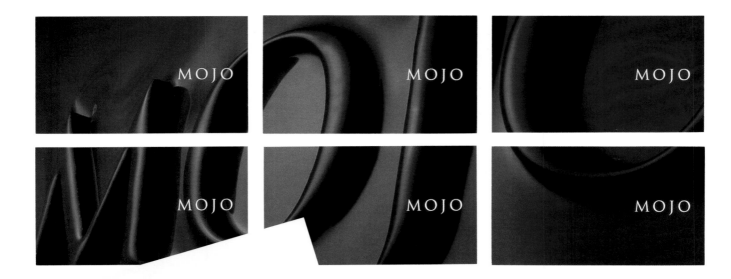

Corey Holms
Art Director - Theatrical Print
cholms@mojohouse.com

MOJO, LLC.
5750 Wilshire Boulevard, Suite 600, Los Angeles, California 90036
323.932.7700 tel 323.932.7701 fax www.mojohouse.com

MOJO

Andrew Percival

Buckslips (opposite page)
Four-colour CMYK, and blue and grey,
on Neenah Paper Classic Crest Solar
White, 80# Cover, duplexed.
'In the print division of MOJO, the
most used piece of stationery is the
buckslip,' says Corey. 'We modified
the business card to promote our work,
again with one uncoated side showing
our logo and name; the reverse is a
crop of a recent poster. It's a good
way to let people know about our
successful collaborations without
sending out a mailer that addresses it
directly. It's also fun figuring out which
poster it's showcasing.'

Website (below)
www.mojohouse.com
The two-aesthetic philosophy
continues on the recently
relaunched website, which mimics
the cooler, corporate aesthetic of
the 'communication' aspect of MOJO's
identity, borrowing type-style and colour
scheme from the stationery. 'A graphic
on the welcome page randomly cycles,
showing a tightly cropped image from
a recent project drawn from across all
divisions of the company, be it a video
game, movie trailer, poster or billboard.'
The site is also a great place to watch
new movie trailers.

CD (bottom)
Digital, in-house.
Features full-colour crop of the
MOJO logo.

NB: Studio

4—8 Emerson Street
London SE1 9DU
United Kingdom
T +44 [0]20 7633 9046
www.nbstudio.co.uk

NB: Studio   London, UK   www.nbstudio.co.uk

Working with major brands, including media corporations such as Channel 4 and high-street retailers such as Mothercare, NB: Studio presents a cool, considered corporate identity, tempered with a programme of promotional projects that hint at wider obsessions and an abiding love of designing for print.

Senior designer Daniel Lock explains the motivation behind these self-published projects: 'Ultimately, the goal is to be at the front of clients' minds, so they think of us first for a new project. It's a way of keeping in contact creatively, and introducing ourselves to new clients too. A lot of our work features unusual print techniques or interesting illustrators that clients may not have seen before, so that we might inspire them.'

So does it work? What sort of reaction do the projects generate? Daniel again: 'We create these projects as memorable gifts, rather than just a direct mailer, so clients are always happy to receive them; particularly if it is designed to sit on their desk, or is a print that could be framed. We aim for longevity, something that people will treasure, and we avoid replicating ideas. Hopefully clients recognize our creative thinking, and will opt to have it applied to their commercial projects.'

NB: Studio Ltd Registered Address: 141 Wardour Street London W1F 0UT Registered Company Number: 3861746

Letterhead (opposite page)
Silver and black foil blocks and black,
on GF Smith Colorplan Pristine White,
die-cut round corners.

Compliments Slip (below)
Silver and black foil block, on GF
Smith Colorplan Pristine White,
die-cut round corners.

Business Card (top right)
Silver and black foil blocks and black,
on GF Smith Colorplan Pristine White
and Black Chromolux, duplexed, die-cut
round corners.

Website (bottom right)
www.nbstudio.co.uk
With a rotating image of the studio on
the homepage, this website offers a
behind-the-scenes glimpse of a busy
design environment. The 'Also' section
contains many of the studio's self-
published projects.

Daniel Lock
Designer

NB: Studio
**4—8 Emerson Street
London SE1 9DU
United Kingdom**

**T +44 [0]20 7633 9046
d.lock@nbstudio.co.uk
www.nbstudio.co.uk**

NB: Studio
**4—8 Emerson Street
London SE1 9DU
United Kingdom**

**T +44 [0]20 7633 9046
mail@nbstudio.co.uk
www.nbstudio.co.uk**

Cards (below)
This Year...
Creative directors: Ben Stott,
Nick Finney, Alan Dye
Designer: Daniel Lock
Illustrators: James Joyce, Anthony
Burrill, Billie Jean, Paul Bower
Conceived as a New Year mailer, the
idea is to create a collectable. The
title 'This Year...' sets the tone with a
prediction, statement or comment on
the year ahead; 2009's highlighted the
collapse of the global economy using
a single dollar bill.

Pack of Cards (right)
Creative directors: Ben Stott,
Nick Finney, Alan Dye
Designer: Alan Dye
Containing images from favourite
projects over the decade, packaged
in an embossed box, this mini-portfolio
(re)introduces the recipient to
NB: Studio.

Book and Invitation
Monsters Ink
Creative directors: Ben Stott,
Nick Finney, Alan Dye
Designer: Jodie Wightman
Illustrator: James Graham
Copywriter: Vivienne Hamilton
A Halloween giveaway promoting
'feeling the fear', this guide to all that's
ghastly and ghoulish cites mythical
monsters from various cultures. Text
and images are screenprinted in white
on to black paper, while the party
invitation is printed in glow-in-the-dark
green ink.

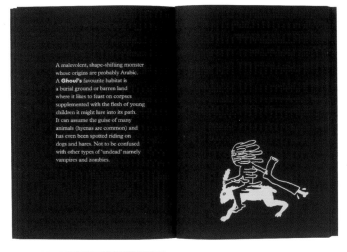

A malevolent, shape-shifting monster whose origins are probably Arabic. A **Ghoul's** favourite habitat is a burial ground or barren land where it likes to feast on corpses supplemented with the flesh of young children it might lure into its path. It can assume the guise of many animals (hyenas are common) and has even been spotted riding on dogs and hares. Not to be confused with other types of 'undead' namely vampires and zombies.

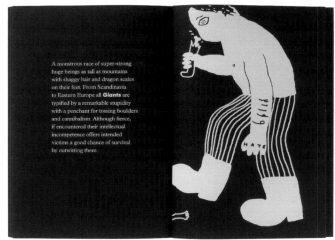

A monstrous race of super-strong huge beings as tall as mountains with shaggy hair and dragon scales on their feet. From Scandinavia to Eastern Europe all **Giants** are typified by a remarkable stupidity with a penchant for tossing boulders and cannibalism. Although fierce, if encountered their intellectual incompetence offers intended victims a good chance of survival by outwitting them.

Originally very beautiful women transformed into hideously ugly monsters, **Gorgons** are identified by the crown of writhing live snakes on their heads. Noted in many classical Greek texts as Queens of the Underworld, their additional features include a round flat face, lolling tongue and sometimes the tusks of a boar. The most famous example of this fearsome creature is undoubtedly Medusa, who, like her sisters, could turn onlookers into stone.

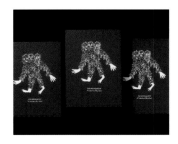

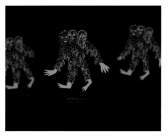

MARTIN NICOLAUSSON
+46 (0)70 789 49 67
INFO@MARTINNICOLAUSSON.COM

Martin Nicolausson   Martin Nicolausson   Stockholm, Sweden   www.martinnicolausson.com

Part of the challenge for a designer working on their own corporate identity is dealing with yourself as a client. If you're in a partnership or shared studio, you also need to please your peers. But when you run your own independent studio, it may be even tougher. Here, Martin Nicolausson voices his concerns and explains his solution.

'Working with a client, there is someone to turn to with questions about the brand or product; someone to have a dialogue with. In my case there was no one that knew the "brand" better than myself, and that's the tricky situation. How to distil myself into an identity? With so many decisions to make, there's often too much information. I could have taken the easy route and gone with a minimalist "say nothing" identity, except I don't feel that fits me.

'Previously, during the process of designing an identity, I've found it hard to feel content, and have grown tired of what I've produced and never finished it. With that in mind, I concluded that it would take an automated or random process to complete my identity, to keep it updated and make it feel dynamic. And I could avoid making decisions as the program would make them for me.

'I have a strong interest in the language of symbols, both those with or lacking meaning. So I established a set of symbols for myself, a library that can be added to, and this is the basis for my identity.

'The symbols are drawn by me, and have significance and meaning in the sense that they represent me as a person, or have some connection to myself or my work. They may be things I like, buildings I've lived in, portraits of friends and family. There are also bits and pieces collected from previous projects.

'Each element of the identity (business card, webpage, stationery) is produced by extracting symbols from the library and placing them on the surface at random, to create a different pattern every time. This is done using a customized computer program. After that, I print and produce each element in-house.

'The more I work on this idea, the more that I feel it's the right path to take, unlike previous attempts to design an identity. I have made nearly every part interchangeable, but kept some things constant for recognition's sake, such as the grid. As everything is flexible, and not set in stone, I won't have that sense of not having finished it.'

MARTIN NICOLAUSSON
BARNÄNGSGATAN 10B
116 48 STOCKHOLM

+46 (0)70 789 49 67
INFO@MARTINNICOLAUSSON.COM
WWW.MARTINNICOLAUSSON.COM

Letterhead and Notepaper
(opposite page and below)
Digital, in-house, black, on white Map
Scandia 2000, 115gsm.
Printed at A4 size for formal
correspondence including invoices
and quotations; printed at A6 size for
informal notes. By printing in-house,
Martin keeps the identity flexible, saves
money and is environmentally friendly.

Envelopes (top right)
Digital, in-house, black, on brown Map
envelopes.
Made from the same stock as regular
brown envelopes, these are assembled
with the rough side turned out: 'so they
can be run through an inkjet printer...
they also look and feel nicer.'

MARTIN NICOLAUSSON
+46 (0)70 789 49 67
INFO@MARTINNICOLAUSSON.COM

MARTIN NICOLAUSSON
BARNÄNGSGATAN 10B
116 48 STOCKHOLM

+46 (0)70 789 49 67
INFO@MARTINNICOLAUSSON.COM
WWW.MARTINNICOLAUSSON.COM

MARTIN NICOLAUSSON
+46 (0)70 789 49 67
INFO@MARTINNICOLAUSSON.COM

Poster (opposite page)
An example of how Martin's language of symbols may be used to create a promotional poster.

Business Cards (below)
Digital, in-house, black, on white Map Scandia 2000, 300gsm.

Website (bottom)
www.martinnicolausson.com
Recently redesigned, the website features random configurations from Martin's set of symbols, alongside an extensive archive.

No Days Off   Patrick Duffy and Teo Connor   London, UK   www.nodaysoff.com

Relaunching his company with a new partner presented an opportunity for an image refresh. 'We came up with a bold, typographic identity based on different phrases about the days that are constantly passing us by. We wanted the identity to be very simple, but to reinforce the name of the company with every execution,' explains Patrick Duffy.

So where does the name No Days Off come from? In the film *24 Hour Party People*, Happy Mondays' frontman Sean Ryder shouts it; and Patrick sported the phrase as a tattoo. When he was struggling to think of a name, a friend suggested using the tattoo, and 'that was that', says Patrick. Words have always been a major part of Patrick's practice; previously he produced *Full Moon Empty Sports Bag*, an independently published literary magazine.

Playing with words around the theme of 'day', the team developed their type-centric approach into a witty and diverse identity. Underlying their print-based approach is a commitment to reduce their carbon footprint. 'Every part of the identity is hand-printed from plates by Adams of Rye, on an original Heidelberg printing press,' explains Patrick. 'Using a traditional letterpress printer reduces paper wastage and ink usage, and made the rebranding as green as possible.'

HAPPY DAYS!

ONE DAY, GEORGE

Patrick Duffy

No Days Off
6 Pinchin Studios
2 Pinchin Street
London E1 1SA

+44 (0)20 7488 9008
+44 (0)7813 800942
patrick@nodaysoff.com
www.nodaysoff.com

Printing: Adams of Rye

Business Cards (opposite page)
and Compliments Cards (below)
Letterpress, 1/1, black on Fenner
Colourset White, 540gsm, 100%
recycled.

Twelve Days of...Christmas Cards
(below right)
2008
Letterpress, 1/0, black or gold on
Fenner Colourset White, 540gsm,
100% recycled.

THANK YOU FOR THE DAY

THE MAN WHO WAS THURSDAY

SHE WAS A DAY TRIPPER!

HOW ARE YOU TODAY?

Hi Liz,

Stationery bits for you.

Cheers
Pat x

With our compliments
—————————————
No Days Off
6 Pinchin Studios
2 Pinchin Street
London E1 1SA

+44 (0)20 7488 9008
info@nodaysoff.com
www.nodaysoff.com

Exhibition
2008
Ada Street Gallery, London
Prints on Fenner Colourset 120gsm,
white, light blue, nero, 100% recycled.
An exhibition of prints launched the new
company: 'it was much more effective
than a mailer could ever be,' says
Patrick. Linking back to the company
identity, the work was about the passage
of time. 'It was a real success, and a
lot of fun; now we're working on some
type paintings using reclaimed metal
and wood, along with a series of zine
collaborations,' he adds. 'We don't see
ourselves as artists, but we like to work
on projects outside client commissions;
it keeps us fresh.'

Exhibition Invitation (top left)
2008
1/1, black, on greyboard, 100%
recycled.

'GONE TODAY
HERE TOMORROW'
NOV. 4, 2008

BONO, THE LEAD SINGER FOR U2, IS PERFORMING A
CONCERT IN IRELAND. AS PART OF HIS PROMOTION FOR
THE ANTI-POVERTY CAMPAIGN IN WHICH HE PLAYS
SUCH A PROMINENT AND IMPORTANT PART, HE STOPS
SINGING AND STARTS CLICKING HIS FINGERS, REPEATING
THE ACTION EVERY THREE SECONDS. THE CROWD FALLS
SILENT, AND AFTER A WHILE, BONO SPEAKS:

'EVERY TIME I CLICK MY FINGERS, A CHILD DIES
UNNECESSARILY FROM A PREVENTABLE DISEASE.'

AFTER HE HAS BEEN DOING THIS FOR A FEW MINUTES
TO A LARGELY SILENT AND TRANSFIXED AUDIENCE,
SOMEONE HELPFULLY SHOUTS OUT:

'STOP CLICKING YOUR FUCKING FINGERS THEN.'

No Days Off ___19___ of 60

NO.

Website
www.nodaysoff.com
Programmer: Pumkin
The splash page features day-related
aphorisms, which are regularly updated:
'it's nice that we can change it, we're
never likely to run out of phrases.'

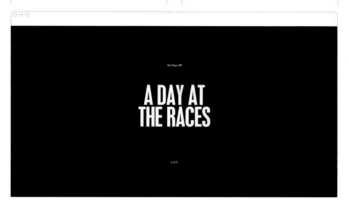

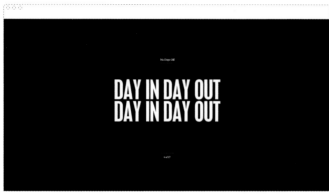

NORM
Dimitri Bruni & Manuel Krebs

Pfingstweidstrasse 31b
CH−8005 Zurich

T 0041 (0)44 273 66 33
F 0041 (0)44 273 66 31

abc@norm.to
www.norm.to

Norm	Dimitri Bruni, Manuel Krebs, Ludovic Varone	Zurich, Switzerland	www.norm.to

This young, independent design team set out with a clear remit. 'We wanted to publish a series of books on norms and standards in graphic and type design,' explains founding partner Manuel Krebs. 'Alongside that, we would offer our services as graphic designers, using the same name. But it turned out that we did fewer books and a lot of design.'

'We reprint all our identity elements every three years, and the new design is usually an improved redesign of the existing one (always in another colour so we can tell the difference). And, of course, we have to use a Norm typeface; we kind of design them for that purpose. The previous corporate identity used Simple; now we use Replica (strictly!).'

Alongside the contact information and the typeface, the current identity includes a number of intriguing grid devices. 'On the reverse of the short letter there are three different grids visible,' explains Manuel, 'which refer to the grid we used to construct Replica.'

Aside from the identity, your first point of contact with Norm is likely to be their website. In an unprepossessing window, one word appears, lowercase, underlined, 'norm', rendered in Simple, the second of their four typefaces. In the frame of that window, 'WELCOME TO NORM' appears as a perfect facsimile of Apple Mac communication. Click on 'norm', though, and all hell breaks loose, with mini pop-up windows littering the screen.

Norm recognize that their website is a product of its time, a moment of playful anarchy when the Internet was still in its infancy. 'We were the first in our design school to work with technology,' explains Manuel; 'we made that site in 1999 when Flash was hot, and we programmed it; that was when you could make a website yourself. We had lots of time, and no commissions.'

'But we love print and typography, we're not web designers; so now we have just two specialisms.' Designing books and creating, marketing and selling their own typefaces, backed up with limited-edition self-published books, is what Norm are known for.

While still students they saw designers such as Neville Brody and the Émigré circle making 'very basic' typefaces, 'so we'd make a new typeface for a flyer'. Commenting on the technology that was available, Manuel explains, 'you could make a pixel typeface in a day or two, constructing letters on a square; it was an okay solution, a thing of its time'.

Their first book, *Introduction*, was themed 'this is us' and accompanied by the typeface Normetica (2000), displaying steadfast feet on the 'i' and a generous bucket to the 'y'. Despite Norm's claims to being 'totally self-centred and self-focused,' their typefaces are playfully pragmatic and beguilingly open, thanks to the addition of 'feet', 'hooks' and 'bowls'.

With book two, *The Things*, Norm explored their next theme, 'this is our world'. A mash of graphs and diagrams are highlighted in process colours; the layers of information are so treacle-thick they defy explanation. 'With *The Things* we made the visuals first, then added the words and realized it didn't work as the visuals lost their impact,' admits Manuel.

Letterhead (opposite page)
1/0, red, on white Biotop, 90gsm.

Business Cards
2/0, red and black, on white Granolux,
240gsm.

Ironically, developed alongside that book was the typeface Simple (2002). Again, it was mono-spaced and with similar family values to Normetica, but a slimmed-down silhouette made it more user-friendly.

Norm's most recent typeface, Replica (2008), is a very different animal. While Simple took three months to design, Replica has taken almost as many years, and although it's been released, the promotional book (on the theme of two-dimensional space) has yet to follow. This time around, Norm adopted a more conventional approach. 'We wrote the words, creating a strict argument. These books are intended to show our work, so we can't hide,' declares Manuel.

Asked why Replica took much longer to develop, he comes back to technology. 'It's a thing of its time so it's more sophisticated. Typefaces look the way they do because of the technology used to make them. We try to really know the software, we use the manual!'

'These days everyone uses the program Fontlab Studio to make typefaces; it's really sophisticated but a little bit didactic, so we decided to create an opposition to technology by restricting the number of grid lines we draw with, using only every tenth line. We want to make something universal, but it needs to have eccentric characteristics in order to be recognized.'

Norm's solution was two-fold. They used the same 'diagonal' bevels for inside curves as for outside curves, 'because print technology is so good these days,' explains Manuel, 'that you don't have to worry about ink traps.' Then they made vertical cuts on all the diagonal strokes, 'so you can set Replica really tight.'

'We test-drive by using, as we're curious to see how a typeface will work. So we sent it to friends, made books and letterheads, and realized that we wanted to make a "virgin" typeface, not a variation on a theme, but a new Grotesk.'

And the name? Again, two reasons: 'From afar, the typeface looks familiar, a replica, but close up you can see that it's something new. Also, the French word "*réplique*" means a harsh, attacking answer, and this is a "*réplique*" to Helvetica, Univers and Unica.'

Making something unique but universal, in a culture that strives for novelty fuelled by technological invention, is a daunting prospect. Norm embrace that technology, but limit it, so as to cut down the endless possibilities and give a more manageable sequence. In the process they have created typefaces, books and stationery that add up to an identity and promotional strategy that has evolved organically, in tune with their career. 'But,' admits Manuel, 'I do think that taking care of the identity of a company called Norm is easier than for some "funky-design-company".'

Stickers (top)
1/0, green, on white sticker stock.

Compliments Slip (below)
3/2, green, red and black, on white
Granolux, 240gsm.

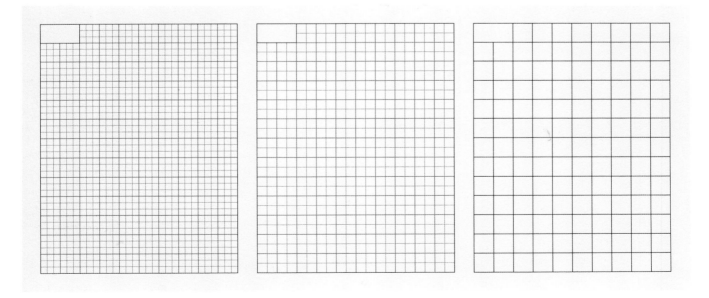

NORM
Pfingstweidstrasse 31b
CH–8005 Zurich
T 0041 44 273 66 33
F 0041 44 273 66 31
abc@norm.to
www.norm.to

CD/DVD Inlay Card (below left)
2/0, blue and black, on Swissboard,
300gsm.

Greeting Card (below right)
2/0, blue and black, on Swissboard,
300gsm.

Website (bottom)
www.norm.to
The playful site is very much 'of its time'.

Playful   Pablo Alfieri   Buenos Aires, Argentina   www.pabloalfieri.com

A graphic designer, illustrator and typographer, Pablo Alfieri created Playful as a space for personal projects; he has fun investigating colour, shape and type, much of it three-dimensional, which he then photographs and manipulates further. Here, Pablo explains why he chose to call his personal showcase 'Playful'.

'I love what I do, and have been really lucky, so I chose a name that represented my ideology, expressed through words like play, enjoy, style...and then I thought of "playful", and that was the beginning of creating "my own way".'

Business Cards (opposite page)
1/0, foil and emboss, gold, silver, iridescent, black, red, violet, blue, on matte black card, 350gsm, and matte white card, 350gsm.
'Another of my "faces" is my business card, which I use at every business meeting because I want to make a good impression. I was inspired by minimalism and simplicity, classic Swiss design and geometry.'

Poster (left)
Play with Shapes
Working with coloured paper, hand-cut shapes and 3D objects, Pablo creates a typeface without using a computer.

Website (right)
www.pabloalfieri.com
'I made a series of photographs (Play at Night; Play with Tools; The 90s) when I was launching my website, to show my ideology and a little of my personal and professional history. The idea was to create different worlds to illustrate these concepts; it was fun to design without the help of a computer. I emailed the images, and posted them on blogs and websites, and the reaction was great! The site received lots of visits and the images were featured in many design books and blogs.'

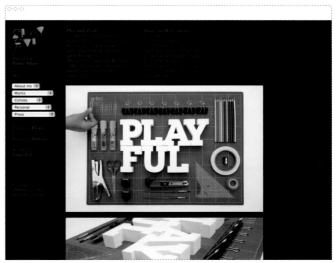

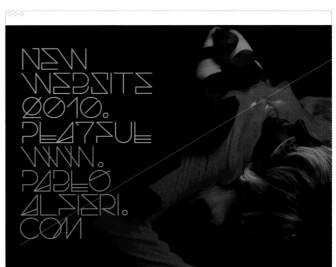

Praline
Letter

Praline | David Tanguy, Robert Peart, Al Rodger, Alex Moshakis, Jean-Marie Orhan | London, UK | www.designbypraline.com

Why Praline? 'Well...it's soft and nutty!' explains Jean-Marie Orhan. 'When we started we were a mix of origins – French, Austrian and Spanish – based in London, so we looked for a name that existed in those three languages, as well as English. It also happens to be the name of a porn magazine in Germany!'

Working across culture, entertainment, publishing and commerce, Praline's client list is a veritable who's who: from Tate Modern and the architect Richard Rogers, to Heston Blumenthal at The Fat Duck, Philips, Nokia and Adidas. Winning awards and appearing in books and magazines, Praline's studio personnel also teach at, and design for, Central Saint Martins College of Art and Design.

Working with so many creative clients, Praline have kept their own corporate identity decidedly non-corporate. Keen print designers, they like to keep in touch with clients via case study brochures (see page 186). Meanwhile, their website contains a vast offering of projects, past and current, efficiently organized, but with a dynamic method of navigation that foregrounds documentary-style photos.

Having recently moved studio, twice, Praline took the opportunity to say hello to friends and colleagues via a special mailer. 'The application of Praline's identity is very organic, evolving with us and our projects,' points out Jean-Marie.

14 Quebec Wharf, 315 Kingsland Road, London E8 4DJ, UK · Phone +44 (0)20 7503 4019
info@designbypraline.com · www.designbypraline.com

Letterhead (opposite page), **Press Release, Estimate, Invoice, and Terms and Conditions** (all below)
Digital, in-house, on olive stock. Employs a palette of coloured headings to differentiate content.

Business Cards (below right)
1/1 and 2/1, yellow or pink and warm grey, on American cotton card; also version with additional name sticker, 2/0 on sticker stock.

Postcard (top right)
City Font
'The postcard was originally a T-shirt graphic, which we designed for fun, and sold via SuperSuperficial,' explains Jean-Marie. 'We had a studio joke about typefaces being named after cities, and when we researched why typefaces for the Macintosh system had such names, we discovered an interesting history. These were designed by Susan Kare in 1983, and Steve Jobs liked the idea of naming them after "World Class" cities. More were designed, but are no longer available, including Cairo, London, Los Angeles, Venice and San Francisco.'

Website (bottom)
www.designbypraline.com
Programmer: Andrea Belvedere, www.byteset.com
Photography: Praline and John Short
Buttons lead you direct to the 'contact' point, or to sign up for the newsletter. Select from a duo of drop-down menus and the screen fills with a mosaic of thumbnails – click on one and more images from that project pop up.

Praline
Press Release

Praline
Estimate

Praline
Invoice

Praline
Terms
&Conditions

2/3

Praline
Yes

Praline
No

Praline

Praline

David Tanguy
Unit 24, 47–49 Tudor Road
London E9 7SN · UK
T +44 (0)20 8525 6648
M +44 (0)7956 921 059
E david@designbypraline.com

designbypraline.com

Al Rodger
14 Quebec Wharf
315 Kingsland Road
London E8 4DJ
T +44 (0)20 7503 4019
M +44 (0) 7968 897 565
E al@designbypraline.com

Richard Rogers Touring Exhibition

Praline
www.designbypraline.com

COSTA NAVARINO

Branding a new luxury experience

Praline
www.designbypraline.com

Energising education

Praline
www.designbypraline.com

Heston in Wonderland

Praline
www.designbypraline.com

Little Chef Popham, lit sign

Little Chef Popham, new menu

A new chef
The first Little Chef opened 50 years ago and soon became the reference in roadside dining. Over the years and after many trials and tribulations, the ailing chain was bought in 2007 by RCapital. In 2008 Heston Blumenthal—the chef behind the Fat Duck at Bray—took on the challenge to reinvent the restaurant-that-time-forgot for the Channel 4 program Big Chef takes on Little Chef. The Popham branch in Hampshire on the A303 was to be revamped according to the vision of one of the best chefs in the world, and Praline was tasked with bringing the graphic identity and expression into the 21st century.

A new exciting place
Praline reviewed the Little Chef identity and graphic system while Ab Rogers Design created the interiors of this new, unique restaurant. A more exciting colour palette was developed, focusing on a spectrum from red through to orange. Charlie, the much-loved brand character of Little Chef is now looking energetic and ready to serve in his new colours and minimised design. Using close crops and silhouettes of his famous profile, he now looks happier and more welcoming than ever.

An instant success
Praline and Ab Rogers Design have created a sophisticated yet humorous identity for this exceptional Little Chef. A generational gap has been bridged: from the new typography to the uniform, from the restaurant to the toilets and signage, every element of the new brand celebrates Little Chef's rich history and places it in a contemporary setting. The relaunch has been an instant success, and through this one operation the overall brand has been revitalised. A recent customer said 'The new design and quality of design has changed my perception of Little Chef for the better'. Charlie's story continues into the 21st century, and beyond.

Kids Menu

Praline Little Chef Popham

Praline Little Chef Popham

Case Study Brochures (opposite page)
Digital, in-house, on white card.
'Every time we finish a major project, we create a case study, and send it to our contacts and potential clients,' explains Jean-Marie. 'It's a nice way to keep in touch, sending something "real", rather than an email. We receive very positive responses, as these tell our clients about other projects by Praline that they're not necessarily aware of.'

New Year Card and Moving Card
Screenprint, white; litho, black, on pink and green card, duplexed.
A double-sided solution, intriguingly created by screenprinting a white frame on both sides of different coloured stock.

2009

GLEEFUL NEW YEAR!

PRALINE HAS MOVED
UNIT 24
47–49 TUDOR ROAD
LONDON E9 7SN

NEW TELEPHONE
+44 (0)20 8525 6648

DESIGNBYPRALINE.COM

2009

ELATED NEW STUDIO!

PRALINE HAS MOVED
UNIT 24
47–49 TUDOR ROAD
LONDON E9 7SN

NEW TELEPHONE
+44 (0)20 8525 6648

DESIGNBYPRALINE.COM

document
KOMMUNIQUE

QUBE KONSTRUKT

Qube Konstrukt   Richmond, Australia   www.qubekonstrukt.com

This mid-sized design studio, with a client list that includes MTV, Coca-Cola and K-Swiss, avoids being typecast by adopting a sophisticated, minimalist approach for their corporate identity. Studio manager James Fotheringham explains; 'Our work is eclectic, so for our own collateral we opted for a subtle approach, which would stand the test of time. It combines old and new fonts, though, reflecting that eclecticism.'

Stressing the collaborative working environment of the studio, their 'unofficial' motto, 'the whole is greater than the sum of the parts', features on a self-published book and DVD, *Consort*, which celebrates their first five years.

Revelling in the possibilities of print, their promotional projects also experiment with elements from the identity. Uncoated black stock, silver and black foil blocking, four-colour black, spot black, gloss and matte varnishes all create effects that play with textures and shadows, appearing chic, mysterious and slightly subversive.

The studio's unusual name adds to the intrigue, and demonstrates their thinking. 'Qube is one co-founder's old graf name and the English translation of the other co-founder's German surname. After a brainstorming session we added Konstrukt, as representative of what we do, because we work in both 2D and 3D; plus we liked the implications of an image, idea or theory formed from a number of elements,' explains James.

The 'Q' became a cube/speech-bubble hybrid, mixed with a typographic system using old and new fonts. Based on the typeface Fishmonger, designed by Tomas Brousil for Suitcase Type Foundry, the letters were redrawn to create a bespoke logotype. 'We are passionate about typography and create our own typefaces, so that each job is unique,' adds James.

---

5 kipling st
richmond vic
australia 3121
T 03 9421 2662
F 03 9429 2993
qube@qubekonstrukt.com
www.qubekonstrukt.com

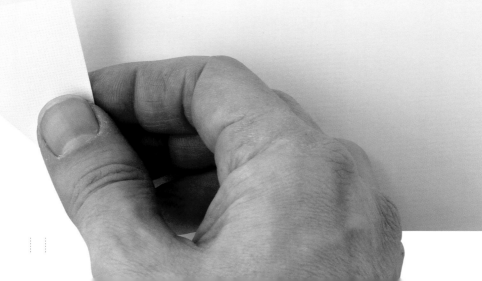

Letterhead (opposite page)
1/0, black, on white stock.

Business Card (below)
Silver and black foil blocks, on uncoated black card.
'Our business cards are our point of contact with clients, so we wanted to create an impression, and people really comment on them. We sourced the thickest black uncoated stock available; the black-on-black theme carries through our book, poster and other promotional material.'

CD Envelope (bottom)
1/1, black, on white card.

Book (top far right)
Consort
Slipcase and cover: silver and black foil block, on Raleigh Notturno, 350gsm. Text pages: four-colour CMYK, plus PMS, satin sealer and black foil block, on Spicers Starbright Smooth, 148gsm and Encore Gloss, 170gsm.
Printed using vegetable-based ink, and featuring client projects, self-initiated and experimental work, this 100-page book explains the studio's methodology by emphasizing collaboration and research across media. This promotional package is sent to agencies and presented at client meetings, as well as selling in local bookshops and via the website.

Poster (top left)
Screenprint, black, on black Raleigh Notturno, hand-scored and folded. A unique folding system secures the book within the poster and negates the need for plastic shrink-wrap.

RINZEN   Rilla Alexander, Steve Alexander,   Brisbane and Melbourne, Australia;   www.rinzen.com
                        Adrian Clifford, Karl Maier, Craig Redman   Berlin, Germany; New York City, USA

As the members of this design/art/illustration collective work in four different locations around the world, a conventional business card – with an address – would be more of a liability than an asset. 'RINZEN kept moving, so we keep our identity fluid, using whatever is appropriate for the application,' explains Rilla Alexander; she's based in Berlin, while others are in New York, Melbourne and Brisbane.

'Our letterheads are printed yellow, full-bleed on the reverse. The front features our icon, used sparingly, but there's no printed address; we add it in the text.' Other elements of the stationery system are yellow too, 'but there's no address, no logo, no icon,' explains Rilla. Designed in 2000, when the collective launched, this flexible identity continues to prove useful. The only change has been to update the business card, to match their redesigned website.

For RINZEN, experimentation is a passion, so they regularly instigate personal and promotional projects, including a series of A5-sized books that are used, 'to promote ourselves, but they don't feature a logo,' explains Rilla. With the widely acclaimed RMX project now in its third incarnation, and a number of published books on the shelf, RINZEN are pro-active, media-savvy members of the design community, who have built a wide network of friends and collaborators.

They regularly showcase these collaborations via exhibitions, producing promotional postcards and stickers. But, to avoid being overly branded, 'if the logo looks too rigid, we design the word RINZEN into the name of the exhibition,' explains Rilla.

'Consequently, some of our illustrations have become part of our identity; for instance, the image of a kangaroo skeleton is so recognizable, it's almost a logo too.' Keeping it flexible, fluid and fun is how RINZEN have constructed a multi-media brand that has gone beyond their commercial work to become a badge of creativity.

Letterhead (opposite page)
1/1, yellow PMS, on white stock.

CD Envelope and Insert Card (below)
2/1, yellow PMS and brown PMS, on
White Matt Celloglaze, die-cut, hand-
finished.
Includes the tagline, 'Enjoy the delight
only possible from RINZEN,' alongside
an illustrated ice-cream cone.

Websites
www.rinzen.com (bottom left)
With five members spread around the
world and a truly international client list,
an effective and comprehensive website
is a must; the colour-coded navigation
device sorts content by type, accesses
an extensive archive and links up to
various sub-sites.

www.rmxxx.com (bottom right)
RMX is a long-running project that
allows 'players' to collaborate by
reinventing each other's content;
RINZEN have revised the rules of the
Dadaists' 'Exquisite Corpse' game for
today's remix culture.

Business Card
Screenprint, yellow and blue, on
white card.
Overprinting yellow and blue ink makes
a third colour: green. The design echoes
the new website's navigation device.

Vinyl Stickers (opposite page)
Multi-coloured vinyl, featuring an array
of images from RINZEN projects.

Postcards (below left)
Four-colour CMYK, on white card.
Promotional postcards for various
events, publications and projects.

Book (below right)
Neighbourhood
2006
Published by Victionary.
The felt cover, complete with sewn-on
patches and an embroidered RINZEN
logo, signals the handmade content,
featuring customized dolls made by a
wide circle of contributors.

A5 Books (top right)
Various formats and materials,
showcasing projects, but never the
RINZEN logo.

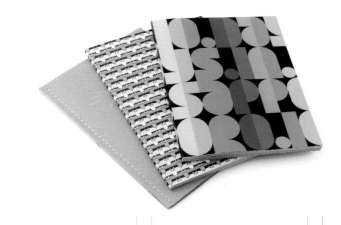

ruiz+company

T +34 932 531 780
F +34 932 531 781
Zamora 45, 5° 2°
08005 Barcelona
www.ruizcompany.com

| ruiz+company | David Ruiz | Barcelona, Spain | www.ruizcompany.com |

A studio of art directors and designers, ruiz+company create branding, communication and advertising for a range of international clients, across fashion, manufacturing and retail. Featured in countless books and magazines, and winning many awards, David Ruiz is a respected member of the international design community.

Creating a corporate identity for a group that operates across disciplines necessitated a flexible system. Avoiding over-design (a conscious stance within the studio), the identity employs the simplest of means, unfussy type and black ink on white stock.

The result is visually dynamic and conceptually complex, presenting a code that needs to be cracked. Four geometric figures embody values such as synthesis and purity, at the heart of each being a discreet plus sign, which was traditionally the symbol for the studio. Each individual element stands alone but hints at more; the addition of others creating a sort of mathematical equation or scientific formula that stands for the whole.

David Ruiz i Marina Company S.L. CIF: B-60719721. R. M. Barna tomo 28105 folio 90 sec. gral hoja 130554 Insc1ª.

Letterhead (opposite page this page, top row)
Screenprint, 1/1, black, on white, Munken Polar, 100gsm.
The large geometric shape is printed on the reverse, creating a subtle, grey show-through.

Business Cards (second row)
Screenprint, 1/1, black, on white, Munken Polar, 400gsm.

Disk Envelopes (third row)
and Document Folders (fourth row)
1/0, black, on white card.

DVD Boxes (fifth row)
1/0, black, on white stock.

Stickers (sixth row)
1/0, black, on white sticker stock.

Envelopes (bottom row)
1/0, black, on white envelope.

Website
www.ruizcompany.com
A portfolio site, with a simple slider navigation, employs the same type and rule treatment as the printed elements of the corporate identity.

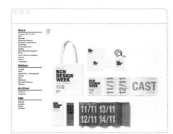

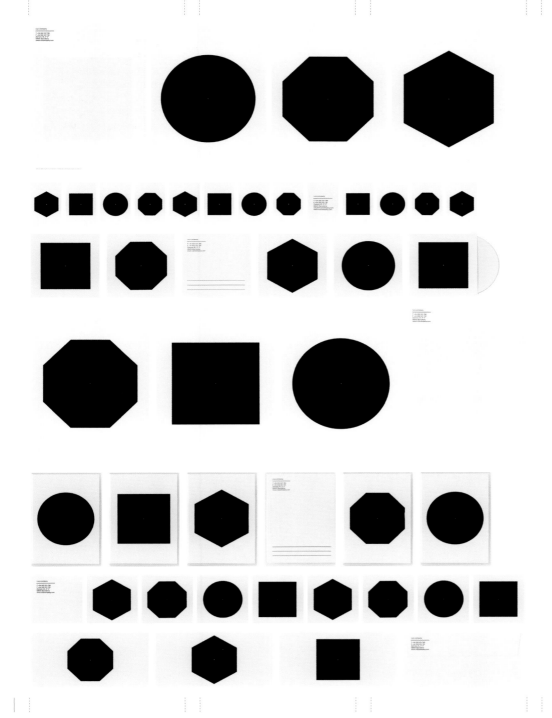

Villa Taman Telaga TJ
1/30. Citraraya
Surabaya, East Java.
Indonesia 60213
+62 31 7096 0798

90 St.Francis Rd. #11-04.
St. Francis Court.
Singapore 328071
+65 96303735

www.sciencewerk.net
hello@sciencewerk.net

| ScienceWerk | Khendi Lee, Danis Sie, Octavia Soebiyanto | Singapore and East Java, Indonesia | www.sciencewerk.net |

Run as a collective, ScienceWerk allows designers, artists, developers and entrepreneurs to collaborate on multi-disciplinary projects without the need to work permanently in one studio. Instead, dual locations are bridged by a shared ethos: '...design has become a lifestyle and platform. We play at work and we work at play.' Occasionally the collective also hang out to brainstorm or implement a design solution.

Small and independent, ScienceWerk declares itself 'a micro-project...we believe design is just like science; it requires experimentation and research, hence the name.' With a tagline that highlights their working method, 'Logic + Aesthetic + Cognition + Research', the aim is to mix functionality, art direction, experience and exploration, to problem-solve a brief across various media.

Similarly, the ScienceWerk identity system continues to evolve, as each designer may print variations on every piece. 'We try to embody our personalities in our corporate identity, playfully mixing wit with thoughtfulness, and creating a complex organism from simple cells.'

Letterhead (opposite page)
Digital, in-house, black, on white
Canford, 100gsm.
Using the most minimal of means,
ScienceWerk adopt a maximizing
approach, mixing icons, marks and
graphic devices to create impact
and develop a comprehensive
graphic language.

Business Cards (below)
Screenprint, black, on Priplak Starlight
Silver 500 micron.
'Each member's personality and style
is represented by their business card,
which shows their design habits, good
or bad.'

Brochure (bottom left)
Laboratory Sheets
Featuring recent projects, the format
allows for each member to regularly
update and digitally print this collective
brochure.

Website (bottom right)
www.sciencewerk.net
A cool, laboratory-style desktop bristles
with fun and functional extras; click
the magnifier cursor on an image for a
closer look.

Envelope (top right)
Digital, in-house, silver
metallic envelope.

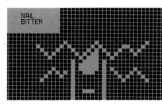

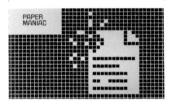

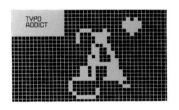
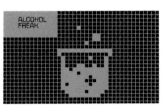
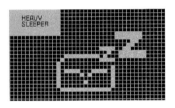
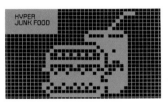

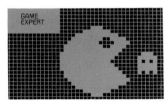

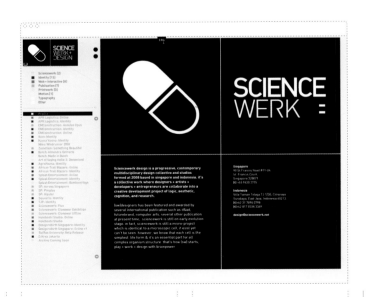

SCROLLAN
WINSSTRASSE 32, VORDERHAUS
10405 BERLIN
TELEFON +49.30.44318790
TELEFAX +49.30.44318799
POST@SCROLLAN.DE
WWW.SCROLLAN.DE
GUTEN TAG

Scrollan   Anne-Lene Proff, Barbara Kotte, Iris Fussenegger, Peter Bünnagel   Berlin, Germany   www.scrollan.de

With projects for international clients in fashion, publishing and cultural institutions, Scrollan's corporate identity has to speak to various audiences, appropriately; plus Scrollan is a partnership, so how do you keep everybody happy?

'Friends who are also designers asked a different studio to do their corporate design, because it's so difficult to do something for yourself,' admits Peter Bünnagel. 'With that in mind we asked our designer, Iris Fussenegger, to do the corporate design for us. Iris had the idea of the folded business card featuring personal text. Then Barbara Kotte, who is a copywriter, suggested there be a different text on each item. Very simple: no fighting.'

The current identity mixes dynamic colour and friendly text with tactile, classic stock and white space. 'The identity is simple, yet playful,' explains Peter. 'And it has elements that communicate with the user, because for us design is all about communication.'

The text is set in a non-hierarchical system, 'basically like you would type on a typewriter, along with a line saying, "Hi",' he adds. The fold hides most of the information, while highlighting 'hello' and the name. All the stationery is printed in three spot colours, which are partially mixed to achieve the final colour range.

Text is central to the identity, so where does the studio name come from? 'A children's book by Astrid Lindgren,' says Peter. 'The name of the youngest child in the story is "Scrollan" (in Swedish, it's Skrållan). A film of the book was on television when we were looking for a name. We liked the idea that the studio has a person's name, but not one of us. So far, we've only met two people who knew where the name comes from.'

And in translation:
Guten Tag = good day, or how do you do?
Schönen Tag = the same, but more informal.
Wie geht's = how are things?
Hallo = hello, or hi.
Bis bald = see you soon.
Ahoi = ahoy (because the studio used to be next to Hamburg harbour).

Letterhead (opposite page),
Business Cards (below left) **and**
Compliments Card (below middle, open
and closed)
Three spot colours mixed, on Colambo
Matt Gletscher, folded.

Address Sticker (below right)
Three spot colours mixed, on
sticker stock.
'The address sticker includes a few
comments,' explains Peter, 'so you
can fold it around the envelope at the
line you consider appropriate for that
correspondence.'

SCROLLAN
GUTEN TAG

PETER BÜNNAGEL
WIE GEHT'S

GUTEN TAG
WIE GEHT'S

IRIS FUSSENEGGER
SCROLLAN
WINSSTRASSE 32, VORDERHAUS
10405 BERLIN
TELEFON +49.30.44318790
TELEFAX +49.30.44318799
FUSSENEGGER@SCROLLAN.DE
WWW.SCROLLAN.DE

SCROLLAN
WINSSTRASSE 32, VORDERHAUS
10405 BERLIN
HALLO
GUTEN TAG
WIE GEHT'S
SCHON GESPANNT
NA DANN
AUFREISSEN
VIELE GRÜSSE
BIS BALD

SCROLLAN
WINSSTRASSE 32, VORDERHAUS
10405 BERLIN
TELEFON +49.30.44318790
TELEFAX +49.30.44318799
POST@SCROLLAN.DE
WWW.SCROLLAN.DE
WIE GEHT'S

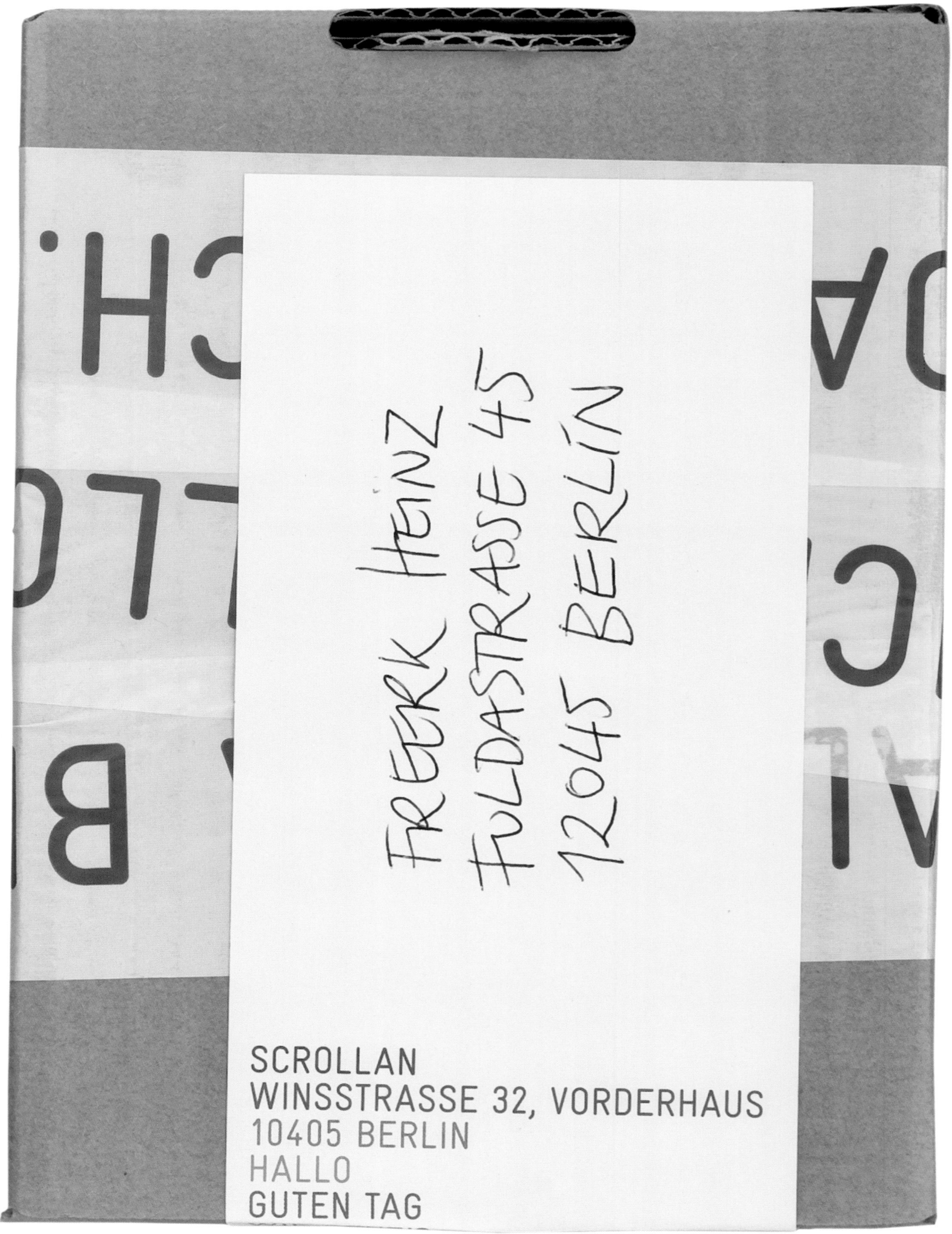

FREDERIK HEINZ
FULDASTRASSE 45
12045 BERLIN

SCROLLAN
WINSSTRASSE 32, VORDERHAUS
10405 BERLIN
HALLO
GUTEN TAG

Packing Tape and Address Sticker
(opposite page)
'The tape is saying, "Hello, here I am".'

Website (below)
www.scrollan.de
Programmer: Christian Kutschan
The website applies the idea of 'no
hierarchy' to a navigation concept that
mixes the 'corporate' colours with other
random ones; it allows navigation but
ignores nearly every usability rule,
and has picked up several prizes for
its innovative approach.

Brochure (top right)
A comprehensive full-colour showcase
of the studio's recent projects for a wide
range of clients, featuring on the cover
a similar type treatment to Scrollan's
high-profile identity.

SCROLLAN
ARBEITEN
ADIDAS Y-3
– +
TEXT

13

SCROLLAN
AHA
MARCUS GAAB FOTOGRAFIERT FÜR DAS DSO
BEIM TDC GEWONNEN
AN DER UNI WUPPERTAL
BEITRAG IN REFLEKTOR 1
DIE AKTUELLE PREISLISTE
DESIGNPREIS DER BUNDESREPUBLIK
PAGE ZEIGT ES
MIT DABEI IN GRAPHIC 12
DESIGNPREIS DER BUNDESREPUBLIK
LEHRAUFTRAG AN DER UDK BERLIN
ZEICHENGESCHICHTEN ERZÄHLT
SCROLLAN WIRD IN ASIEN VORGESTELLT
AUSSTELLUNG STUCK ON ME
MEHR...
ARBEITEN
TEAM
KONTAKT

Sell! Sell!   Andy Palmer and Vic Polkinghorne   London, UK   www.sellsell.co.uk

Sell! Sell! is an independent creative agency boasting a 'no bullshit' approach. Partners Andy Palmer and Vic Polkinghorne work with large and small clients, including The Disney Channel, Krispy Kreme, O2 and Friends of the Earth.

First off, why the name? 'We were looking for an identity that would set us apart from any typical creative agency, which usually either feature the partners' names or are daft and random,' explains Vic. 'Sell! Sell! is an obvious choice; after all, that's what clients come to us for.'

Aiming for the identity to be eclectic and adaptable to suit their varied work, the name appears in many guises, but is backed up with a simple symbol, '...that we could use consistently where appropriate,' Vic adds. 'The starburst is normally an overused cliché...with an "amazing" offer inside. So we thought it would be fun to reappropriate it for our logo. It shows that we don't take ourselves too seriously. The three signature colours – bright pink, orange and green – are a deliberate choice to soften our approach, which can come across as quite bold and in-your-face.'

The chosen typeface, Garage Gothic (designed by Tobias Frere-Jones for Font Bureau), underlines that boldness, but with a softened, vintage edge. Similarly, the various sustainable paper stocks, with their tactile, flecked surfaces, mute the colours and rough up the imagery.

'We're conscious of keeping the identity fluid, interesting and relevant; so we incorporate photography, old matchbook advertising images and bold graphics, if we think they fit into the piece we're making,' explains Vic.

And the reaction? 'Clients are for the most part normal human beings, just like us, so they find the fun stuff fun.'

SELL! SELL!
8 PRINTING HOUSE YARD,
HACKNEY ROAD, LONDON E2 7PR
TELEPHONE 0207 0333 999
EMAIL DOUBLES@SELLSELL.CO.UK
VISIT SELLSELL.CO.UK

SELL! SELL! IS THE TRADING
NAME OF SELL SELL LIMITED
REGISTERED IN ENGLAND NO.5437218

Design: Vic Polkinghorne

Letterhead (opposite page and below)
Four-colour CMYK, using vegetable inks, on sustainably produced paper. Photography: *Old Man* by Bela Tibor Kozma; *Girl* by Justin Horrocks.
The letterhead is used mainly to present scripts and ideas, 'so we wanted something that had an element of playfulness that captured the Sell! Sell! spirit of "poking a finger in the eye of the industry"; we believe in doing things our own way.' says Vic. The photography is sourced through iStock, recoloured and retouched, 'to achieve an eye-popping look.'

Business Cards (bottom)
1/1, various colour vegetable inks, on sustainably produced board.
The cards are intended to convey the spirit of the company. Adapting vintage matchbook images, they incorporate some fun slogans. 'One of the cards offers the holder "good luck", which is something we think is essential in business.'

Postcard (top right)
1/1, various vegetable inks, on sustainably produced board, die-cut with vintage-style serrated edges. This promotional postcard was intended 'to show our appetite for putting energy into even the smallest job.'

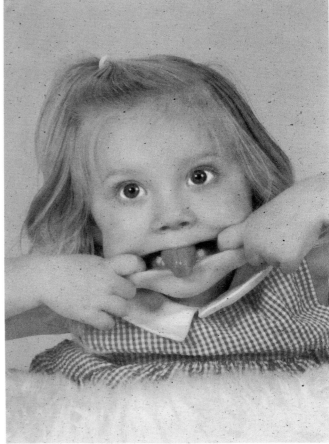

Poster
Bullshit Free Zone
1/1, pink, on 100% recycled newsprint.
Created as a fun mailer with a bold
message, this poster proclaims Sell!
Sell!'s message in the clearest possible
way. Printed in signature pink, on the
reverse is a repeat pattern of their
starburst logo. 'Newsprint was used
because we didn't want the poster to
feel too "precious"; we want people
to put them up on the wall, not keep
them rolled up in a tube.' Available for
free from the website, 'they're proving
very popular!'

THIS IS A
BULLSHIT
FREE ZONE.

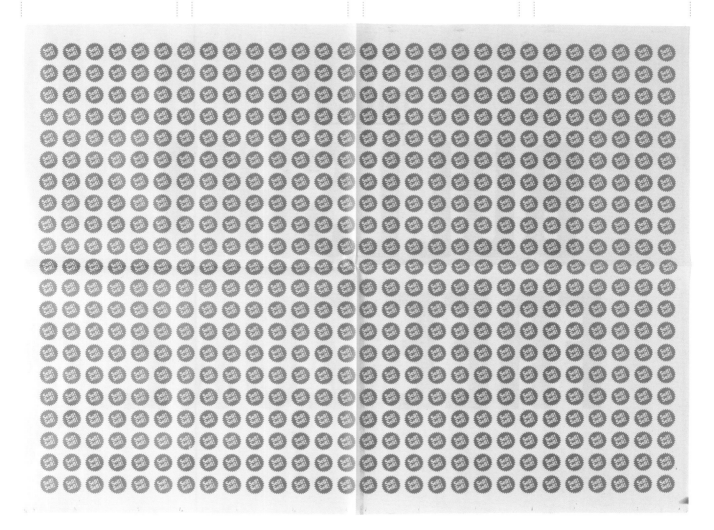

Signage (below)
Powder-coated steel, Perspex,
illuminated.
'It's like a starburst "stuck" on to our
old building.'

Website (bottom)
www.sellsell.co.uk
This portfolio site features a simple
type menu, white background and
instinctive navigation.

Case Study Cards (top right)
Success Story
Digital, four-colour CMYK, on
sustainably produced paper.
This constantly updated set of case
studies, now numbering 18, tells the
stories of Sell! Sell! successes.

Brochure
What's the Point of Advertising?
1/1, vegetable inks, on sustainably produced paper, stickers.
Keeping costs down, this one-colour, 20-page brochure explains the company's approach and uses stickers to add branding.

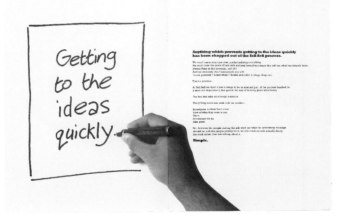

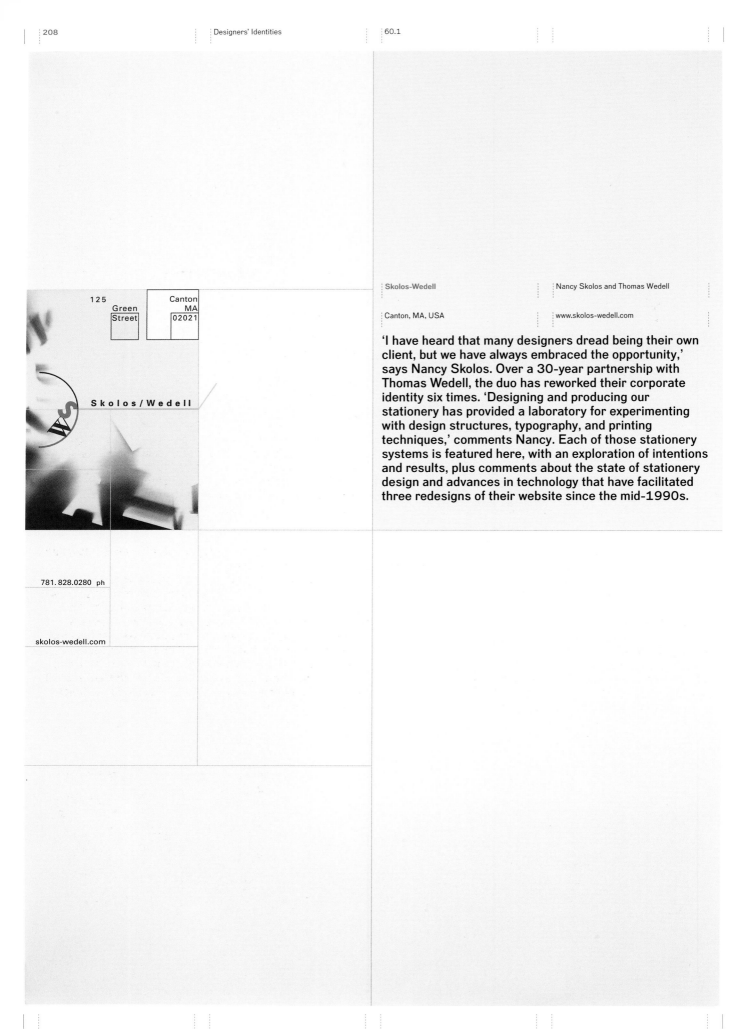

125 Green Street

Canton MA 02021

Skolos / Wedell

781.828.0280 ph

skolos-wedell.com

Skolos-Wedell

Nancy Skolos and Thomas Wedell

Canton, MA, USA

www.skolos-wedell.com

'I have heard that many designers dread being their own client, but we have always embraced the opportunity,' says Nancy Skolos. Over a 30-year partnership with Thomas Wedell, the duo has reworked their corporate identity six times. 'Designing and producing our stationery has provided a laboratory for experimenting with design structures, typography, and printing techniques,' comments Nancy. Each of those stationery systems is featured here, with an exploration of intentions and results, plus comments about the state of stationery design and advances in technology that have facilitated three redesigns of their website since the mid-1990s.

Letterhead (opposite page)
Envelope (bottom left) **and**
Business Card (bottom right)
'We moved studio to our home/studio
in Canton. This letterhead is a bit of
a compilation, a greatest hits from
the previous versions (see pages
210–213). We kept the "SW" logo from
1996, but recalibrated the stationery
design to be more holistic. Even though
it looks different from the original 1979
stationery, it has some of the same
concepts going on, using proportion
to map the entire page in a similar way
to which the grid activated the earlier
design. Again, we work elements
with and against the structure. The
photographic element is a photogram
that has letterform-like shapes in it.'

Website (top right)
www.skolos-wedell.com
A chronological archive site displays a
career's-worth of posters filed by year
and access by enticing visual slivers.

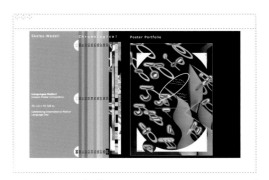

Liz Farrelly: You use an array of print techniques and finishes; do you think the 'art' of designing stationery has been affected negatively by the use of digital printers in design studios over professional printing?

Nancy Skolos: There are still a lot of small letterpress and screenprinting shops that specialize in fancy techniques and finishes, but in commercial offset printing shops the level of finishing at that larger scale has definitely fallen off. In the 1980s it wasn't uncommon to see 12-colour jobs with spot varnishes and lamination, die-cuts and embossing. I'm not sure if it's because of digital printing, but the budgets just aren't there and if they are, there are more efficient and effective ways to disseminate information.

LF: Your stationery looks and feels expensive; are you setting out to impress clients? Is the intention to showcase your aesthetic and skills? Do you think that your clients expect to see a virtuoso solution from their designer?

NS: Yes, we always thought of our letterhead as a marketing piece and a frame for our letters and proposals. If we weren't willing to value and showcase our aesthetic skills, how could we expect our clients to? We have designed many intricate letterheads for clients. One of them, which we designed 25 years ago, was reprinted this year. It took me a few days to translate the design from its original mechanicals to digital; even the typeface had to be modified slightly because it had originally been 'phototype'.

LF: Each time you've changed your stationery, do you feel there are elements that you want to retain or continue to explore?

NS: The fun part about developing our identity over the years was that it was an evolution. We never started from scratch but rather just let it evolve.

LF: You've developed a very sophisticated and eloquent graphic vocabulary, a whole range of elements that you use and reuse throughout your work. Is the changing identity a sort of personal experimentation with these forms?

NS: The stationery is a nice way of marking time, and monitoring where we are in our visual thinking and vocabulary.

LF: Apart from the stationery, what other elements make up the corporate identity?

NS: Other promotional pieces that have accompanied the stationery over the years include small mailing pieces, a poster in the early days, and now the website. Our first website in the mid-1990s used JavaScript to create an illusion of a tactile page with die-cut windows that became the menu for seeing the portfolio. Our second website was programmed in Flash ActionScript, to make spinning wheels of thumbnails, each representing a different area of the portfolio. We now have a simple HTML website that is laid out as a timeline of our work.

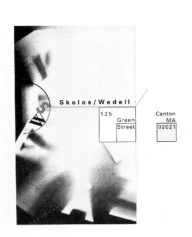

Letterhead and Envelope with First Day Cover of Stamp designed for US Mail
1996
'In this version, we worked to express technology in a conceptual way, repeating our address and phone data as a map that found its location by emphasizing one final version of the information in a bolder font. We also included a photographic image with a texture that mirrors the rhythms in the type.'

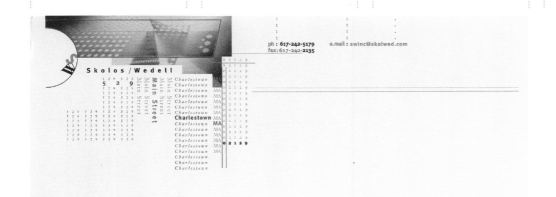

ph : **617-242-5179**   e.mail : swinc@skolwed.com
fax: 617-242-**2135**

Skolos / Wedell

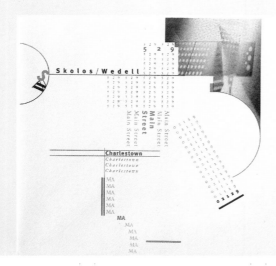

Skolos / Wedell

32
Computer
Technology

USA

FIRST DAY OF ISSUE

ABERDEEN PROVING GRND
OCT 8
1996
21005

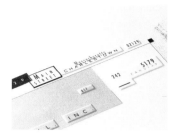

New Partnership Letterhead (below and left)**, Business Card and Envelope** 1990

'This design was necessitated when our partner, Ken Raynor, left the studio. It was difficult to design the letterhead without his name, so we came up with something that married the "S" and "W". The design was generated in Aldus FreeHand and has a bit of a clunky distortion. The design itself was mannered and very overwrought. The purple ink was metallic, reflecting a printing trend of the early 1990s. This design featured in the Cooper-Hewitt Triennial.'

Letterhead (below and right), **Business Card and Envelope**
1985: Skolos, Wedell + Raynor
'We moved studio from our apartment into a large industrial space. This stationery reflects the golden era of 1980s graphic design. Print production was pushed to the limit, with blind embossing registering with four colours. The graduated colours allude to the photographic quality we were exploring in our work. The gradations were created using airbrushed black and white artwork that was photographed and printed in the darkroom at various sizes to produce varying fades.'

**Letterhead, Business Card and
Envelope** (below left)
1982: Skolos, Wedell + Raynor
'This version of our stationery was a
variation on the structure of the first.
Inspired by de Stijl and the dawn of
deconstruction, the bars begin to break
away from the edges of the page, and
intervals between elements are less
predictable. We added more colour,
to express the liberating spirit of the
early 1980s.'

**Original Letterhead, Business Card
and Envelope** (below right)
1979: Skolos, Wedell + Raynor
'Simple and precise. Every element
on the page set up an alignment
or signalled a place to type (with a
typewriter), or to fold. We always
considered the letterhead to be a
critical piece of design that introduced
our sensibilities to potential clients and
framed our proposals. In our first set
of office stationery, we even designed
our own bank cheques. Unfortunately,
we don't have any samples left.'

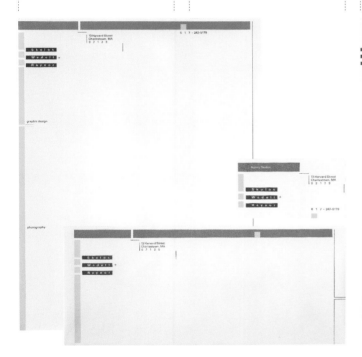

We_want_to_conserve card.ai   150.00 lpi   45.00°   3/23/09   11:37:45 PM
Process Black

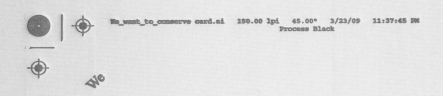

Frauke Stegmann   Frauke Stegmann   Cape Town, South Africa   www.ineedtimetothinkaboutwildlife.org

Having grown up in Namibia, surrounded by unspoilt nature, Frauke Stegmann decided to use her corporate identity and stationery to spread a message that is close to her heart. Starting with a URL-as-declaration, Frauke explores ways of raising awareness around wildlife conservation. Part of a large-scale, multiple-media project undertaken in collaboration with designers at various events, it's a work-in-progress, but with already tangible results. Here she explains her motivation.

www.ineedtimetothinkaboutwildlife.org

Letterhead (opposite page and below)
and Notepaper (bottom)
Letterpress, 1/0, red, on various
coloured card.
The letterhead is simply the untrimmed
version of the notepaper; by showing
the trim marks, Frauke highlights
the wastage inherent in conventional
printing processes. She offers an
alternative – don't trim and you'll have
more paper to use.

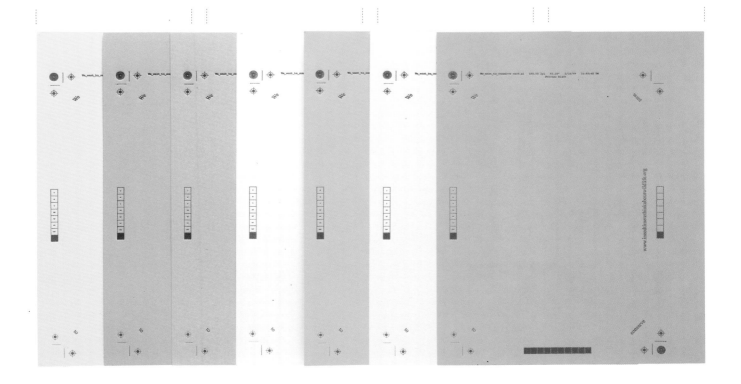

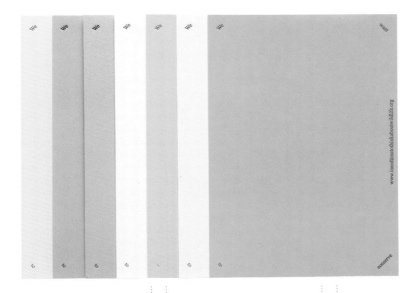

Letterhead
2001: Letterpress, 1/0, gold foil
block, on pink stock. Made using a
pre-existing plate.
The extravagant aesthetic may seem
to contradict the ethics of reuse;
alternatively, it may be considered a
comment on the restricted palette often
adopted for eco-friendly projects.

Envelopes (below)
Letterpress, 1/0, black, on
various envelopes.

Liz Farrelly: Tell me about the name you've chosen to work under, and your fascination with wildlife; how did it come about?

Frauke Stegmann: As an intuition; in its simplest form this 'project' is about a fascination, respect and admiration for nature, and wanting to use my position as a graphic designer to promote an awareness of accountability for our, humanity's, collective actions. In 2003, I made a poster for the Graphic Europe conference in Barcelona, using the opportunity to focus on the endangered Iberian lynx, which lives in the cork forests between Spain and Portugal. This was a collaboration with the design studio åbäke. The drawing of the Iberian lynx appeared on sweatshirts, and was the first in a series publicizing this cause; back then the project was called 'Forget me not'. It's a very slow-moving project, because if you start asking questions such as, 'is selling sweatshirts a good way of creating awareness?', then being spontaneous becomes tricky.

Then in 2004, at the Victoria and Albert Museum's Village Fete (organized by Scarlet Projects), I introduced 'I need time to think about wildlife'. In collaboration with Chosil Kil of Jan Family, we cut stencils of foliage and reptiles, spraying images onto cotton bags, and included leaflets on endangered species.

I began to think about how wildlife and nature function as a backdrop to our cultural, historical and scientific activities in the West. Seen objectively, nature is free of culture, history and science, but it can also become emblematic, used within symbols of power by nations and multinational companies; those various activities are laid on top of wildlife, fauna, flora and geology. And as it is outside society, the disconnected place, nature can be a rich source for the imagination.

I'm interested in how those two categories relate to each other, or don't: the culturally, historically and scientifically advanced, and the 'primitive', the outside, which constitutes wildlife and nature.

LF: The first letterhead you made, the gold embossed version, is a beautiful object; what sort of reaction does it get?

FS: The letterhead was created using a pre-existing work by someone else; it's the most basic form of appropriation. I found something that was already out there instead of making something new. I chose the type of gold and the particular pink paper and reprinted the image with the existing plate. And although it is an overtly 'pretty' object, and the reaction is nearly always 'how extraordinarily beautiful', the fact that it makes use of a found object means that it is very utilitarian, despite its over-the-top, almost kitsch, aesthetic.

LF: By contrast, the business card that features pencil shading is very banal. What's the idea behind that one?

FS: That's about creating something with as little means as possible, or whatever is closest to hand; only working with whatever is lying on your desk. It's a practical application of 'less is more'.

Frauke Stegmann
f_stegmann@hotmail.com
07947 180 320

+1.646 336 0500, 86 forsyth street, nyc 10002
www.stilettonyc.com, info@stilettonyc.com

Stiletto nyc   Stefanie Barth and Julie Hirschfeld   New York City, NY, USA and Milan, Italy   www.stilettonyc.com

Stefanie Barth and Julie Hirschfeld are Stiletto nyc, a design studio based in New York and Milan. 'We think of the company as one place that happens to have two offices,' explains Julie. That duality goes deeper, though, reflecting the partners' backgrounds and the variety of projects that pass through their studio.

Stefanie studied design in Germany, while Julie studied painting and Russian in the United States. After college, Stefanie designed for print and Julie worked in motion graphics; now the studio applies their wide-ranging skills to projects in both fields, and for clients in media, publishing and fashion.

'We always approach work from a conceptual basis rather than being media-specific,' explains Julie. 'We start by brainstorming an idea, then work individually, but passing the project back and forth until it's done. In that way, it's more "Stiletto" than personal, and it's especially interesting to add print knowledge to our motion work, which ends up being more editorial and textural rather than overly technical.'

Stiletto nyc's identity mirrors that dual approach, with images appearing both on screen and in print, and stationery that includes textures ranging from smooth white to glossy purple and raw greyboard.

And the name? 'It means both a knife and a high heel. We liked the double meaning – it's feminine with an attitude,' suggests Julie. Realized as a hand-drawn logotype and bespoke typeface, the slimline 'Stiletto' often appears in purple foil block, adding a hint of flash to an otherwise understated aesthetic.

Letterhead (opposite page)
1/0, purple, on white stock.

Business Card and
Compliments Card (below)
1/1, purple, on white stock, duplexed.

CD, Envelope and Sticker (top right)
1/0, purple, on white sticker stock for
the disk, and on white card envelope.

+1.646 336 0500, 86 forsyth street, nyc 10002
www.stilettonyc.com

Presentation Folder (right)
Purple foil block, on greyboard,
one colour; purple, on coated stock
(interior), duplexed.

Folded Poster and Reel Title (below)
An atmospheric photograph of dancing
helium ballooons with a summery New
York as the backdrop, hints at Stiletto's
combination of fun, glitz and invention.
The poster is printed on uncoated stock,
and folded for posting.

Reel Stills (below)
The balloon fun continues...

Website (bottom)
www.stilettonyc.com
A picture-led format, with images
ranged left on a white screen,
resembles an editorial magazine page.
Click on an image to access the project.
A 'Mac-style' pull-down menu offers
alternative navigation.

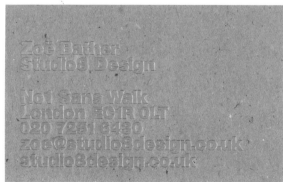

Studio8 Design   Zoë Bather and Matt Willey   London, UK   www.studio8design.co.uk

Renowned editorial and print designers Studio8 are decidedly low-key when it comes to their corporate identity. 'Rather unusually, we don't have printed letterheads (not very professional), but we do have a "way" of doing Studio8 "stuff",' explains Matt Willey, adding with a degree of reticence, 'I could ramble on about materials and process and the sort of aesthetic that produces....'

The stationery and promotional brochures they do produce, however, eloquently speak of their vast knowledge of different print techniques and materials, and a pragmatic, hands-on attitude to making that yields up projects that are both eye-catching and tactile. Zoë Bather sums up their approach: 'We've got a duty as a print-based design studio to advise our clients on how to use paper in an environmentally responsible way, and probably save some money too. And we apply the same logic to our own stuff.'

Compliments Slip (opposite page, top)
1/1, black and blue, on Omnia, 120gsm.
'This was printed on an unused bit of
sheet from another job,' explains Zoë.

Business Cards (opposite page,
bottom)
1/0, gold foil block, on greyboard,
750 microns.
'This greyboard was going spare; it's
more usually used as protective filler
for packaging other paper stock.'
With its fibrous texture and random
colour speckles, the greyboard offers
a dynamic contrast to the luxurious
foil lettering.

S81 Pamphlet
Four-colour CMYK, on Brand X FSC,
115gsm.
This 20-page, self-cover, loose-leaf
pamphlet featuring the studio's work
was printed on the same sheet as
another job so as to use 100 per cent
of the sheet.

A booklet and poster produced to raise awareness of the
destruction of the Amazon rainforest for the US-based charity
Rainforest Action Network (RAN).

Client: Rainforest Action Network

Established 25 years ago, Royal Academy Magazine is the UK's
leading arts quarterly and has the largest circulation of any art
magazine in Europe. We redesigned the magazine – the new look
launched in Autumn 2005 – and continue to be responsible for
the design and art direction of each new issue.

Client: Royal Academy of Arts

'Mexico' documents the influence of American consumerism
on Mexican visual culture. The book features images by Magnum
photographer and collector extraordinaire, Martin Parr.
Designed in collaboration with Nick Bell.

Client: Chris Boot Publishing

S81 Brochure
Text: digital, four-colour on White
Marizion Ultra, 90gsm, 52 pages.
Cover: Colourset Nero, 120gsm,
4 pages.
Dust Jacket: letterpress, 1/0 black or
gold, on Redeem 130gsm.
Text and cover are single leaves,
stab-stitched, with black binding cloth
wrapping the spine. 'This brochure
is printed in short runs of 50 copies,'
explains Zoë, 'but we use litho paper to
retain the tactile and high-quality feel.
The dust jackets are printed, trimmed
and folded by us. The brochure size is
dictated by the largest single leaf we
could get out of a sheet (SRA3) that
would fit on to the digital press.'

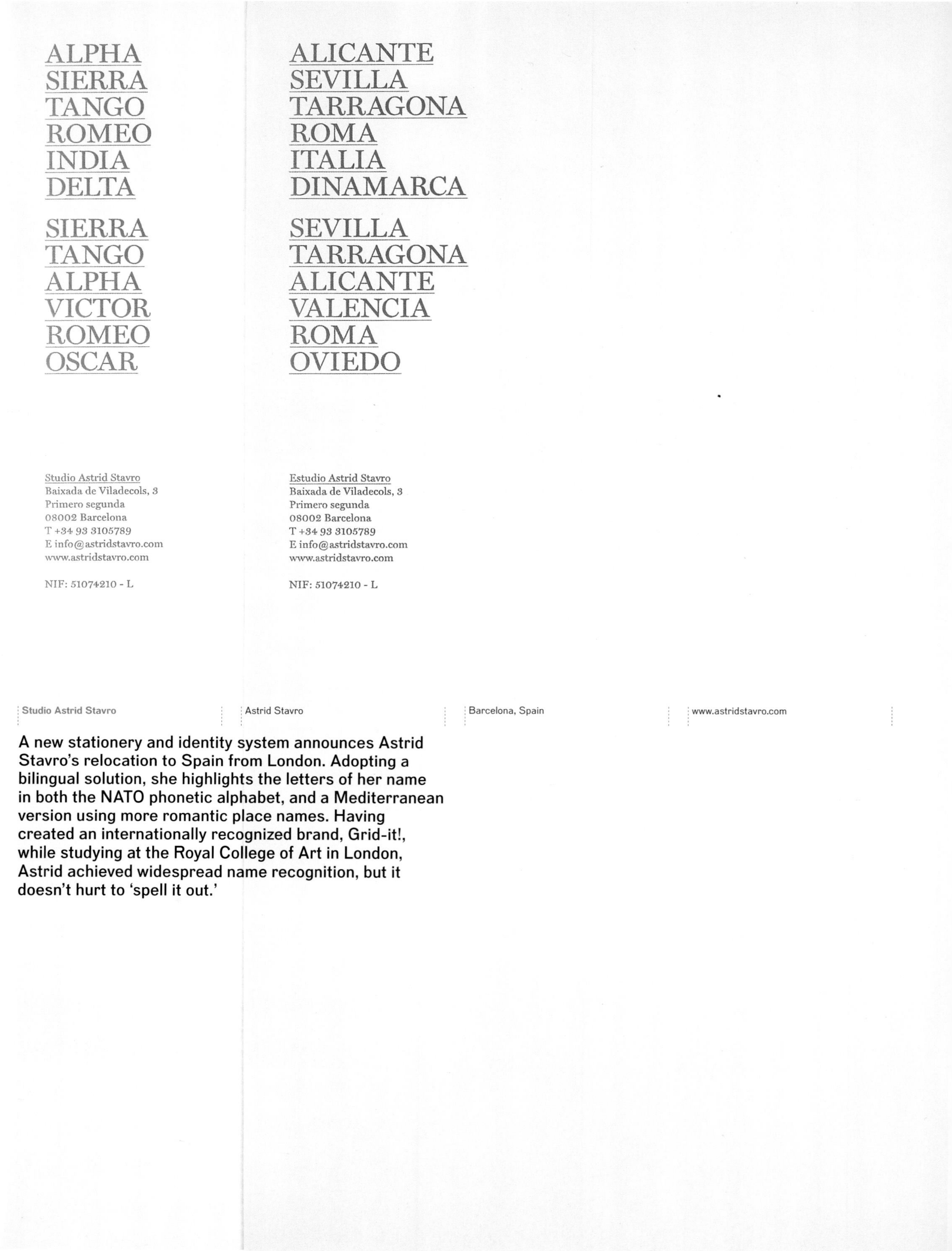

ALPHA
SIERRA
TANGO
ROMEO
INDIA
DELTA

SIERRA
TANGO
ALPHA
VICTOR
ROMEO
OSCAR

ALICANTE
SEVILLA
TARRAGONA
ROMA
ITALIA
DINAMARCA

SEVILLA
TARRAGONA
ALICANTE
VALENCIA
ROMA
OVIEDO

Studio Astrid Stavro
Baixada de Viladecols, 3
Primero segunda
08002 Barcelona
T +34 93 3105789
E info@astridstavro.com
www.astridstavro.com

NIF: 51074210 - L

Estudio Astrid Stavro
Baixada de Viladecols, 3
Primero segunda
08002 Barcelona
T +34 93 3105789
E info@astridstavro.com
www.astridstavro.com

NIF: 51074210 - L

Studio Astrid Stavro · Astrid Stavro · Barcelona, Spain · www.astridstavro.com

A new stationery and identity system announces Astrid Stavro's relocation to Spain from London. Adopting a bilingual solution, she highlights the letters of her name in both the NATO phonetic alphabet, and a Mediterranean version using more romantic place names. Having created an internationally recognized brand, Grid-it!, while studying at the Royal College of Art in London, Astrid achieved widespread name recognition, but it doesn't hurt to 'spell it out.'

Letterheads (opposite page)
2/0, spot colour, on white stock.

Postcards (below left)
1/1, black, on white, 400gsm, by
Trucard.

Business Cards (below right)
1/1, black, on Fedrigoni Splendorlux,
300gsm.

Invoice (bottom left)
3/0, spot colour, on white stock.

Sticker (bottom middle)
1/0, black, on white sticker stock.

Envelope (bottom right)
Black stock.

ALPHA SIERRA TANGO ROMEO INDIA DELTA

SIERRA TANGO ALPHA VICTOR ROMEO OSCAR

ALICANTE SEVILLA TARRAGONA ROMA ITALIA DINAMARCA

SEVILLA TARRAGONA ALICANTE VALENCIA ROMA OVIEDO

ALPHA SIERRA TANGO ROMEO INDIA DELTA

SIERRA TANGO ALPHA VICTOR ROMEO OSCAR

ALICANTE SEVILLA TARRAGONA ROMA ITALIA DINAMARCA

SEVILLA TARRAGONA ALICANTE VALENCIA ROMA OVIEDO

Grid-it! Notebooks (right and below)
Seven different notebooks to scale,
each with 60 tear-off sheets, printed
in cyan on off-white 120gsm stock,
shrink-wrapped, red sticker.
Manufactured by Miquelrius.

Business Card (bottom)
2/1, spot colour, on cream stock.

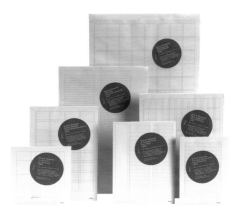

Astrid explains how she came up with the idea for Grid-it! and how she brought it to market. 'Originally, it came from tutor Alan Kitching's Gridlock course at the RCA. I designed a book based on *The Devil's Dictionary* by Ambrose Bierce, which broke the grid, and I got obsessed with grids in general. Then one day, while in the letterpress department, I stared at the boxes holding metal and wood blocks, and that's when inspiration kicked in.'

With the degree show looming, Astrid needed a project for the exhibition; 'Reproducing famous grids on notepads seemed like a witty idea, with endless possibilities; the grids could even be transformed into shelving units and other 3D products.'

How did you research the grids, and choose which to use? 'Working with Birgit Pfisterer, we made a list of iconic books and magazines, and got in touch with editorial and grid designers, including Derek Birdsall, Phil Baines, Robin Kinross, Alan Kitching, Hamish Muir and Pablo Martín. We wanted to test the list and get some feedback, and little by little, we cut it down to five grids.'

Launched in London, the first print run of 500 sold out in a day, inspiring Spanish company, Miquelrius, to sign a three-year deal to manufacture and distribute the notebooks. Now Astrid is ready to add more grids to the series, and is in talks to produce a shelving unit with a world-renowned manufacturer. Both an 'homage' and a useful product, Astrid's idea succeeds because it functions so well on many levels; plus the notebooks appeal to a diverse audience, from design geeks to stationery fans, and anyone who just likes to be organized.

Grid-it! has won countless awards, been lauded by a host of design glitterati, earned column inches in both the design and mainstream media, and been exhibited in museums across Europe and the United States. As a self-promotional exercise it has more than worked.

Astrid Stavro MA RCA
+44 (0) 792 973 8667
astrid@griditnotepads.co.uk
astrid.stavro@alumni.rca.ac.uk
www.griditnotepads.co.uk
www.communication2005.com

Shelving units (below and right)
Art of the Grid.
Birch plywood, painted, prototypes.

Business Card (bottom)
1/2, spot colour, with pencil addition, on
cream stock.
Made in a limited edition as a college
project.

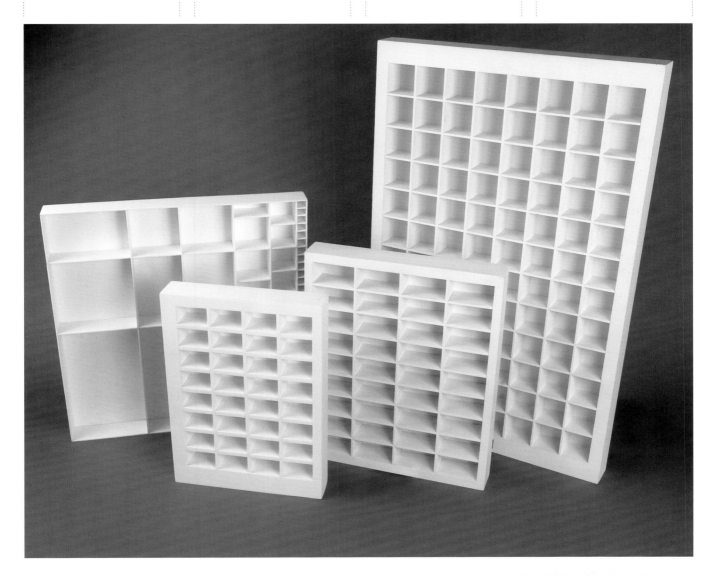

Limited edition business card

Astrid Stavro MA RCA
+44 (0) 7929 738 667
astrid.stavro@alumni.rca.ac.uk
pavlovita@hotmail.com
www.griditnotepads.co.uk
www.communication2005.com

74 / 500

studio
parris wakefield

parriswakefield.com
01379 783048

Willow Byre The Common
Mellis Suffolk IP23 8EF

| Studio Parris Wakefield | Sarah Parris, Howard Wakefield, Simon Griffin, Maria Farrugia | Suffolk, UK | www.parriswakefield.com |

Using their stationery to showcase their work, Studio Parris Wakefield's corporate identity also emphasizes the connection between this recent redesign and their extensive, archival website.

Sarah Parris explains, 'Howard Wakefield has a long history of using Photoshop and pioneered many techniques during his time with Peter Saville; this studio continues to explore those infinite possibilities. We wanted to see how much we could distort a city's skyline while allowing it to remain beautiful and recognizable. Working with our client, Kvadrat, we created a series of images celebrating an event at the Milan Furniture Fair. It was an enigmatic approach to representing the city, and led to creating imagery for further projects and events in different cities.'

The series features ten cities; the New York cityscape was created for KrvKurva's La.Ga bag, launched at New York's International Contemporary Furniture Fair (I.C.F.F.) in 2008. These dynamic images are teamed with the typeface Alto, designed by Thomas Thiemich for FontShop.

Registered Office
United House 23 Dorset Street London W1U 6EL
Registered in England & Wales No 4481594
Directors Sarah Parris & Howard Wakefield

Designers: Howard Wakefield and
Maria Farrugia.
Cityscape images: Sarah Parris

Letterhead (opposite page)
Digital, in-house, 2/0, black and grey
on white, Atlas Photo Quality Matt,
170gsm.
'We print our stationery in-house to
be flexible, economic and green; this
means we can frequently change the
stock with no wastage.'

Compliments Slips (below)
Digital, in-house, on white, Atlas Photo
Quality Matt, 170gsm.
'On the reverse of the compliments slips
and business cards we're showcasing
recent Studio Parris Wakefield designs
and plan to periodically change them.'

Websites (bottom)
www.parriswakefield.com
www.parriswakefieldadditions.com
Design: Studio Parris Wakefield
Programmer: Tui Interactive Media
A cool, grey ground and grey
text link these webpages to the
stationery system and connect the
current corporate identity with this
comprehensive showcase and archive.
A second website offers graphic
design products for sale and a blog,
extending the brand while using the
same design elements.

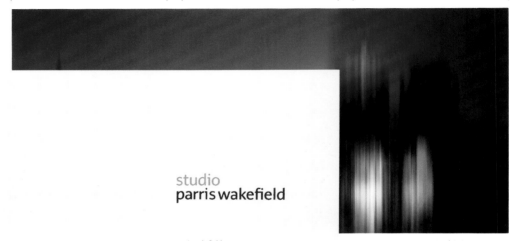

studio
parris wakefield

parriswakefield.com
01379 783048

Willow Byre The Common
Mellis Suffolk IP23 8EF

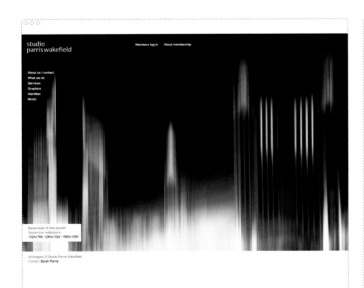

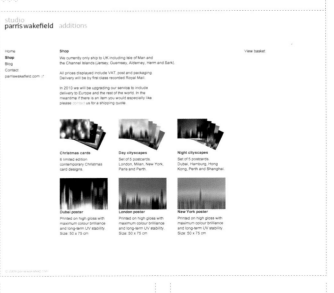

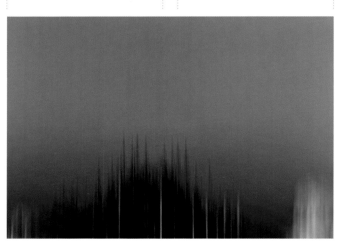

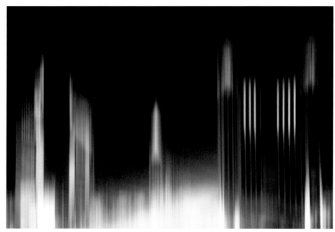

Business Cards
Printed by MOO
Four-colour CMYK, on MOO Classic,
UV matte laminate.
'The "Printfinity" option produces
a different image on every card in a
pack, at no extra cost. MOO's stock is
sourced from sustainable forests, and
is elemental chlorine-free (EFC).'

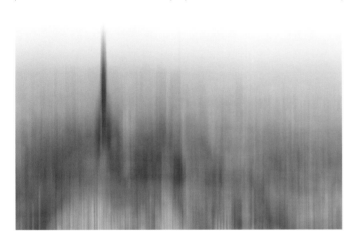

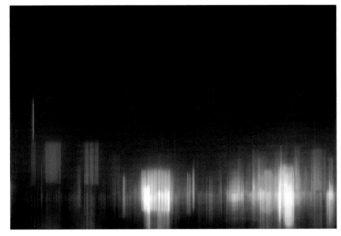

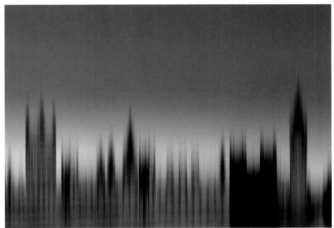

Howard Wakefield
Creative Director
howard@parriswakefield.com

studio
parris wakefield

parriswakefield.com
01379 783048

Willow Byre The Common
Mellis Suffolk IP23 8EF

Studio Tonne | Paul Farrington | Brighton, UK | www.studiotonne.com

'I find it funny when people ask me whether or not I still do experimental work,' says Paul Farrington of Studio Tonne, '...everything we do is experimental.' Whether it's collaborating with long-time client Moby, creating his own computer-based music, designing a digital audio toy for the website, or working with organizations such as Vodafone or Imperial College, Paul is happy creating on-screen solutions and working with print and 3D installations.

'I used to want to be seen as a larger organization, but not anymore. I like the fact that we're a small studio, like a family, and clients are part of that,' explains Paul.

For his corporate identity he's opted for a bold mix – a large-scale logotype in high-contrast yellow and grey. 'I pick colours that I feel are right, colours that I would wear...yellow is optimistic,' he adds. 'Also, the palette is based on a logical printing decision; I can print yellow and grey cheaply if I need to; the yellow will look the same whether it's printed four colour or spot colour.'

Letterhead (opposite page, below and top right)
2/2, yellow and grey, on white stock. Using a super-light stock enables Paul to send out each letterhead folded into a square (this page, top), which playfully abstracts the logo, writ large on the reverse. Fold guides are printed on the yellow front.

Business Card (bottom)
2/2, yellow and grey, on white card.

Paul Farrington

studio@studiotonne.com
07941 351649

Tonne
Studio 1.1, 11 Jew Street,
Brighton, BN1 1UT, UK

studiotonne.com
01273 311208

Designs for a deaf audience
Sonic typography

A series of typefaces created from recordings of regional british accents.

Interactive music game
Digital installation

Players create music and visuals by hand and body movements.

ENA Stick

Packaging solution for a multi-functional kitchen device for prolonging vegetable life and purifying water. A simple, diecut, glueless solution was reached that could be freestanding or hung from a point of sale device.

Foundation for Art and Creative Technology

A modular identity created to group the project strands together under the FACT brand.

FOUNDATION FOR ART & CREATIVE TECHNOLOGY

Various Events

Real time visuals that respond to a live music performance.

Royal College of Art CRD Research group
Publishing / Identity / Book design

Sound Polaroids
Institute of Contemporary Arts

Visitors to the gallery interact with images of London by making sound in the space. On tour the installation became a performance, where cities are filmed and manipulated live.

Grizedale Arts
Forestry Commission

Identity and art direction for all marketing materials and print items produced by the artists in residence.

Opening Night Visuals
Sonar 2000

Music visuals for the Barcelona based electronica festival's opening night.

Michael Nyman / Klangpark
Ars Electronica
CD packaging

Produced as part of the Ars Electronica festival for Michael Nyman, this graphic score is based around the way he worked on Klangpark - deconstructing the work of seven musicians and creating a single score from the composite parts.

Sound Unit
Lovebytes Festival

A suite of generative soundtoys, sequencers and music machines allows music to be made using a simple graphic interface.

Interactive:
The Internet for Graphic Designers
Electronics
Authour / Publishing

Tonne founder, Paul Farrington, was the author of this book as well as the designer. The book explores ways of inspiring print designers to create work for the internet and digital spaces.

Live Here Now

Identity for a company who record live music shows.

Sonic Arts Network

We have designed a wide range of promotional material, ranging from posters and the identity, through to monthly newsletters. Small budgets with high impact printing using recycled stock.

12 Months
Prada / IDEO / OMA

A 500 page book that told a behind the scenes story of Prada stores. The book featured pull outs, fold outs, hidden sections, and a debossed foil cover.

TWELVE MONTHS

Book covers

arthouse

Arthouse
University of Brighton

Spin 'n' Groove
Channel 4 / DfE
Digital sequencer

An online multi-user musical sequencer created to allow 6–11 year olds to create and share musical ideas.

Music Studio / www.gridclub.com
Channel 4 / DfE

A music studio covering the key-stage two curriculum. This project won three awards including an interactive BAFTA.

2 x 12 Soundtoy
Hip-Hop
Music software / Album

Musicians diversify their working methods in using the Soundtoy software to generate new music. Featuring work by Håkan Lidbo, Scanner, Si-Cut. Db and Tonne, this hybrid CD presented works by the artists as well as an additional CD-ROM element.

Hospital digital festival
Lighthouse Arts

A programme of events, invites, and marketing.

Atlantic Waves Festival
Calouste Gulbenkian Foundation
Identity / Marketing

We have provided the complete identity across all media for the last five years. Each year has a different abstract theme based on water.

Depeche Mode Remixer
Mute Records
Digital sequencer

A remix tool that accompanied the release of a remix box set.

Cinecity Film Festival

Since 2003 we have provided visual identity for the festival that runs across a range of media including the festival programme, flyers, website and a daily festival newspaper.

VIA
Identity

A creative studio for moving image projects. The logo is based around a one line play on the companies acronym.

Fear Factory Films
Identity

FEAR FACTORY FILMS

Noisetoy
Mute Records

A soundtoy for the 'distract' area of the Mute website.

Time:Tone musical clock
Mute Records

This downloadable toy plays music (from the extensive Mute back catalogue) based on inter-vals of time. Different sounds play on the year, month, week, day, hour, etc. It also automatically downloads news, releases, and live event information on the Mute stable.

Lanatos
Simon Fisher Turner
Digital instrument

A musical instrument that allows music to be made through a visual score.

Lilium / Tonne
Kliteture Records

Debut album that balances deep, seductive grooves with a delicate digital effluvium.

Eyestorm

EYESTORM

Books that Fly

Aerobic, Reaktor
Native Instruments
Interface design

User interface design for music software.

www.mobyhotel.com
Mute Records
Digital campaign / website / marketing

Digital campaign to support the release of Moby's album, Hotel.

Fragile Identities
William Kentridge
Catalogue / Marketing / Exhibition design

Catalogue, website, exhibition design and marketing material.

Digital snowflake
Mute Records

The Mute logo took the form of a snowflake for this digital Christmas card.

Pedro Amaral
Calouste Gulbenkian Foundation

Casebound CD/book utilising recycled stock and a debossed cover.

salvia

Salvia / XL recordings

www.4ad.com
4AD Records
Interface

Interactive interface for exploration through the label's 25 year back catalogue.

Noticeboard system
Imperial College walkway, London

This large scale artwork and noticeboard system was designed to allow college wide notices and events to be housed in specific locations. The system covered 196 metres of walkway at Imperial College.

Modelling State
Association of Computer Machinery

Alumni RCA
Royal College of Art

Annual publication which interviews college alumni from around the world to investigate how studying at the RCA has affected their working practice.

Solidified Light
New Scientist magazine

Resilica
Identity

resilica

Modular Seating System
Imperial College, London
Product design

A modular seating system for the college's main courtyard.

Power in your hands
Vodafone / Bartle Bogle Hegarty
Illustration

Campaign illustration created on the theme of the phones multimedia power.

Incredible power is in your hands

Colour Wheel
Dan Rose Music Consultancy
Online music library

An online music library that gives a select advertising based clientele access to a database of music that can be played, shared, saved to the users own library.

Sean Henry
Osborne & Samuel Gallery

Ward Enhancement Scheme
NHS Plymouth hospital

Large scale illustrations to revitalise the children day ward.

POP!
www.wemakestories.com
Puffin / Penguin
Pop up storybook maker

An interactive tool that allows children to create pop-up stories, view them onscreen, print and make them.

Digital fish tank
NHS Plymouth hospital
Interactive installation

Interactive fish tanks placed in waiting rooms encourage interaction from children of all ages. The tanks use a webcam to place the child in the underwater environment allowing them to play and feed shoals of fish.

Arborescent
Fuse Leeds 09 festival
Music score

Taking inspiration from musician Xenakis' creative approach, we where commissioned to create a graphic score that was performed at the festival.

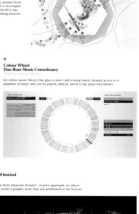

Folding Poster (opposite page)
Limited edition of 500.
'I wanted to make a printed piece
showing highlights from the last ten
years, and send it to people we wanted
to work with. The process revealed
a visual journey of common themes,
and that my work has developed but
remained consistent through the use of
colours and typefaces; for example, you
can see how a seating project relates to
a website for Moby.'

Website
www.studiotonne.com
'I think that 99 per cent of our work
depends on the personality of the
designer and how well we work with
a client. First meetings are really
important for telling somebody who
we are; the website is another way of
representing ourselves in both a playful
and a professional manner.' To that end,
you'll find digital games, group portraits,
a 'day in the studio', and an extensive
news and work archive on the website.

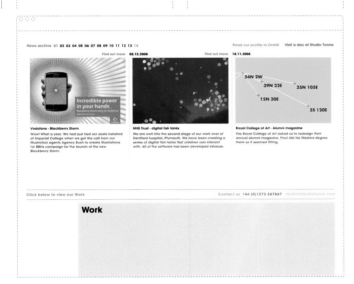

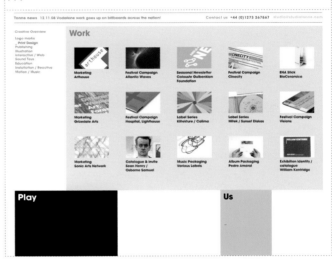

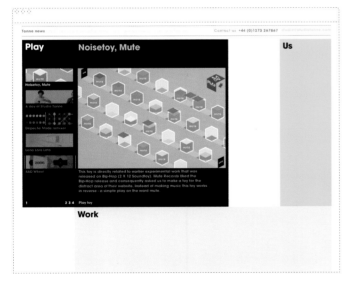

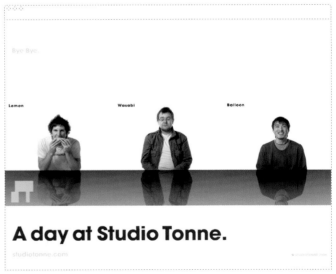

from **Daryl Tanghe** *to*

46367 Snowbird Drive
Macomb, MI 48044

tags

help These tag boxes have been provided for your reference.
Fill them in with anything you'd like to remember about me.

subject

date *body*

Daryl Tanghe   Daryl Tanghe   Bellevue, WA, USA   www.dtanghe.com

Recent graduate Daryl Tanghe created his corporate identity while still at college, with the aim of better navigating the competitive job market.

'I realized that my strong point as a designer was in creating relationships between research, concepts and visuals,' says Daryl. With an interest in interactive design, he created a visual metaphor for 'reference' and 'interactivity'.

'Tagging was a natural choice,' he explains. 'I thought it would be interesting to bring that interactive element back to reality, to my stationery. So the identity allows people to "tag" me, in order to remember things about me.'

Intending his work, rather than the identity, to be the focus, he has kept the design elements low-key. 'I used black and grey typography with a dash of small blue type to draw attention to information titles, and yellow to highlight text and create a visual hierarchy.'

sincerely **Daryl Tanghe**

586.491.6415
dtanghe@gmail.com
AIM fd5daryl

Letterhead (opposite page)
Digital, in-house, on white stock.
'The letterhead was fun to create; I tried to figure out how somebody might store it in a filing cabinet.' Having tagged the document based on content, particular correspondence could be easily located. Printing yellow on the reverse 'highlights' Daryl's letter in a stack of white paper.

Business Card (below left)
Digital, in-house, on white card.
'This is the most important part of my identity. It has six boxes on the back, referring to text boxes from an Internet browser, and includes a simple explanation (for if I'm not present). It also uses the term "help", another Internet reference.'

Envelope (bottom left)
Digital, in-house, on white stock.
'I used the tagging boxes to write the name and address of the recipient, thinking this would hint at the idea of using the blank boxes.'

Website
www.dtanghe.com
The homepage includes the main navigation and thumbnails of work, and a system for visitors to tag Daryl's designs, eventually accumulating into a list of key words below the description of each project. Clicking on a tag loads all the images similarly labelled.

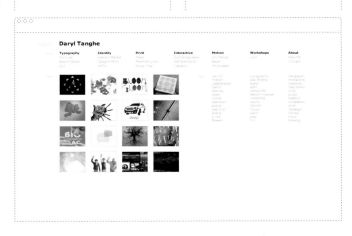

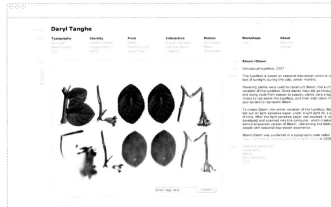

tags

help These tag boxes are here for your reference. Use them to jot down anything you'd like to remember about me in the future.

designer **Daryl Tanghe**

contact 46367 Snowbird Drive
Macomb, MI 48044
586.491.6415
dtanghe@gmail.com
www.dtanghe.com
AIM fd5daryl

Daryl Tanghe
46367 Snowbird Drive
Macomb, MI 48044

There.

| THERE | Simon Hancock and Paul Tabouré | Sydney, Australia | www.there.com.au |

This boutique design agency specializes in identity, branding and environmental design. The founding partners, Simon Hancock and Paul Tabouré, have clocked up years of industry experience, working both in Australia and overseas, and their client list, past and current, bristles with big names. From multinationals to start-ups, the diversity of clients is what Paul Tabouré credits with 'keeping our work and approach fresh and exciting.'

Paul explains: 'Put simply, we turn problems into ideas and ideas into reality, helping brands get from where they are, to where they want to be.' With a practice-what-they-preach attitude, THERE adopted the tagline, 'Design that moves you'.

'We describe how we can help clients solve their business marketing issues; we call it "the shift". Then we create a strategic "roadmap", to enable the transition from the present (here today) to the possibilities in the future (there)', explains Paul.

Leading by example prompted a redesign of THERE's own brand collateral. 'It needed to work on a number of levels. Create a cohesive look and play on the company name, and be contemporary yet understated, so as not to alienate any potential client sectors.'

With clever copy, an eye-catching palette, and a simple but solid logotype, these dynamic building blocks have proved to be very flexible. So, what sort of reaction does the new identity get? 'Staff and clients like the bold simplicity and the playful humour in the written approach, and the business cards never fail to raise a smile.'

Letterhead (opposite page)
Silver foil block, on white stock; and
2/0, grey and black, on white Dogett's
Expressions Super Smooth.
Both of these multi-functional sheets
may be overprinted in-house with
various details, for presentations,
tenders and quotes. A series of
templates for internal messaging
uses clever headlines.

Print Specs Form (below left)
Digital, in-house, black on white stock.

Fax Header (below, middle)
Digital, in-house, black, on white stock.
Minimized for transmission, the fax
header combines a bold typeface to
provide clear information, with outline
letterforms, to reduce call times.

Compliments Slip (below right)
Red and grey, on white stock.

Business Cards (bottom left)
2/2, red, grey, black, on
white Dogett's Expressions Super
Smooth, 352gsm.

CD Case (bottom right)
Screenprinted, 1/0, white, on opaque
plastic case; 2/0, red and grey, on
white stock, folded.
The paper insert is printed only on
one side.

Identity Range
Showing the extent of THERE collateral,
including the second version of the
letterhead (bottom right), and the disc,
which is screenprinted white with text
highlighted by the disc surface
(bottom left).
The range also features two notebooks
2/0, red and white, on red board cover;
2/0, grey and black on white, spiral
bound.
Complete with clever taglines, and data
template on each sheet.

Signage
As environmental graphics and signage
systems are part of THERE's offerings,
the studio is suitably flagged up.

Website
www.there.com.au
The corporate colours of grey, red and
white look equally strong translated
from white paper to a black
background onscreen.

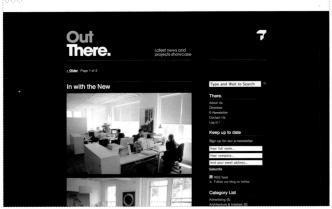

thirst / a design collaborative

1440 w hubbard floor 2   chicago illinois 60622 usa   т 1 312 334 2550   ғ 1 312 334 2549   w 3st.com

Thirst/3st   Rick Valicenti   Chicago, IL, USA   www.3st.com

Alongside a playfully elegant logotype, the letters piled up, truncated, extended, and finished off with extravagant slab serifs, a tagline reiterates that Thirst enjoys a wider agenda than most commercial studios and announces itself as 'a design collaborative'.

Running a busy studio, with clients ranging from fellow creatives (photographers and architects) to opera companies, landmark buildings and trade fairs, Rick Valicenti and his colleagues also take time to design and publish a series of research projects, lecture and event posters, and editorials (featuring in the design press and mainstream media), all lavishly printed and avidly collected.

'Thirst pursues its own curiosities, social commentary and process innovations, for no other reason than passion,' they explain. Made possible with 'contributed energy...from printers and programmers', these 'process innovations always seem to migrate into commercial commissions.' The end products are sent to more than 250 designers and commentators on Thirst's select mailing list, and are distributed at public lectures.

Letterhead (opposite page)
Designer: John Pobojewski
Engraved, 1/0, PMS 801, Mohawk
Superfine, Ultra White Smooth, 28#
Writing, blind deboss.
Subtle touches, including debossing,
laser-cutting and printing via the
method of engraving, provide this
stationery system with a unique mix of
tactile qualities, and demonstrate an
avid attention to detail.

Business Card (below)
Designer: Rick Valicenti
Engraved, 1/0, PMS 801, Mohawk
Ultrafelt, Black, 100# Cover, laser-cut.

Envelope (bottom)
Designer: John Pobojewski
Engraved, 1/1, PMS 801 on Square
Flap, Via, Light Grey Smooth, 70# Text.

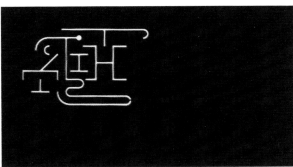

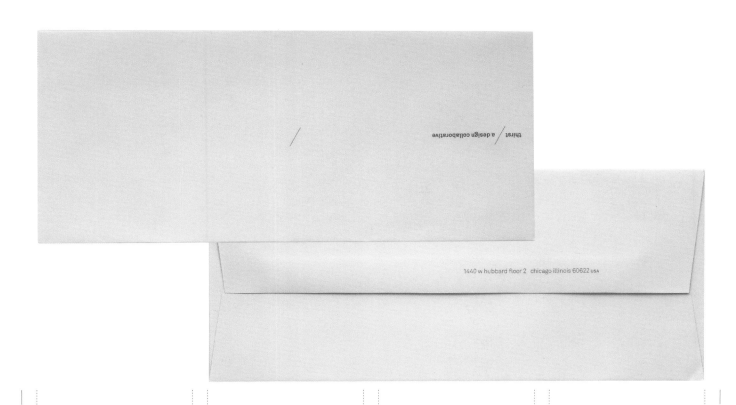

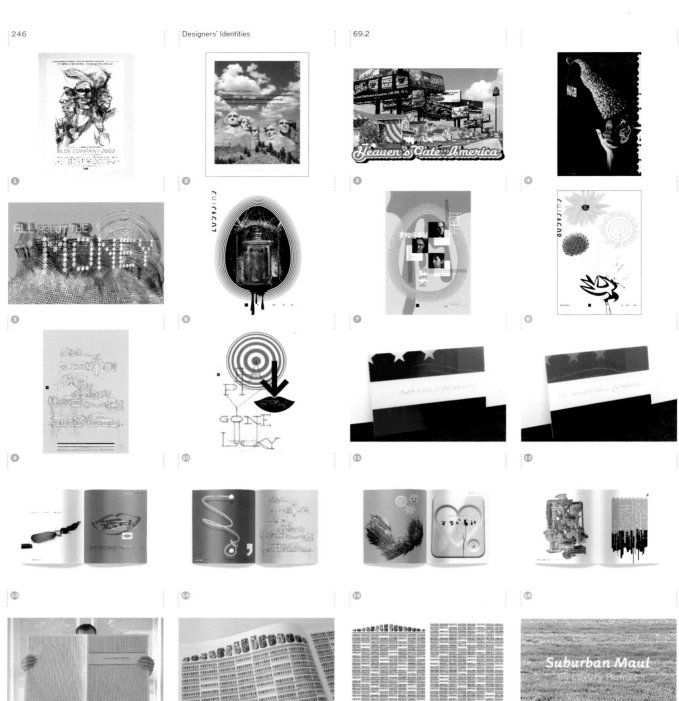

Blue Company (opposite page, 1)
2003
Art director and designer: Rick Valicenti
Content: Rob Wittig

Mount Rushmore (2)
2009
Art director and designer: Rick Valicenti
3D rendering: Bill Cornman

Heaven's Gate (3)
2003
Image: Bill Valicenti and Rick Valicenti

Posters (4, 9 and 10)
Lecture Series

All About the Money (5)
2003
Art director and designer: Rick Valicenti
Image: Matt Daly

AIGA Fresh Talent Posters (6–8)
2007–08
Art director and designer: Rick Valicenti

Designer: Bud Rodecker
3D rendering: Bill Cornman

Mr. Rogers Tribute (11–12)
2004
Art director and designer: Rick Valicenti
and John Probojewski

i4 Design (13–16)
2008
Art director and designer: Rick Valicenti
Programmer: John Probojewski
3D logotype: Matt Daley
An editorial portfolio highlights 'Rick's
secrets to a fulfilling life as seen
through the Thirst prism, with John's
code giving new dimension to Rick's
favourite expressions.'

Intelligent Design (17–19)
2007
Art director and designer: Rick Valicenti
and John Probojewski
Programmer: Robb Irrgang and
John Probojewski

Self-published tabloid based on
intersecting issues, for example,
consumerism, politics and religion.

Suburban Maul (20)
2003
Art director and designer: Rick Valicenti
Photo retouching: T. J. Blanchflower

Visual Rattle (21–24)
2008
Art director and designer: Rick Valicenti
Images: Rick Valicenti and Real Eyes

Book (this page, below)
Emotion as Promotion: A Book of Thirst
2004
Hardcover, 280 pages
Art director and designer:
Rick Valicenti
Publisher: Monacelli Press

Websites
www.3st.com (bottom left)
Art director: Rick Valicenti
Designer and programmer:
John Probojewski

Blog (bottom centre)
happenings.3st.com
Art director: Rick Valicenti
Designer: Bud Rodecker
Programmer: John Probojewski

Notes to Self (bottom right)
www.rickvalicenti.com
Art director and artist: Rick Valicenti
Designer: Bud Rodecker
Programmer: Robb Irrgang
Over 575 journal entries, using Sumi
ink applied through a syringe or with a
foam brush to Rives BFK paper.

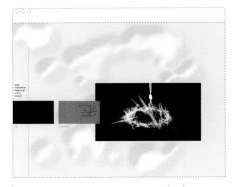

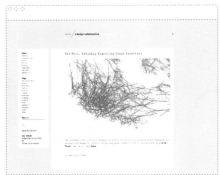

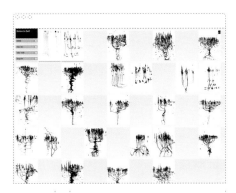

[TOM HINGSTON STUDIO]

Tom Hingston Studio Ltd
76 Brewer Street
London W1F 9TX

T +44 (0) 20 7287 6044
F +44 (0) 20 7287 6048
info@hingston.net
www.hingston.net

Tom Hingston Studio   Tom Hingston   London, UK   www.hingston.net

The five-strong team at Tom Hingston Studio produces graphics, moving image, advertising and branding solutions for A-list clients from the worlds of music, fashion, beauty and media. With such a discerning audience, the studio's corporate identity, and in particular the stationery system, needs to impress.

'We were keen to bring a level of refinement and tactility to the stationery,' explains Tom Hingston. 'So we've created a series of contrasts through restrained means; the result is minimal yet luxurious.'

The stationery uses a mix of processes: duplexing, debossing, foil blocking and offset litho. Tom explains, 'Essentially, the research and experimentation had already been undertaken, as we've been fortunate enough to employ these processes for clients. Combining them into one print job was the tricky aspect. We worked closely with the printer, Generation Press, to achieve this level of finish, and every element of stationery was sampled several times in small quantities before printing the whole job.'

And the reaction? 'Really positive. Handing out a business card that has a certain weight and quality still resonates with people.'

Registered Office
76 Brewer Street
London W1F 9TX
Company No 4339617
VAT No 7078 5287 25

Letterhead (opposite page)
Text is debossed; the reverse features a fine, close pinstripe.

Business Card (top right)
Text is debossed out of a super-gloss front, while the reverse is smooth but matte.

Postcards, two versions (below)
Playing with elements from the letterhead and business card, here they are arranged into different combinations. The reverse of each card is black, but with subtle differences: one features a high-tech honeycomb texture, while the other resembles an impasto paint surface.

All stationery printed by Generation Press

Website (bottom)
www.hingston.net
An elegantly monochrome site, with the addition of a high-visibility, neon pink navigation button.

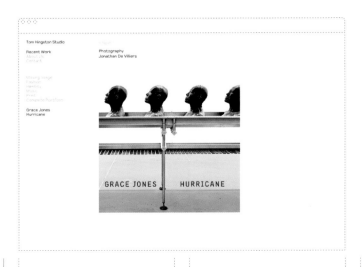

```
===============================
N: TwoPoints.Net
   International Bureau of
   Communication
-------------------------------
```

```
-------------------------------      -------------------------------
> Laurence King Publishing Ltd      A: Via Laietana 37
  361-373 City Road                    4ª Planta / Despacho 32
  London EC1V 1LR                      08003 Barcelona
  United Kingdom                       España
                                     ...............................
                                     T: 0034 93 318 53 72
                                     M: 0034 646 37 10 55
                                     ...............................
                                     E: Info@TwoPoints.Net
                                     U: TwoPoints.Net
                                     -------------------------------

                                     ---------------------------------------------------------------
                                     S: Letterhead
                                     D: 31.08.2009
                                     ...............................................................
```

TwoPoints.Net   Lupi Asensio and Martin Lorenz   Barcelona, Spain   www.twopoints.net

Founded by Lupi Asensio and Martin Lorenz, TwoPoints.Net was set up as a place for experimentation; it's a small company that thinks big, and on an international scale. With a network of collaborators that includes musicians, photographers, software developers and writers, they're able to offer clients a one-stop shop of creative solutions.

So where does the name come from? Martin Lorenz explains: 'TwoPoints refers to the colon found in German and Spanish that marks the transition between the speaker and his message. We see our visual communication as the two points between the sender and the receiver.' He adds, 'the "Net" demonstrates that, in spite of being a small office, we oversee large-scale projects that involve professionals from diverse fields; different teams according to each project.'

With such a flexible working practice, the issue was how to sum that up. 'We thought no corporate identity or logo would ever be able to express our stylistic diversity,' Martin admits. 'Our work is who we are, so why not use all our work as our corporate image? So every December we make an installation of that year's work.' The first thing you notice is the diversity of look and media. 'We try very hard not to have one style,' comments Martin. Then they print an A5 postcard, featuring an image of the installation, and cut half the print run into business cards. Looking back, Martin notes, 'it's interesting to see how our company is changing.'

```
---------------------------------------------------------------
Doppelpunkt, S.L. / CIF B-64433824 / Registro Mercantil de Bar-
celona, Tomo 39270, Folio 63, Hoja B-343749, Inscripción 1
```

Letterhead (opposite page)
Digital, in-house, black, on yellow stock.

Business Cards (below) **and A5 Postcard** (top right)
'We print the background of the installation with a Pantone silver, overprint the image of our office in black and print the work in CMYK. On the reverse, the text is printed in black and sealed with a UV varnish.' As each business card is a 'fragment', their fans like to collect the entire set. 'Often we end up giving eight business cards to one person...I'm just waiting for the day our clients and contacts meet to exchange cards.'

Websites (bottom)
www.TwoPoints.Net
www.DesignBy.TwoPoints.Net
www.ProjectsBy.TwoPoints.Net
www.WorkshopsBy.TwoPoints.Net
www.ProductsBy.TwoPoints.Net
Emphasizing their collaborative network, the TwoPoints.Net web presence is suitably diverse, with a main site and 'departments' that showcase commissions, projects, workshops and collaborations, as well as an e-commerce site for products and limited editions.

```
=======================
TWO
POINTS.
NET
-----------------------
N > MARTIN LORENZ
-----------------------
T > 0034 933 185 372
M > 0034 646 371 055
-----------------------
E > MARTIN@TWOPOINTS.NET
-----------------------
A > C/ BERTRELLANS 4, PPAL 2ª
    08002 BARCELONA
-----------------------
U > TWOPOINTS.NET
    DESIGNBY.TWOPOINTS.NET
    PROJECTSBY.TWOPOINTS.NET
    WORKSHOPSBY.TWOPOINTS.NET
```

Design
The Department of Design

Websites (opposite page, left to right,
top to bottom)
UnderConsideration
Logo and Website

Speak Up
Logo and Website

Brand New
Logo and Website

Quipsologies
Logo and Website

UnderConsideration   Bryony Gomez-Palacio and Armin Vit   Austin, TX, USA   www.underconsideration.com

The work and life partnership of Bryony Gomez-Palacio and Armin Vit launched Speak Up, one of the first graphic design blogs, back in 2002. Since then they have established another five sites, and written and designed a number of books, as well as running a busy practice, the Department of Design. Here, Armin Vit answers questions about that experience, and how publishing, online and in print, can build a designer's corporate identity into a promotional tool.

Liz Farrelly: In your last post on Speak Up, you mentioned how at the start of your career you wanted to be well known, and said that the blog helped achieve that status. What gave you the idea that a blog could do that, way back at the beginning of the 'blogging revolution'?

Armin Vit: 'To be honest, at the beginning I had no idea that a blog could actually work as a means of self-promotion or a soap box; it simply felt like a fresh alternative to publishing. I had no connections to magazines or book publishers, so blogging was the perfect medium to start a design stream of consciousness that lasted seven years, in the form of Speak Up. Along the way, people took notice. I think it was the uncensored nature of the blog that was so attractive. We changed strategies every year, if not every other month; there was no model, we were reacting to things going on in the industry, the level of involvement from our audience and our own interests and ambitions.'

LF: Speak Up was your first and principal blog and brand; you developed a visual identity on a completely new platform, and promoted yourselves via a world-wide network by adopting a revolution means of communication. Did Speak Up feel like it became a community rather than remain personal? Did you feel like you'd lost 'ownership' of it? When you closed it; did it allow you to go in a different direction with your other blogs and brands?

AV: 'Speak Up went through various phases and it went full circle in terms of being a very personal endeavor. When it started there was only me writing, and perhaps five or ten people making comments, one being my Dad. As we gained more readers and expanded with more authors, Speak Up became, as you say, a community-driven enterprise. By 2004, I could go on vacation and the site would stay active with various people leading discussions and keeping things (relatively) under control. This was Speak Up's heyday. We had Debbie Millman, Marian Bantjes, Tan Le, Gunnar

Swanson, Mark Kingsley, and other authors, running at full speed, along with me and Bryony, and we were driving some of the most heated discussions online, every day, multiple times a day. There was even a point where other authors took Speak Up, and me, as the subject of their posts; it was pretty weird.

'By 2006, the energy from both the authors and the commentators had waned, in part because of the larger number of blogs that demanded everyone's attention. So it came back to me being the main content generator; and by the time we launched Brand New and Quipsologies, Speak Up wasn't the sole obsession. By 2008, it had almost become a hindrance, with declining traffic and a lower number of comments. I would struggle to write two pieces a week, Bryony would do one or two a month and we would cross our fingers that a guest editorial would come through. It became very personal again, and demonstrated that it was always our responsibility. The decision to close it was a relief and, indeed, allowed us to move on to other things.'

LF: Explain UnderConsideration and how that works as an umbrella brand.

AV: 'We originally bought the underconsideration.com domain name because speakup.com and all close derivatives were taken. We thought UnderConsideration was a funny complement to the ethos of Speak Up; to always question everything and look at other points of view. When we launched The Design Encyclopaedia (TDE), we realised that UnderConsideration would become the parent company of all these things and that the simple premise of taking everything under consideration would fuel all of our ventures. Now every blog we launch, or are currently running, is "A Division of UnderConsideration", or "A Product of...". For us, it's reassuring to know that we can use that identifier and designers will see it as an extension of the quality and vibe we have established. The logo itself is the most softly spoken of all the ones we have, since it must exist alongside other logos, and it serves as an endorser. It's also fairly classic, and carries an air of seriousness that offsets the playfulness or bluntness of some of our other logos. Bryony made the elongated "R" and it really is one of my favourite details of all the things we've done.'

UNDER CONSIDERATION LLC

FORMED 2007
ESTABLISHED 2001

WHAT THIS IS

A growing network and enterprise dedicated to the progress of the graphic design profession and its practitioners, students and enthusiasts. At times intangible, its purpose is to question, push, analyze and agitate graphic design and those involved in the profession. *More about UnderConsideration...*

THINGS TO DO AROUND HERE

1 / Browse our design work at the Department of Design
2 / You could learn about the hard-working founders
3 / Get an idea of what our ADV×3 advertising is all about
4 / Maybe follow us on Twitter?
5 / Or just enjoy the lively sites that make up this corner of the internet by scrolling down, reading and clicking where necessary

THE UNDERCONSIDERATION ONLINE NETWORK / INFO · RECENT ACTIVITY

BRAND NEW

underconsideration.com/brandnew
Displaying opinions, and focusing solely on corporate and brand identity work.
More about Brand New...

RECENT ACTIVITY / RSS

Aether is the New Black
On Jul 20.2009

Rounded Letterforms Arrive in Perú
On Jul 17.2009

The Great White Discount
On Jul 16.2009

Update on the Week's Progress
On Jul 16.2009

Mystery Product Revealed
On Jul 16.2009

FPO *for PRINT only*

underconsideration.com/fpo
Celebrating the reality that print is not dead by showcasing the most compelling printed projects.
More about FPO...

RECENT ACTIVITY / RSS

Oh & Ah Business Card
On Jul 20.2009

Today Is Not a Dress Rehearsal Poster
On Jul 17.2009

The National Repertory Orchestra Poster
On Jul 16.2009

underconsideration.com/quipsologies
Corralling the most relevant and creative on- and off-line bits that pertain to the design community.
More about Quipsologies...

Quipsologies | From the Authors

Vol. 31 | No. 47
OiL!, a Flickr set of "A portion of my Dad's [...]

Vol. 31 | No. 46
NHL Patches. No need for more description other than the [...]

Vol. 31 | No. 45
In case you have missed out on the heated topic [...]

Vol. 31 | No. 44
The three-dimensional typographical stylings of Andrew Byrom. (Be sure to [...]

Quipsologies | From the Community

Vol. 31 | No. 34
A Better World by Design, a student-run conference at Brown [...]

Vol. 31 | No. 33
A rare glimpse into the process of seminal poster artists [...]

Vol. 31 | No. 32
Before: Pepsi | After: Pecsi Pepsi changes its spelling [...]

Vol. 31 | No. 31
A Quaker-WordPress-eBay-Rolling Stones-Twitter-YouTube keyboard. Quipped by <a href="http://theplamen.blogspot.com" rel="nofollow">Plamen</a> [...]

Vol. 31 | No. 30
Desperation by Josh Summers Quipped by <a href="http://www.imagekind.com" rel="nofollow">Nate</a> on [...]

NEWS

August 2009
/ STA
Armin will be judging the The Society of Typographic Arts' AnnualXX in Chicago on August 28, while enjoying a meet-and-greet the night before with fellow judges and designers.

July 2009

Graphic Design, Referenced
Our third book as authors and designers, published by Rockport Publishers, is now on the market. Graphic Design, Referenced: A Visual Guide to the Language, Applications, and History of Graphic Design. We've also put together a one-page preview with details and sample content.

/ TypeCon 2009: Rhythm
Armin will be speaking at TypeCon in Atlanta on July 18 about the identity design for the conference created through the Department of Design.

June 2009
/ Mano-a-Mano
UnderConsideration will be hosting a special event at the 2009 HOW Design Conference, battling to determine who knows the most about graphic design history and practice, mano-a-mano.

May 2009
/ Portfolio Center
Bryony will be speaking at Portfolio Center in Atlanta on May 26.

/ WebVisions
Armin will be speaking at WebVisions in Portland, OR on May 22.

/ FPO: For Print Only
Our newest, yet oldest, obsession is the subject of UnderConsideration's new blog, FPO: For Print Only.

April 2009
/ Austin, TX
The headquarters of UnderConsideration are now located in Austin, TX, leaving behind frosty ol' Brooklyn. We will miss you.

/ ProfiMWP
Bryony and Armin will be speaking at ProfiMWP on April 17 as part of their 2008–2009 Visiting Artist Lecture Series.

March 2009
/ Opinion on the Recovery.gov Logo
In the article "Recovery: The Brand" for the The Los Angeles Times, writer Adam Tschorn tagged Shepard Fairey and Armin to discuss the merits of the new logo for The American Recovery and Reinvestment Act issued by Obama's administration.

Speak Up

Speak Up

an archived division of
UNDERCONSIDERATION

Maintained with the continued support of our ADV×3 partners

Search Archives [Go]
Archives by Month
Archives by Category
Full archive list

The Archives,
August 2002 – April 2009

HELLO (AND, WELL, GOODBYE)

After nearly seven years of blogging, Speak Up has ceased publication. While this may not be a remarkable amount of time in the world of print and online publishing, the intensity with which we — founders, authors and readers alike — undertook it made it seem as it had been decades. For a thorough description on the reasons to close Speak Up, you may read this post, so as not to take much more space here. This web site is a bare-bones version of the archives for quick and easy perusal of more than 1,600 posts — a replica of Speak Up, as it was on closing day, can be found here, and at any point you can add "as-it-was/" after "speakup/" to the URL to see the original version. Comments on both sites have been closed.

To the right you will see all of our categories with a brief description of what you may find. Above it you can access all archives by month, category or as a laundry list of everything, and you can still search the content.

Below are some highlights from our time spent blogging. In somewhat chronological order.

We hope all this helps maintain the legacy of Speak Up frozen in digital time and that it may be of some use to passersby. Thank you all for your continued support and interest.

Bryony and Armin
Principals, UnderConsideration LLC

THE RISE AND FALL (AND RISE) OF LOGO DISCUSSION
On March 25, 2003 UPS announced that, after 42 years of service, it would do away with its bow-tied logo designed by Paul Rand in 1961. In return, Futurebrand gave UPS a glossy shield. The design industry, in return, was vociferous about the change and Speak Up served as one of the most prominent platforms at the time to voice the discontent. From that moment on, reviewing corporate and brand identity changes became a staple of Speak Up. Ironically, this theme and the ensuing conversations about logo changes — that, for the most part, were rarely in favor of the new design — irked many Speak Up readers the wrong way and some complaining ensued. In October of 2006 we launched Brand New, a site devoted to corporate and brand identity redesigns with full-time critiques of logos. Twice ironically, Brand New is now our most popular and trafficked web site.

RANTING ABOUT RANT
In 2003, Emigre magazine changed its physical format to pocketbook and its content to writing and criticism. Co-published with Princeton Architectural Press the first issue in this format was titled Rant, an acknowledged provocation to challenge young designers and writers "to develop a critical attitude toward their own work and the design scene in general." It worked. A lengthy discussion on Speak Up, representing the

BOOK REVIEWS
One of the biggest perks of running a design blog was that we, and some of our authors, received complementary review copies of dozens of great design books. Truth be told, we sure earned them, with plenty of reviews.
Browse Book Reviews Archives

BUSINESS
Speak Up was only as useful as its authors and devoted readers made it to be, and when we banded to discuss the business aspects of design great advice was given and relatable stories were told.
Browse Business Archives

CRITIQUE
Perhaps "critique" was the basic modus operandi of the blog, with everyone critiquing everything relentlessly, but these archives are as vivacious as a good classroom crit.
Browse Critique Archives

DESIGN ACADEMICS
Since Speak Up attracted eager students and weathered teachers alike, sprinkled with a heavy dose of professionals, education matters constantly proved worthwhile.
Browse Design Academics Archives

ESSAYS
While the writing on Speak Up was generally short and to the point, every now and then the authors flexed their theoretical, analytical and grammatical muscles to engage in some more considerate writing.
Browse Essays Archives

INTERVIEW
Funnily enough, the early interviews with some of the industry's heavy hitters was what gave us plenty of credibility and attention. After that, it was just fun to poke other people

BOOK RECOMMENDATIONS
Over the years we made an ever-growing list of recommended design books. There was never any shortage of content for this section.
Browse Book Recommendations Archives

BOOK CLUB
A brief and limited attempt at coordinating our audience to read one book at the same time and then discuss. It kind of worked.
Browse Book Club Archives

BRANDING AND IDENTITY
Whatever we say about this category will not make it justice to the impact it had in the industry. From the moment UPS said bye-bye to its Paul Rand logo, Speak Up became the de facto destination for discussions on branding and identity. It eventually became part of our downfall, but that's another story.
Browse Branding and Identity Archives

BUSINESS ARTICLES
For a short period of time we attempted to do exclusive business articles for a specific firm or designer and Chicago-based designer Steve Liska leading the charge.
Browse Business Articles Archives

DESIGNER / DESIGN FIRM PROFILE
Every now and then it was interesting to turn our attention to a specific designer and see what others thought.
Browse Designer / Design Firm Profile Archives

DISCUSSION
Ah, "discussion." Wow, did we discuss. The majority of Speak Up's most heated and followed conversations can be found in this category.

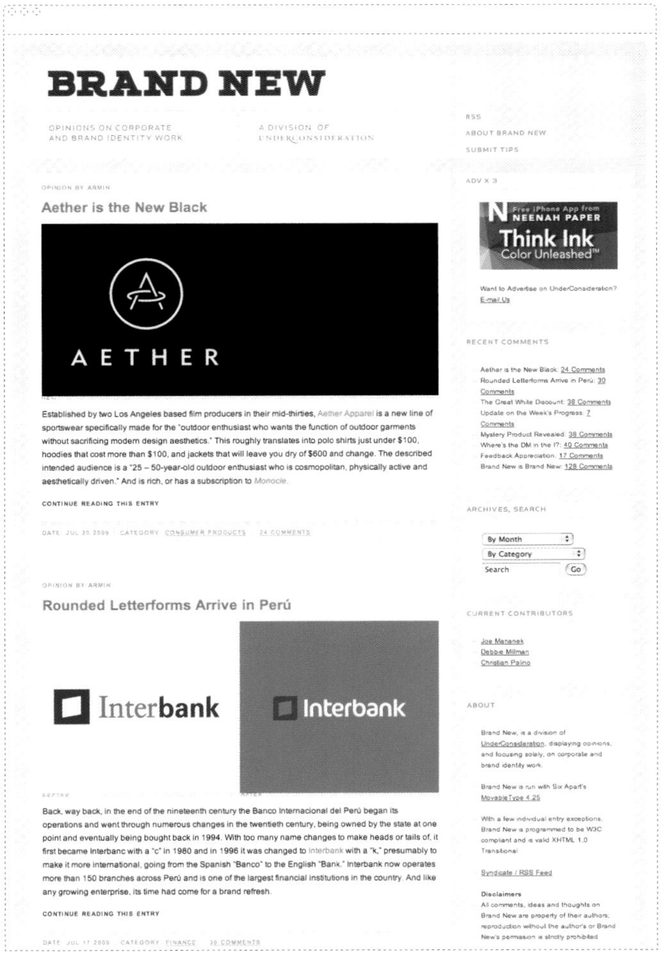

BRAND NEW

OPINIONS ON CORPORATE
AND BRAND IDENTITY WORK

A DIVISION OF
UNDERCONSIDERATION

RSS

ABOUT BRAND NEW

SUBMIT TIPS

ADV × 3

Want to Advertise on UnderConsideration?
E-mail Us

OPINION BY ARMIN

Aether is the New Black

Established by two Los Angeles based film producers in their mid-thirties, Aether Apparel is a new line of sportswear specifically made for the "outdoor enthusiasts who wants the function of outdoor garments without sacrificing modern design aesthetics." This roughly translates into polo shirts just under $100, hoodies that cost more than $100, and jackets that will leave you dry of $600 and change. The described intended audience is a "25 – 50-year-old outdoor enthusiast who is cosmopolitan, physically active and aesthetically driven." And is rich, or has a subscription to Monocle.

CONTINUE READING THIS ENTRY

DATE: JUL 20 2009 / CATEGORY: CONSUMER PRODUCTS / 24 COMMENTS

OPINION BY ARMIN

Rounded Letterforms Arrive in Perú

Back, way back, in the end of the nineteenth century the Banco Internacional del Perú began its operations and went through numerous changes in the twentieth century, being owned by the state at one point and eventually being bought back in 1994. With too many name changes to make heads or tails of, it first became Interbanc with a "c" in 1980 and in 1996 it was changed to Interbank with a "k," presumably to make it more international, going from the Spanish "Banco" to the English "Bank." Interbank now operates more than 150 branches across Perú and is one of the largest financial institutions in the country. And like any growing enterprise, its time had come for a brand refresh.

CONTINUE READING THIS ENTRY

DATE: JUL 17 2009 / CATEGORY: FINANCE / 30 COMMENTS

RECENT COMMENTS

Aether is the New Black. 24 Comments
Rounded Letterforms Arrive in Perú. 30 Comments
The Great White Discount. 38 Comments
Update on the Week's Progress. 7 Comments
Mystery Product Revealed. 38 Comments
Where's the DM in the ?. 40 Comments
Feedback Appreciation. 17 Comments
Brand New is Brand New. 128 Comments

ARCHIVES, SEARCH

By Month
By Category
Search [Go]

CURRENT CONTRIBUTORS

Joe Marianek
Debbie Millman
Christian Palino

ABOUT

Brand New, is a division of UnderConsideration, displaying opinions, and focusing solely, on corporate and brand identity work.

Brand New is run with Six Apart's Movable Type 4.25

With a few individual entry exceptions, Brand New is programmed to be W3C compliant and is valid XHTML 1.0 Transitional

Syndicate / RSS Feed

Disclaimers
All comments, ideas and thoughts on Brand New are property of their authors; reproduction without the author or Brand New's permission is strictly prohibited

---

QUIPSOLOGIES, A DIVISION OF UNDERCONSIDERATION, IS BENT ON KEEPING THE DESIGN COMMUNITY AWARE OF AS MANY THINGS AS POSSIBLE THROUGH AN EVER-GROWING CLUSTER OF CREATIVE MORSELS FOUND ON- AND OFF-LINE.

RSS › FROM THE AUTHORS

No. 47
OiL!, a Flickr set of "A portion of my Dad's oil can collection." Amazing. [Via Drawin']
QUIPPED BY ARMIN
Jul.20.2009

No. 46
NHL Patches. No need for more description other than the site is a pain in the ass to navigate. [UniWatch]
QUIPPED BY ARMIN
Jul.20.2009

No. 45
In case you have missed out on the heated topic of embedding fonts for the web, I Love Typography has a good summary of what has happened so far.
QUIPPED BY ARMIN
Jul.20.2009

No. 44
The three-dimensional typographical stylings of Andrew Byrom. (Be sure to check Grab Me).
QUIPPED BY ARMIN
Jul.16.2009

No. 43
Trop50, the last remainder of the Arnell Group redesign of Tropicana, gets redesigned.
QUIPPED BY ARMIN
Jul.16.2009

No. 42
iQ Font, the first (and presumably only) typeface drawn by a car.
QUIPPED BY ARMIN
Jul.16.2009

No. 41
Students of Heather Shaw at UMass Dartmouth turn design classics by Jan Tschichold and Herbert Bayer into HTML/CSS typographic masterpieces.
QUIPPED BY ARMIN
Jul.16.2009

No. 40
"The Story about Stop Motion" told in, of course, stop motion. [Via Motionographer]
QUIPPED BY ARMIN
Jul.16.2009

No. 39
Roger Black, famed magazine and newspaper designer, has a kick-ass vacation home in West Texas made of recycled shipping containers. [Via HOW]
QUIPPED BY ARMIN
Jul.16.2009

QUIPSOLOGIES
FINDING THE CREATIVE IN THE EVERYDAY
A DIVISION OF UNDERCONSIDERATION
Vol. 31
July 2009

Archives

ADV × 3 PROGRAM
REGISTER NOW!
AIGA Design Conference
MAKE THINK
October 8–11, 2009

Want to Advertise on UnderConsideration?
E-mail Us

See all ADV×3 Ads

QUIPPING RULES

First and foremost, the editors will edit without mercy and at their sole discretion.

Do not Quip to your own site. If you think you have something interesting to share, e-mail us, we will decide.

Quipsologies are intended to revolve around design but be broadly-themed. Creativity, art, architecture, branding, business, music, movies, museums, books and the such are fair game.

Quipsologies is not about conversation, refrain from commenting on other contributions.

Keep it short and to the point.

Events may be posted, but please limit the entry to a very brief description, the title, place and time.

If you are selling something (fonts, stock, gadgets, etc.), stop. You can't. E-mail the editors if you would like to promote.

Quipsologies is about sharing your interests, recommendations and intrigues. Keep it useful and fun.

ABOUT QUIPSOLOGIES

QUIPSOLOGIES ACKNOWLEDGES THAT THERE IS STRENGTH IN NUMBERS AND INDIVIDUAL INTERESTS; EVERYONE IS INVITED AND ENCOURAGED TO ADD THEIRS. QUIP RESPONSIBLY.
(JUMP TO THE BOTTOM TO QUIP.)

FROM THE COMMUNITY › RSS

No. 34
A Better World by Design, a student-run conference at Brown & RISD, October 2-4. Speakers include Jan Chipchase, Bill Drenttel, Emily Pilloton, and Nathan Shedroff among many others!
QUIPPED BY WV
Jul.17.2009

No. 33
A rare glimpse into the process of seminal poster artists The Heads of State.
QUIPPED BY MR
Jul.17.2009

No. 32
Before: Pepsi | After: Pecsi
Pepsi changes its spelling to Pecsi in Argentina to accommodate the local idiom.
QUIPPED BY PLAMEN
Jul.17.2009

No. 30
Desperation by Josh Summers
QUIPPED BY NATE
Jul.16.2009

No. 29
Ever wanted to learn all the guitar fretboard notes? Here's the best chart I ever found, seriously! It's that Good!
QUIPPED BY BRYAN
Jul.16.2009

No. 28
Nice post about how funny webdesign studios can get more clients?
QUIPPED BY ALINNE
Jul.16.2009

No. 27
Exchange program for all of you creative professionals that want to travel but keep your job: Link SwapYourShop
QUIPPED BY JENNIFER WRIGHT
Jul.15.2009

No. 26
Nice Photoshop actions for product showcasing Product shot covers (Use the contact form with the code "zooff", and you'll be sent a link worth $20 off) - doesn't tell anyone ;)
QUIPPED BY GRAPHICS = GOOD
Jul.15.2009

the design encyclopedia

THE BEST WAY TO STAY UPDATED WITH THE DESIGN ENCYCLOPEDIA
IT THROUGH OUR RSS, WHICH WILL LET YOU KNOW ANYTIME
THERE ARE CHANGES AND ADDITIONS. CLICK HERE TO GET THE URL

A DIVISION OF
UNDERCONSIDERATION

INDEX   LOGOUT   EDIT THIS PAGE   OLD REVISIONS   SEARCH

ADV × 3 PROGRAM

Trace › Welcome to the design encyclopedia › Wolfgang Weingart

Wolfgang Weingart

TABLE OF CONTENTS ▲

Wolfgang Weingart
  Sample Work
  Link
  Related Links
  Books

Want to Advertise on
UnderConsideration? E-mail Us
See All ADVx3 Ads

NEWEST ENTRIES

Wolfgang Weingart
Frank O. Gehry & Associates
TWA Terminal
Kansas City Art Institute
Michael Graves
Libby Perszyk Kathman
Knoll
Cooper Hewitt National Design
Museum
Print
Trollback + Company

RECENT CHANGES

Rushton Phillips
April Greiman
AIGA
ESDI
The Playground
Memefest
Wishlist
adblock
Society for News Design
Fred Smeijers
ALL RECENT CHANGES

ABOUT TDE

Introduction
Wishlist
Details, Facts and More
Contact
Advertising with TDE

WIKI FUNCTIONALITY

A Quick Glimpse
How to Start a Page
Syntax
Playground

JOIN OUR MAILING LIST

Name (required)

1941: Birth

1958: Enrolled at Merz Academy in Stuttgart, Germany.

1960: Graduated from Merz Academy, and began a three-year apprenticeship at Ruwe Printing.

1964: Encouraged by his apprenticeship mentor Karl-August Hanke, Weingart joined the Basel School of Design in Switzerland.

1968: Joined the Advanced Class of Graphic Design faculty at Basel.

2001: Weingart published his book *Wolfgang Weingart: My Way to Typography.*

Sample Work

Edit

1998. University of California at Los Angeles catalog

WORD IT

ONE WORD   A DIVISION OF UNDERCONSIDERATION   ENDLESS POSSIBILITIES

ABOUT WORD IT

LAST MONTH'S WORD
Drought

THIS MONTH'S WORD
Fly

NEXT MONTH'S WORD
To Be Announced

All Words

SUBMISSION GUIDELINES
SUBMISSION FORM

Search (names only)   Go
FOR TAG SEARCHES USE THE TAG LISTINGS OR
BROWSE THE ENTIRE TAG ARCHIVE

RECENT COMMENTS

(2) on Aurora M.'s Fly
(2) on Jen Harders's Fly
(3) on Kyle Stewart's Fly

ADVx3 [SEE ALL]

Want to Advertise on
UnderConsideration?
E-mail Us

BY
Gabe Chai

IN
Fly

ON
July 19, 2009

COMMENTS
0

THIS WORD IT'S PERMALINK

CLICK ON WORD IT FOR
AUTHOR'S LINK, IF PROVIDED

TAGS
+ Gabe Chai
airbus
airplane
bear
black and white
florida
photography

SEE ALL TAGS

BY
Marina Holshevnikoff

IN
Fly

ON
July 19, 2009

COMMENTS
0

THIS WORD IT'S PERMALINK

CLICK ON WORD IT FOR
AUTHOR'S LINK, IF PROVIDED

TAGS
+ Marina Holshevnikoff
birds
blue
clouds
frame
sans serif
sky
typography

SEE ALL TAGS

FPO

for PRINT only

rss

a division of
UNDERCONSIDERATION

about FPO   submit to FPO

Oh & Ah Business Card

BY BRYONY / ON / JUL.20.2009 / IN / BUSINESS CARDS

ADV × 3

Want to Advertise on UnderConsideration?
E-mail Us

· project OVERVIEW

DESCRIPTION
Oh & Ah Business Card

CLIENT
Self Promotion

DESIGN CREDITS
Oh & Ah

PRINT CREDITS
Uncredited printer in Malaysia

· production DETAILS

QUANTITY PRODUCED
1,600

PRODUCTION COST
RM81 (Malaysia Ringgit) (US$21)

PRODUCTION TIME
2 days

DIMENSIONS · WIDTH · HEIGHT · DEPTH
90 mm. × 50 mm. (3.54 in. × 1.96 in.)

PRINT METHOD
Thermography and offset

PAPER STOCK
Kraft paper 300 gsm

NUMBER OF COLORS
1 spot color (black)

OTHER
First there was offset printing, followed
by cutting the cards to size before
adding thermography at the end of the
process.

· jump to FULL POST

THIS POST HAS 0 COMMENTS

IT HAS BEEN TAGGED WITH / KRAFT PAPER / OFFSET / THERMOGRAPHY

Today Is Not a Dress Rehearsal **Poster**

Recent Comments

Today Is Not a Dress Rehearsal Poster [3]
The National Repertory Orchestra Poster [2]
Brand New Sketchbook [6]
Alex Parrott Postcard [11]
Vegas Vic Self Promotion [9]
Pretty Sure Poster [11]
AQoodid Business Card [6]
Justine Ungaro Business Cards [17]

Archives and Search

Search   Go
By Month
By Category
By Tags

About

FPO is a division of UnderConsideration
LLC, celebrating the reality that print a not
dead by showcasing the most compelling
printed projects.

FPO is run with Six Apart's MovableType
4.2

Syndicate

RSS Feed

Disclaimers
All comments, ideas and thoughts on FPO
are property of their authors, reproduction

UNDERCONSIDERATION LLC

UC.DOD

UnderConsideration's Department of Design provides creative services for
corporate and brand identity work as well as full development of printed and
digital matter, through consistent management, careful attention to detail, and
consideration for each project's requirements and context. UC.DOD is also
responsible for the development of UnderConsideration's online and offline
applications, including the design and coding of all blogs, and design and
production of all books, promotional materials and supporting identities.

PROJECTS

Graphic Design, Referenced Type: Book | Client: UnderConsideration | Project Link

Our third book as authors and designers, published with Rockport Publishers, is
*Graphic Design, Referenced: A Visual Guide to the Language, Applications, and
History of Graphic Design*, a 400-page visual and informational guide to the most
commonly referenced terms, historical moments, landmark projects, and influential
practitioners in the field of graphic design.

See Full Project

JCJ Architecture Identity Type: Identity | Client: JCJ Architecture | Project Link

JCJ ARCHITECTURE

With offices in Boston, Hartford, Los Angeles, New York, Phoenix and San Diego and
expertise in civic, corporate, education, hospitality and science & technology markets,
JCJ Architecture is a highly prolific firm that designs and builds at the local, regional
and global level. UnderConsideration was brought in to revitalize their identity in a
way that marked an evolution from their 2006 name change and identity.

See Full Project

TypeCon 2009: Rhythm Logo Type: Identity | Client: TypeCon | Project Link

**DEPARTMENT
OF
DESIGN**

WORK

· View by Type
 Book
 Identity
 Poster
 Print
 Web

· View by Client
 AIGA
 Alliance for a Healthier Generation
 Caesars Golf
 Creativity
 JCJ Architecture
 New York University School of Law
 Office for Urbanism
 Rizzoli
 Soap Foundation
 TypeCon
 UnderConsideration
 VisionSpring
 William J. Clinton Foundation

PARTNERS

Bryony Gomez-Palacio and Armin Vit
Born and raised in Mexico City both are graphic designers
and co-founders of UnderConsideration, each with a
decade of experience in various disciplines including
corporate and brand identity, annual reports, business
collateral, web design and programming, packaging, as
well as magazine and book design. They are the authors
of *The Word It Book* and *The Women of Design* and F+W
Publications, and of Graphic Design, Referenced, a 400-
page book, with Rockport Publishers.

They concept, produce and oversee all the work
processed through UC.DOD.

Full bios... Bryony, Armin

CONTACT

UnderConsideration LLC
5818 Shoalwood Ave
Austin, TX 78758
p. (917) 755-0750
f. (718) 228-6720
e. info@underconsideration.com

OTHER

· Related Links
 UnderConsideration
 Principals
 Speak Up
 Brand New
 FPO
 Word It
 Quipsologies
 The Design Encyclopedia

· Books
 The Word It Book: Speak Up presents a gallery of
 interpreted words
 Women of Design: Influence and Inspiration from the
 Original Trailblazers to the New Groundbreakers
 Graphic Design, Referenced: A Visual Guide to the
 Language, Applications, and History of Graphic Design

· Good Code
 UC.DOD is W3C compliant and is valid XHTML 1.0
 Transitional

UC.DOD

Websites (opposite page, left to right, top to bottom)
The Design Encyclopedia
Logo and Website

Word It
Logo and Website

For Print Only
Logo and Website

The Department of Design
Logo and Website

Logotypes (right)
Bryony and Armin have created a family of logotypes for their expanding portfolio of websites, blogs and editorial projects, as well as their over-arching company, UnderConsideration. Each logo is available in multiple versions, for use at different scale, both in print and online, and in monochrome and colour.

UNDER CONSIDERATION

Speak Up   UC.DOD

+)Ξ   WORD IT
the design encyclopedia

BRAND NEW   FPO
                 for PRINT only

LF: Why did you decide to create multiple blogs and sites, with all the attendant needs for building separate brands and logos? Do you think people got confused? How do you mitigate against that?

AV: It was very organic. We didn't set a goal to have five new blogs in five years. The first extension, in 2005, was The Design Encyclopaedia (TDE), a wiki. It is a very different model to the original blog and showed us the potential of eventually having a network of websites, under the UnderConsideration umbrella. After TDE, there was no clear direction for a new blog, until 2006 when we started Brand New as a spin-off from Speak Up. That came about when we realized there was an endless supply of logos to discuss and an audience happy to discuss them. Quipsologies and Word It followed in 2007 and 2009 respectively, as offshoots of Speak Up. Our latest, For Print Only (FPO), dealing with projects on paper, was another digression.

So now we have a network that shares a distinct DNA in its design and philosophy. We are designers first, so our impetus is to design things, and creating logos and websites for each blog is fun, and allows us to push ourselves to build shells where we can deploy content. The separate and strong brands we've created are exactly for the purpose you mention; to help differentiate one from the other, especially at their inception when we are setting them apart from the 'mothership', Speak Up. Each blog has its own editorial format, so along with their unique identities, they don't leave much room for confusion.

LF: Are there special issues to consider, like colours or size, when designing a logo for a website or blog? Or does it give you more freedom, in that you're able to frequently change details and customize them, making it more fun?

AV: The main attraction is that we can do whatever we want. We design a lot of logos for clients, so we try new things with our own work. Logos should work online and offline, so it's about creating striking identities that look great no matter where they are. Plus, if you've noticed, we like to run our logos big, so size is never an issue!

LF: About the books that you create with publishers; do you feel you've been able to keep a consistent identity working with outside publishers? Have you had to take into consideration any branding or design requirements set by those publishers?

AV: Other than the limitations of production (for example, all text must be on a fifth black plate to enable translation) we have been very lucky to produce books that are a natural extension of our writing, editing and design sensibilities. Both of our publishers, HOW Books and Rockport Publishers, have placed a lot of trust and confidence in us, so that we produce books we are very proud of. It's not all rainbows and unicorns, of course; for the three books we've published we've done between 15 and 20 different covers or cover variations, and we've had to come up with dozens of minutely different subtitles and justify why our books will sell, but they are minor things that you would expect in any collaborative project.

LF: Do you consider your books to be part of your promotional endeavors, and an effective part?

AV: I wouldn't necessarily call them promotional...We see them like any project, with their own unique challenges, deadlines and nuances. In the end, unlike a logo for a client, they do carry our name with them, so they become promotional. The flip side is that they set us up as experts in the field, and we would be dumb if we didn't play up these books when we try to land a new client. We make sure to mention it, so they understand that we know what we're talking about and that it's worth paying us thousands and thousands of dollars for their project!

LF: Do you think you can deliver a different message using print and paper, rather than over the Internet? Is the Brand New Sketch Book the first stationery item you've created? Do you consider that to be a self-promotional tool too?

AV: *Stop Being Sheep* was our first printed product; these were mini anthologies of the best comments from each of the first four years on Speak Up. They were a great extension of the online world, and they served as mementos that celebrated the people, the commentators, who made Speak Up great. We are always thinking about physical objects that we can make, but as you know, they are more expensive to produce and you are taking a gamble, not knowing if people will buy it. With online blogs, you can take risks at much lower costs, sometimes even for free.

Universal Everything

Universal Everything   Matt Pyke   Sheffield, UK   www.universaleverything.com

Based in a log cabin studio in Sheffield, Matt Pyke is a cross-media artist and designer; he uses just about every media available to realize creative projects – from pencils to generative programming. He also animates, directs and produces, curates and lectures. He formed Universal Everything in 2004. 'I wanted to work under a name that could express an ideal; of the biggest blank canvas in the universe, to go anywhere and try anything,' he explains. Tapping into a network of colleagues and friends, designers, programmers, musicians and artists, Matt helms a diverse collective that crosses the traditional divides between design, art and technology.

'Everything we release to the public has an aim beyond entertaining people, to express how we work (as a network), how we think (including many influences outside graphic design), and where we want to go (forever exploring and reinventing our approach),' says Matt.

Whether that's a commission for a blue-chip client (Apple, Audi, Nokia, London 2012 Olympics); an installation at the Victoria and Albert Museum, New York's Museum of Modern Art, or Paris's temple of cool, Colette; or a self-published project, such as the series of Advanced Beauty: Sound Sculptures DVDs, Matt considers each iteration as representative of Universal Everything's collective identity.

The main portal to Universal Everything is via three websites, which appear on the website as different coloured folders, with tab-button links. Matt explains the structure: 'Universal Everything shows art and commercial commissions, basically our client work. Everyone Forever documents our findings, because we want to share our thinking with the world. Advanced Beauty presents self-initiated audio-visual content, and is our area for research and development.'

Designer: Matt Pyke
Printer: Benwell Sebard

Letterhead (opposite page) **and Compliments Slip** (below right)
Pantone black, holographic foil, on Stephen Sultry Grey, 100gsm. Marrying a dramatic flash of foil with a tactile, self-coloured stock, the logotype is central to Universal Everything's identity. Matt describes it as, 'a handmade studio signature based on customized Avant Garde, with a calligraphic flourish.' (Avant Garde was originally designed by Herb Lubalin in 1970 for ITC.)

Notepaper (below left) **and DVD Cover Insert** (top right)
Pantone black, holographic foil, on Stephen Sultry Grey, 100gsm. The paper size that fits a standard DVD box is also used for informal correspondence.

Business Card (bottom left)
Pantone black and holographic foil, on Stephen Sultry Grey, 350gsm.

Sticker and Envelope (bottom right)
Sticker: Pantone black, Pantone grey and holographic foil, on Linebacker Solid Back Non-Perm Self-Adhesive. Envelope: Black matte stock.

DVD and Case (top right)
Printer: Wewow.
The addition of an acid yellow plastic case creates an eye-catching package.

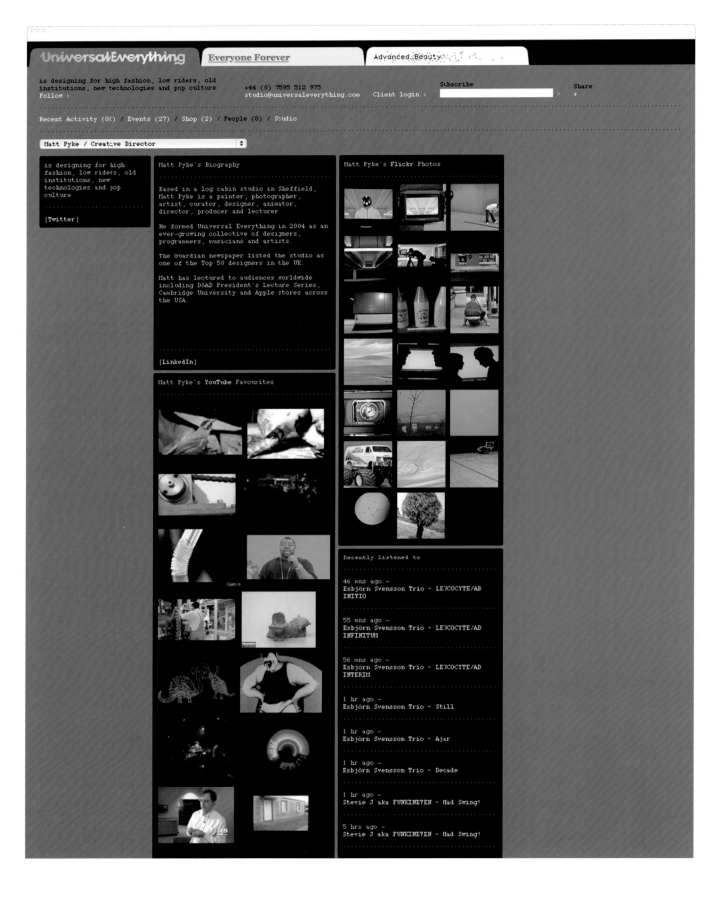

Websites
www.universaleverything.com
www.everyoneforever.com
www.advancedbeauty.org/blog
A multi-layered and forever expanding
archive, this multi-site logs the
network's online activity, including
recent videos, current studio activity on
Twitter, music listened to, photographs
snapped and YouTube favourites. Also
available are listings of upcoming
lectures and events organized by and
featuring network members. Three
'folders' with tab-buttons aid navigation
and accent the connectivity of these
three 'worlds'. With an automated
content generation function, frequent
project updates vie for attention
alongside the 'live self-portraits' of the
network's collaborators, 'as we listen,
travel, watch, think and talk'.

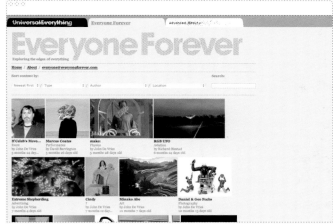

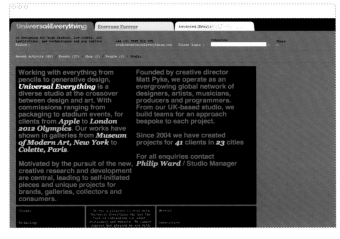

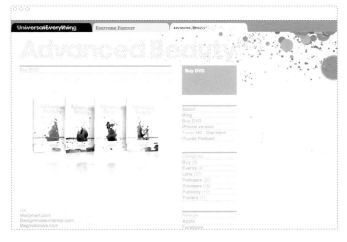

VIER5   Paris, France   www.vier5.de

Declaring their approach to be 'based on a classical notion of design', VIER5's corporate identity combines the restraint of a black and white archival website with energetic, hand-rendered mark making, and a self-publishing programme. Comprehensive and diverse, the corporate identity does not include a letterhead.

FAIRY TALE is the studio's biannual magazine. 'One reason for publishing a magazine in the spring and autumn is our interest in fashion and the relationship between graphic design and fashion,' explain VIER5. They describe the magazine as, 'a free work of design, from the cover to the last page, not simply a series of fashion photographs between a large number of adverts.'

VIER5 admit to previously having avoided using images; but after working on a collaborative catalogue with the American photographer, Lewis Baltz, 'which gave us a new view on how we could work with pictures,' they took on the magazine project, as an antidote to their client-based design work. Consequently, the magazine attracted a new type of client, and VIER5 have since incorporated photography into their practice.

As a document of their theory-based methodology, *FAIRY TALE* demonstrates VIER5's approach. They often work with cultural institutions and publish these projects, alongside discussions with curators, interviews with artists, and the 'transformation' process of turning design work into magazine content.

More recently, VIER5 have published an eponymous book, featuring an archive of photographs from before their move to Paris. 'The pictures are research into our own time and society, and this is the basis of most of our work,' they explain. The photographs display odd details, strange lighting, 'or show some kind of destruction.'

'The difference between the book and *FAIRY TALE* is that the book is a reflection of "inside": it's about us. The magazine reflects the "outside"...Our hope is that people get a sense of the possibilities of design, and the freedom of choice you can have as a designer.'

Book (opposite page, top)
VIER5

Magazine (opposite page, bottom)
FAIRY TALE

Business Card (top right)
1/0, blue, on cream card.
As if written with a slightly damaged
pen, the letterforms are accompanied
by shadowy traces.

Compliments Slip (below)
1/1, cream and green, on greyboard.
Again, the distinctive handwritten logo
appears, with a jagged line traversing
the card.

Websites (bottom)
www.vier5.de
www.v5-warehouse.com
The site features a screen-wide, gently
flashing cursor, which divides the menu
from the image field.
A second website features a wide
range of fashion and accessory
projects which are bringing VIER5
to a widening audience.

Vier5
139, rue du Faubourg St.Denis
75010 Paris
++33 | 42 05 09 90
contact@vier5.de

The work of Vier5 is based on a classical
notion of design.
Design as the possibility of drafting and
creating new, forward-looking images in
the field of visual communication.
A further focus of our work lies on designing
and applying new, up-to-date fonts.
The work of Vier5 aims to prevent any
visual empty phrases and to replace them
with individual, creative statements, which
were developed especially for the used
medium and client.

work:
-poster, exhibition cornelius cardew
-poster, bauhaus universität
-two posters, cac bretigny
-fairy tale; issue 'architecture and interieur'
-two posters, cac bretigny
-poster, exhibition franz erhard walther
-poster, ecole des beaux arts bordeaux
-poster, exhibition rainer oldendorf
-poster, exhibition roman ondak
-three posters, cac bretigny
-posters, exhibition 'the void'
-poster, exhibition david lamelas
-book; 'the deaths in newport'
-posters, exhibition atelier van lieshout
-poster, douglas coupland

-website rmn (reunion des musees nationaux)
-guiding system documenta 12
-ci museum für angewandte kunst frankfurt

If you would like to have more information
about the work of Vier5 please send an
email or call.

POSTER, LECTURE HFK BREMEN

FT 'NATURE', AW2009/10

VIER5 HANDBUCH

Vier5 WAREHOUSE
139, rue du Faubourg St.Denis
75010 Paris
++33 | 42 05 09 90
contact@vier5.de

WELCOME to the VIER5 WARHOUSE!

this is the webshop of VIER5 all products
you can find here are designed and produced
by VIER5 for your pleasure.

PRODUCTS
-fashion
-accessores
-jewellery
-books/magazines
-posters

CONDITIONS/SHIPPING

ORDER
>

LINKS
www.vier5.de
www.fairytale-magazine.com

jewellery:

"HEART" necklace
material:
-heart: black plexi glass
-chain: metal silvered
size:
heart: 3,8 x 3,8 cm
chain: 82 cm
price: 125 euro

"CHEWING-GUM" necklace
material:
-chewing gum: solid silver (925),
-chain: silver (925)/gold (333)
size:
-chewing gum: 0,7 x 2 cm,
-chain: 58,5 cm
every piece is handmade and
unique.
"MUST HAVE".
price: 180 euro

VIER5-MONOGRAM-brooch
(red)
material: transparent plexi glas,
silver, two diamonds
size: 8,5 x 5 cm
original size look at
www.vier5.de
every piece is handmade and
unique.
price: 470 euro

VIER5-MONOGRAM-brooch
(white)
material: white plexi glas, silver,
two diamonds
size: 8,5 x 5 cm
original size look at
www.vier5.de
every piece is handmade and
unique.
price: 470 euro

CROWNCAP pin
material: metal earrated
size: 2,5 x 2,5 cm
please look at: www.vier5.de
set of two pins: 20 euro

there is also a version in solid
silver. for more information
please ask.

Alvin Yeung   Alvin Yeung   Tokyo, Japan   superpowerups.com

When Alvin Yeung was in his final year at the School of Visual Arts in New York City, circumstances required him to move halfway around the world to Tokyo. Realizing that he needed to communicate with a new audience, with different cultural expectations of him as a designer, and using a foreign language, he chose to raise his profile and make an impact – in one of the most competitive design communities on earth – by adopting a number of unconventional methods.

'I had a few personal projects, not knowing what field of graphic design to concentrate on. The results were bordering on artworks, but all the thought processes, the parameters, grids and consciousness about typography were design-focused,' explains Alvin. 'I think every passionate graphic designer can relate to wanting to make something about their personal experiences. So I decided to use these projects to reveal to others, and to myself, what kind of designer I wanted to be.'

はじめまして。
nice to meet you.

カイブツ の、
kaibutsu of,

アルヴィン ヤン と、
alvin yeung and,

もうします。
what has been said.

ニューヨーク
new york

からきました。
came from.

グラフィックデザイナーです。
graphic designer.

カイブツ
kaibutsu

105-0003

東京都
tokyo

港区
minato-ku

西新橋
nishi-shimbashi

3-15-12

ケミカルビル
chemical building

6F

k +81-3-5733-6886
a +81-80-3578-7720
f +81-3-5733-6887
alvin@kaibutsu.jp

Business Cards (opposite page)
1/1, purple foil block, on
white card.
To present his interest in clouds,
Alvin created a pattern using
interlocking 'puffs'.

3/3, red, blue and black, on
white card.
In three different languages, Alvin
explains that he's a designer from New
York, living in Tokyo, and that it's 'nice
to meet you.'

Stickers
Admitting to having a thing for
clouds, and inspired by Tibetan and
other oriental motifs, Alvin set out to
investigate graphic mark-making.
'I started to sketch clouds, and
developed a comfortable line and curve
style for the initial cloud mark.' The
challenge of incorporating all sorts of
interesting objects with clouds, from
ice-cream to bunnies, to mohawks
to poop, created variations on the
cloud puff. He printed a batch of vinyl
stickers 'to paste around the world...
The Japanese response was very
positive due to the fact that they almost
always love anything puffy and cute.'

Promotional Posters (below)
On short trips back to New York, Alvin screenprinted a series of posters to use as promotional pieces. He gave the posters to new friends from Tokyo's design scene. His goal was 'to incorporate some hint of transition and flight in these posters,' as a document of his nomadic lifestyle. In editions of 25 and 60, each poster was printed using single screens and gradient flooding to achieve a graduated colour scheme, in various colourways.

Screenprinted Masks (bottom left)
A set of masks was printed on to handkerchiefs in limited editions of 25. 'This promotional piece helped me connect to other designers and geeks who love geometry, tribal art and loud colour palettes,' explains Alvin. Printing on cloth made it portable 'for meetings and various design events.'

T-shirt (bottom right)
A block of 3D type advertises that Alvin is looking for a job. Anyone willing to take a chance can email him.

Wallpaper (below)
Disseminating the cloud-based identity
further, these wallpapers promote
Alvin to friends, acquaintances and
new followers. Here he explores ideas
around how small colour changes affect
symmetry, and how pixels can create
more iconic images.

Websites (bottom)
www.superpowerups.com
After hours of teaching himself Flash,
Alvin built a site using ActionScript 2.0.
It features commercial and personal
projects against a themed background
of cloud motifs. 'I wanted to give the
site a presence, an identity, instead of
keeping it neutral.'

www.al.vvvvv.in
This site runs on HTML using a blog
platform, the aim being to create a web
presence that is easily updated, to
showcase new and ongoing projects.

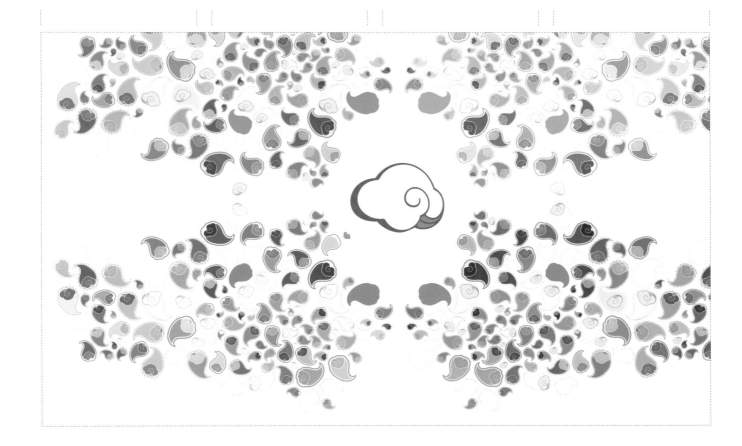

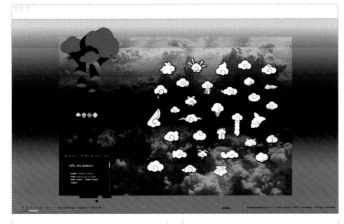

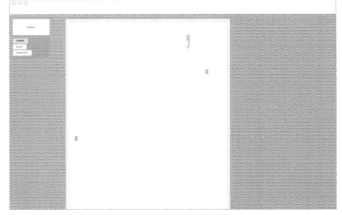

DESIGN
BRANDING   ZÜRICH **TOKIO**™
WERBUNG

+
47° 22' 53" N | 08° 32' 10" E

ZürichTokio   Daniel Donati, Laura Donati, Karin Glarner,   Zurich, Switzerland   www.zurichtokio.com
                     Stefan Lemberger, Niels Schäfer, Fabian Widmer

Having been part of a successful design company, code.ch, for over a decade, Daniel Donati explains why he went against received wisdom and adopted a new name after his partner left. 'If you have a successful brand, no expert would recommend that you change it; but that's exactly what we did, even though we were well known for excellent graphic design, and were successful. Moving on was what we decided to do.' He continues, 'We've also found new influences by travelling with open eyes.'

Even though they don't have an office in Japan, it's implied in the company name – why? 'We're based in Zurich; Tokyo is a symbol for our fascination with creating new worlds.' That explorative instinct is showcased in the new company's corporate identity, which features photographs of the entire crew in some very out-of-the-way places. Additional map co-ordinates reveal them to be an independent bunch. Daniel describes his colleagues as 'strong individuals, restless, interested in everything that is eye-catching in content and form. Curiosity does not kill the cat, it's our engine and it doesn't start at nine, nor does it stop at five.' And, of course, they take their own photographs too.

Letterhead (opposite page and below)
2/0, black and grey, on white stock.
Uniquely, the contact details are on
the reverse while the front features
the studio's global co-ordinates.

Business Cards (bottom and top right)
Four-colour CMYK, on white card,
perforated.
Featuring an outdoor portrait of each
staffer, the perforations mean the card
may be folded to create meeting-table
namecards. Each individual's job
description or special skill is also noted.

Compliments Slip (below right)
2/2, black and grey, on white card.

Envelope (middle right)
Four-colour CMYK, on white
window envelope.
A beautiful view may be glimpsed
through the 'window'.

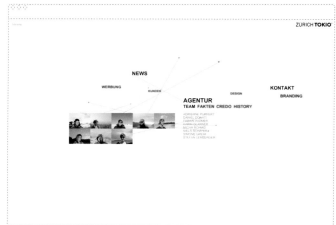

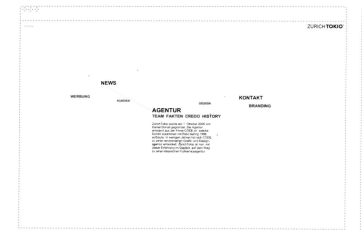

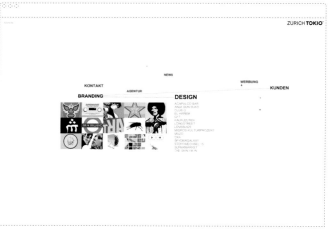

Website
www.zurichtokio.com
'Our MiniSite is a "short trip" through
our world. Fast, informative and for
those who don't have the time for a
"long trip", which is on our MaxiSite.'
Both are easily accessible from
the same URL. They feature the
photographic elements found on the
designers' business cards, along
with rotating hand-held video clips on
the intro page, showing destinations
around the world. Bold graphic arrows
accentuate a sense of direction.

MINI SITE

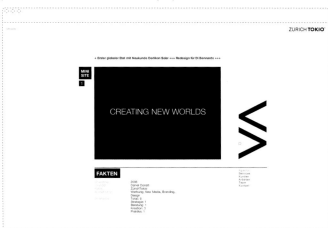

THE LIBRARY
TOWER HAMLETS COLLEGE
POPLAR HIGH STREET
LONDON E14 0AF
0207 510 7763

Contributor Contacts

344 Design
www.344design.com
Stefan G. Bucher

abc–xyz
www.abc-xyz.co.uk
Julian Morey

Aboud Creative
www.aboud-creative.com
Alan Aboud

Abraka design
www.abraka.com
Carine Abraham

Absolute Zero Degrees
www.absolutezerodegrees.com
Merryl Catlow, Mark Hampshire,
Keith Stephenson

AdamsMorioka, Inc.
www.adamsmorioka.com
Sean Adams and Noreen Morioka

Airside
www.airside.co.uk

Akatre
www.akatre.com
Valentin Abad, Julien Dhivert,
Sébastien Riveron

almost Modern
www.almostmodern.com
Jorn de Vries and Markus Rummens

Alter
www.alter.com.au
Jonathan Wallace and Dan Whitford

AmoebaCorp
www.amoebacorp.com
Mike Kelar and Mikey Richardson

Richard Ardagh
www.elephantsgraveyard.co.uk

ATTAK Powergestaltung
www.attakweb.com
Casper Herselman and Peter Korsman

BANK™
www.bankassociates.de
Sebastian Bissinger and Laure Boer

Fabien Barral
www.fabienbarral.com

Battery Battery
www.battery.nl
Yurrian Rozenberg

Alexandre Bettler
www.aalex.info

Bunch
www.bunchdesign.com

Bureau Ludwig
www.bureau-lidwig.com
Birte Ludwig

Burneverything
www.burneverything.co.uk
David Hand, Matt Lewis, Sam Wiehl

Coboi
www.coboi.ch
Katharina Reidy

Deanne Cheuk Design
www.deannecheuk.com
Deanne Cheuk

designjune
www.designjune.com
Julien Crouïgneau

deValence
www.devalence.net
Alexandre Dimos and Gaël Étienne

Dextro.org
www.dextro.org
Dextro

dress code
www.dresscodeny.com
Andre Andreev and G. Dan Covert

EightHourDay
www.eighthourday.com
Katie Kirk and Nathan Strandberg

EMMI
www.emmi.co.uk
Emmi Salonen

Mario Eskenazi
www.m-eskenazi.com

FL@33
www.flat33.com
Agathe Jacquillat and Tomi Vollauschek

Form
www.form.uk.com
Paula Benson and Paul West

FoURPAcK
www.fourpack.nl
Tessa Hofman and Richard Pijs

Malcolm Goldie
www.malcolmgoldie.com

Hans Gremmen
www.hansgremmen.nl

Grundini
www.grundini.com
Peter Grundy

Alina Günter
www.alinaguenter.ch

HarrimanSteel
www.harrimansteel.co.uk
Julian Dickinson and Nick Steel

Hexaplex
www.hexaplex.nl
Micha Bakker and Cheryl Gallaway

**Ian Lynam
Creative Direction
and Graphic Design**
www.ianlynam.com
Ian Lynam

Inkahoots
www.inkahoots.com.au
Joel Booj, Kate Booj, Jason Grant,
Mathew Johnson, Ben Mangan,
Robyn McDonald

Kapitza
www.kapitza.com
Nicole Kapitza and Petra Kapitza

KOI
www.koi.li
Krispin Heé and Peter Jaeger

Made In Space, Inc.
www.madeinspace.la
April Greiman

Magpie Studio
www.magpie-studio.com
David Azurdia, Ben Christie, Jamie Ellul

MARC&ANNA
www.marcandanna.co.uk
Marc Atkinson and Anna Ekelund

MINE™
www.minesf.com
Christopher Simmons

MOJO
www.mojohouse.com
Michael Kahane and Jeff Lamont

NB: Studio
www.nbstudio.co.uk

Martin Nicolausson
www.martinnicolausson.com

No Days Off
www.nodaysoff.com
Teo Connor and Patrick Duffy

Norm
www.norm.to
Dimitri Bruni, Manuel Krebs, Ludovic
Varone

Playful
www.pabloalfieri.com
Pablo Alfieri

Praline
www.designbypraline.com
Alex Moshakis, Jean-Marie Orhan,
Robert Peart, Al Rodger, David Tanguy

Qube Konstrukt
www.qubekonstrukt.com

RINZEN
www.rinzen.com
Rilla Alexander, Steve Alexander,
Adrian Clifford, Karl Maier,
Craig Redman

ruiz+company
www.ruizcompany.com
David Ruiz

ScienceWerk
www.sciencewerk.net
Khendi Lee, Danis Sie,
Octavia Soebiyanto

Scrollan
www.scrollan.de
Peter Bünnagel, Iris Fussenegger,
Barbara Kotte, Anne-Lene Proff

Sell! Sell!
www.sellsell.co.uk
Andy Palmer and Vic Polkinghorne

Skolos-Wedell
www.skolos-wedell.com
Nancy Skolos and Thomas Wedell

Frauke Stegmann
www.ineedtimetothinkaboutwildlife.org

Stiletto nyc
www.stilettonyc.com
Stefanie Barth and Julie Hirschfeld

Studio8 Design
www.studio8design.co.uk
Zoë Bather and Matt Willey

Studio Astrid Stavro
www.astridstavro.com
Astrid Stavro

Studio Parris Wakefield
www.parriswakefield.com
Maria Farrugia, Simon Griffin,
Sarah Parris, Howard Wakefield

Studio Tonne
www.studiotonne.com
Paul Farrington

Daryl Tanghe
www.dtanghe.com

THERE
www.there.com.au
Simon Hancock and Paul Tabouré

Thirst / 3st
www.3st.com
Rick Valicenti

Tom Hingston Studio
www.hingston.net
Tom Hingston

TwoPoints.Net
www.twopoints.net
Lupi Asensio and Martin Lorenz

UnderConsideration
www.underconsideration.com
Bryony Gomez-Palacio and Armin Vit

Universal Everything
www.universaleverything.com
Matt Pyke

VIER5
www.vier5.de

Alvin Yeung
superpowerups.com
al.vvvvv.in

ZürichTokio
www.zurichtokio.com
Daniel Donati, Laura Donati,
Karin Glarner, Stefan Lemberger,
Niels Schäfer, Fabian Widmer

Author's Acknowledgements

All that's left now is to say thank you to
everyone who contributed to this book.

And to Nathan Gale at Intercity; to
Laurence King, Jo Lightfoot and
Susie May at Laurence King Publishing.

Also to Michael Dorrian for inspiration.
Especially to Gregg Virostek for
inspiration, help and everything.

Liz Farrelly, 2010

Credits

p. 185 (bottom right) Praline and John
Short; p. 189 (top right) Sebastian
Golling; p. 203 (left) Bela Tibor; p. 203
(right) Justin Horrocks; p. 220, p. 221
Chris Jones; p. 228 Mauricio Salinas.
All other photographs are credited
where they appear.

Studio photoraphy by
PSC Photography.
www.pscphotoraphy.com

This book is set in Dada Grotesk
by deValence (see pages 82–85).
www.devalence.net